Cauldron of Changes

Cauldron of Changes

Feminist Spirituality in Fantastic Fiction

Janice C. Crosby

McFarland & Company, Inc., Publishers
Jefferson, North Carolina, and London

> The present work is a reprint of the softcover edition of Cauldron of Changes: Feminist Spirituality in Fantastic Fiction, first published in 2000 by McFarland.

LIBRARY OF CONGRESS CATALOGUING-IN-PUBLICATION DATA

Crosby, Janice C., 1962–
    Cauldron of changes : feminist spirituality in fantastic fiction / by Janice C. Crosby.
        p.   cm.
    Includes bibliographical references (p.) and index.

    ISBN 978-0-7864-7376-2
    softcover : acid free paper ∞

    1. Fantasy fiction, American — History and criticism. 2. Feminism and literature — United States — History — 20th century.   3. Women and literature — United States — History — 20th century.   4. American fiction — Women authors — History and criticism.   5. American fiction — 20th century — History and criticism.   6. Feminist fiction — History and criticism.   7. Spiritual life in literature. 8. Spirituality in literature.   9. Feminism in literature. I. Title.
PS374.F27C76   2013
813'.0876609'0082 — dc21   00-25625

BRITISH LIBRARY CATALOGUING DATA ARE AVAILABLE

© 2000 Janice C. Crosby. All rights reserved

No part of this book may be reproduced or transmitted in any form or by any means, electronic or mechanical, including photocopying or recording, or by any information storage and retrieval system, without permission in writing from the publisher.

Cover image © 2013 PhotoDisc

Manufactured in the United States of America

McFarland & Company, Inc., Publishers
  Box 611, Jefferson, North Carolina 28640
    www.mcfarlandpub.com

To all the Goddesses
I have met on the path

Acknowledgments

Many persons have been instrumental in developing and shaping the vision manifested in this work. Among the many women who have helped me along the path of the Goddess, I would especially like to thank Selena Fox, Starhawk, and Luisah Teish for their works, teaching, and encouragement. I also thank attendees of the Reclaiming Summer Intensive of 1989, and those of several PSGs; you have shown me how these principles can manifest themselves within groups and communities. And to all my Craft sisters and brothers, many thanks.

I also wish to thank my colleagues at Southern University, Baton Rouge, for their continued support and encouragement. Special thanks go to Joyce Jones, Daisy Latimer, David Porter, and Tom Morgan for knowing what it took.

A huge thanks to Randi Gray Kristensen for serving as the reader of several chapters and responding so perceptively.

My continued thanks to those who served as the first readers of this text: Rosan Jordan, Robin Roberts, Carolyn Jones, Veronica Makowsky, and Carl Freedman. In particular, I would like to credit Rosan for her patient feedback, Carolyn for her role as devil's advocate, and Veronica for her perceptive questions, which contributed greatly to the formation of this work. I also wish to acknowledge Robin Roberts for her belief and encouragement in *Cauldron* as an academic project.

Deep thanks also to Robin Reid, Don Palumbo, and other members of the PCA Science Fiction/Fantasy area group: we are not alone, and the truth *is* out there!

To Phyllis Le Feaux, Jo Hanna, and Francis Dodick, wise women and healers, I offer my deepest gratitude for their light and love. Among the many friends who supported me, I am most indebted to Randi Kristensen and Kendra Hamilton. I also thank Tim Whittemore, who knew the Goddess before I did and supported my journey, and Susan Gaharan along with the other CUUPS, Lionesses, and Birds.

Finally, this work could not have been completed without the loving encouragement of my mother, Dorothy Wood Crosby, and my sister, Iris Crosby McQuain.

Contents

Acknowledgments		vii
Introduction		1
1	Toil, Trouble … and Joy: Feminism and Spiritual Reclaiming	7
2	Rewriting History and Legend	30
3	Finding and Defining Personal Power	71
4	The Quest for the Goddess	108
5	Wise Women and Healers	137
6	Conclusion	164
Notes		169
Annotated Bibliography		175
Index		203

Introduction

Feminist literary criticism has been slow in incorporating the insights of the feminist spirituality movement into its discussion of women's literary works, both noncanonical genres such as science fiction and fantasy and more "traditional" literatures. One of the first major works to begin filling the gap between literary studies and feminist spirituality was Carol Christ's *Diving Deep and Surfacing: Women Writers on Spiritual Quest* (1980). In her discussion of Adrienne Rich, Margaret Atwood, Ntozake Shange, and Doris Lessing, Christ notes how the religious elements of these authors' works have been overlooked due to their variance from the traditional, male-defined concept of spiritual quest as a journey through trials, which, when overcome, result in a transcendent experience. In contrast, the authors in Christ's study depict their [female] protagonists' peak religious experiences as climactic moments which integrate them into the natural world. Her study reflects one of the goals of feminist literary criticism, which is to help find alternatives to androcentric experience and analysis in order to more accurately interpret women's texts.

Since Christ's study, only a few critics have further explored feminist spirituality in women's literary texts: Gloria Orenstein, for instance, devotes only one chapter to literature in her study of Goddess spirituality in women's art, *The Reflowering of the Goddess* (1990); Annette Van Dyke, in *The Search for a Woman-Centered Spirituality* (1992), situates her discussion of feminist spirituality in novels in the larger context of lesbian criticism.

The purpose of this study is to further connect the discourses of feminist literary critics and theorists of feminist spirituality by showing how an understanding of the recent projects of feminist spirituality is necessary to contextualize and interpret the appearance of Goddess worship, earth-based spirituality, and psychic phenomena in fictional works by contemporary American women novelists who write speculative or fantastic fiction. I use "speculative" and "fantastic" fiction as umbrella terms which include the genres of science fiction, fantasy, and magical realism.[1] My focus is on the feminist struggle to reclaim history/herstory and to articulate feminist methods of personal and social power based on immanent value and interconnection.

In terms of feminist literary criticism of mainstream literature, my work follows in the tradition of archetypal criticism as exemplified by Annis Pratt's *Archetypal Patterns in Women's Fiction* (1981). Like Pratt, I consider thematic patterns and repeating figures, though I differ from her by not framing my discussion of them in strictly Jungian terms. While her discussion of women in nature, rape trauma, and the female quest as found in women's fiction demonstrates a perceptive analysis of the mainstream fiction on which she focuses, Pratt notes that science fiction literature provides exceptions to the aforementioned archetypes. I consider these exceptions in the texts I discuss. Another important difference in our approaches is my reference to contemporary women's experience versus a more abstract, theoretical approach.

In terms of speculative/fantastic fiction, the novels discussed tend more toward the genre of fantasy, away from "hard" science fiction with its reliance on known scientific principles (Wolfe 51). Although Sarah Lefanu in *Feminism and Science Fiction* (1989) and Robin Roberts in *A New Species* (1993) are primarily concerned with feminist appropriation of science fiction rather than fantasy fiction, I share with these writers the view that speculative fiction, while originally misogynistic, lends itself to feminist questioning and vision in a way that realism cannot. The open-ended ground rules of fantastic fiction, which free the writer to answer "What if?" any way she chooses, make room for both social criticism and the depiction of what Marleen Barr calls "heroic fantastic femininity" (*Alien to Femininity* 83). However, unlike Barr, the connections I draw between fantastic fiction and the feminist spirituality movement recast heroic femininity as a spiritual exercise.

My analysis of the contemporary feminist spirituality movement also distinguishes this work from criticism such as Thelma Shinn's *Worlds Within Women: Myth and Mythmaking in Fantastic Literature by Women* (1986) and Charlotte Spivack's *Merlin's Daughters: Contemporary Women Writers of Fantasy* (1987). While these studies discuss the significant revisions women writers of fantastic fiction have wrought in myth and legend, Shinn and Spivack fail to examine the actual experiences underlying such revisions. In fact, the feminist revision of myth is integrally tied to a similar project which sprang from contemporary spiritual feminists' search for woman- and life-affirming mythologies and symbol systems, as I will demonstrate. Thus, Spivack's view of magic as metaphor (5) must be modified when faced with actual women who see themselves as magicians, able to shape their worlds through magic. An additional difference in my work is the inclusion of more recent authors whose body of works deserves note: Mercedes Lackey, Gael Baudino, Starhawk, and Patricia Kennealy. While I do include authors about whom a fair amount of critical material has been written, such as Toni Morrison, Marion Zimmer Bradley, Octavia Butler, and Joan Vinge, I find it important to examine these authors in connection with new authors who continue to reshape the direction of speculative fiction.

Another purpose behind this book is the study of popular culture, both in the fictional texts I have selected, which include popular works of genre fiction as well as some considered "literary" fiction, and in the articulation and examination of feminist spirituality as a living, contemporary cultural manifestation. Because popular culture studies have at best only glossed over this connection, my work covers a neglected aspect of American culture. My thematic study is made possible through a dialogue between academic and grassroots perspectives, both literary and theoretical. By including the perspectives of everyday women who explore feminist spirituality, the study contains a grassroots element.

The major trends in feminist spirituality discussed in the first chapter, "Toil, Trouble ... and Joy," underscore the several related themes appearing in literature which incorporate a female-focused spirituality: rewriting history and legend, finding and defining personal power, the quest for the Goddess, and wise women and healers. Although I will discuss each work of fiction I have selected in terms of only one of these themes, let me state now that this thematic strategy is a convenient oversimplification. Thus, I treat a novel like *The Mists of Avalon* primarily as an example of a feminist retelling of history and legend, while recognizing that the story of Morgaine, the protagonist, has everything to do with defining the nature of power, especially one's own, and also with discovering the true meaning of the Goddess. Like the practices of feminist spirituality itself, my categories overlap and reinforce each other, creating a dialogue of influences and concerns.

The second chapter, "Rewriting History and Legend," begins my analysis of literary works, and describes the feminist literary project of rewriting and retelling the history and legends of western culture. Viewed another way, some of these authors contribute a first writing and recorded telling, for the woman's perspective may have always been absent or otherwise silenced in patriarchal narratives. As Carol Christ puts it, "Women's stories have not been told. And without stories there is no articulation of experience.... Without stories [a woman] cannot understand herself. Without stories she is alienated from those deeper experiences of self and world that have been called spiritual or religious" (*Diving Deep and Surfacing* 1).

However, in rewriting legends such as the Arthurian saga, women writers are doing more than speaking where once there was a void; they are writing against the hegemonic discourses of western patriarchy, an essential tool of suppression. These writers do not simply assume an alternative "herstory," but actively attack the assumptions and erasures of patriarchal history. This is an activity made possible by feminist research, and new narratives of the fall from Goddess-focused culture parallel feminist anthropological and archaeological discoveries. Marion Zimmer Bradley's *The Mists of Avalon* and *The Firebrand*, as well as Kim Chernin's *The Flame Bearers*, portray the clash of matrifocal and patriarchal religions and values as seen through the eyes of a female protagonist who is challenged by herself, other women, or the Goddess to maintain a strong female identity and preserve matrifocal tradition. Alice Walker's *The Temple of My Familiar* adds an Africentric[2] perspective to this discussion, and includes both female and male focal characters. As these texts challenge patriarchy as manifested in the Judeo-Christian and classical foundations of western culture, they also invite readers to identify with the protagonist and participate in the author's creation of a new, matrifocal history.

My third chapter, "Finding and Defining Personal Power," reflects my conclusion that the overwhelming concern of the spiritual feminist enterprise is the search for and definition of a personal power which finds its basis in an ethic of interconnection rather than domination. This concern becomes a major motif in contemporary women's fantastic or speculative fiction like Mercedes Lackey's *Oathbound* and *Oathbreakers*, Patricia Kennealy's *Keltiad* trilogy, Gael Baudino's *Strands of Starlight*, and Octavia Butler's *Wild Seed*. In most of these novels, the female protagonists generally face a spiritual or existential crisis which sends them on a search to discover their own strengths. In doing so, the women must heal themselves from injuries frequently depicted as inflicted by a patriarchal society. The protagonists achieve a true glimpse of the power of feminist interconnection only after rejecting offers to join in forms of patriarchal exploitation. For white writers, this situation reflects European American women's double position of oppressed and oppressor, and offers the hope that through an awareness of the uses of power, European American women can use their power to heal rather than exploit, thus fighting racism. For African American female writers, sexism and racism are exposed as dangerous constructs affecting the lives of black women.

Chapter 4, "The Quest for the Goddess," builds on the insights of the previous chapter while focusing on how the figure of a Goddess can be integral to a woman's spiritual quest, as found in Marion Zimmer Bradley's *City of Sorcery*, Lynn Abbey's *Daughter of the Bright Moon* and *The Black Flame*, and Joan Vinge's *The Snow Queen*. Carol Christ argues that "[t]he expression of women's spiritual quest is integrally related to the telling of women's stories" and that "[i]f women's stories are not told, the depth of women's souls will not be known" (*Diving Deep and Surfacing* 1). Therefore, to understand the significance of female spiritual quests which involve a Goddess, the reader needs to know how the Goddess works for contemporary women. As deity, symbol, fiction, self, or some combination of all these things, a wealth of literature attests to the difference she makes in both fictional and real women's lives. In these novels, protagonists' discoveries about the Goddess are integrally tied to the process of self-discovery.

In Chapter 5, "Wise Women and Healers," protagonists who have arrived at a new sense of female power display powers of healing which hearken back to a time when women's power was legitimized as a necessary force in the community as a whole. Arguing that this tradition has been more readily accessible to African American authors because of distancing from the dominant European-based culture, I discuss Toni Morrison's *Beloved*, Gloria Naylor's *Mama Day*, and Ntozake Shange's *Sassafras, Cypress, and Indigo* in this framework. Pagan/Jewish writer Starhawk's *The Fifth Sacred Thing* is then examined as a forward-looking work which epitomizes the multicultural dimensions of spiritual healing in a world which embraces immanent spirituality as the foundation of life and activism.

The structure of this book itself forms a microcosm of the female spiritual journey I have found in the texts and in the experience of spiritual feminists. At some point, a woman connects with the feminist spirituality movement, and finds that it offers her a type of nourishment previously lacking in her life. She then discovers a new history and a new mythology, which help create a backdrop against which she can reconceptualize her spiritual self as a valuable female self. As she does so, a woman realizes that she can neither play nor submit to the power games of patriarchy in her own life; in fact, she must write new rules about what constitutes power. At some point in her exploration, she comes to a personal understanding of Goddess, of female deity.[3] Having found healing in her journey, she spreads that healing in the world around her.

Each day, women begin and continue this journey. And, each day, more women seem to be incorporating the experience of spiritual feminists into their literary works. While not every spiritual feminist writes about her journey, almost all read fiction and nonfiction literature embodying spiritual feminist principles (Eller 33–34). An understanding of these ideas, which I treat as themes, is necessary for an informed understanding of the fictional texts. In analyzing these texts, I acknowledge women reading these novels as active participants in creating meaning and connecting it to their own lives.

By approaching these texts thematically, the connections between them will become apparent in a way which no single methodology could reveal. Also, the thematic approach clarifies how each text comments upon feminist spiritual empowerment as derived from European, African, and Jewish racial and ethnic traditions. Rather than articulating a unilateral viewpoint of the works under discussion, I wish to expand the conversation taking place between author, reader, critic, and culture in and through these texts. However, without wishing to universalize women's experience, as early feminist criticism tended to do, I do wish to emphasize commonalities at the same time I note differences, especially those related to race. Linking the grassroots feminist spirituality movement with concerns articulated by academic feminists, and the texts of popular culture with concepts in religious studies, I hope to weave the strands of women's spiritual practice into a web which can challenge a long-standing view of these elements as separate and isolated.

My title, *Cauldron of Changes,* plays on this interweaving of spirituality and literary study. The phrase originally comes from a pagan chant:

> Cauldron of changes,
> Blossom of bone
> Ark of Eternity
> Hole in the stone[4]

which combines resonant images of life, death, eternity, and transformation. In my usage, the cauldron, symbol of death and rebirth, is language, the container for the articulation of our perceptions of reality. The writers I discuss are the wise women, the witches who combine the varied ingredients of myth, history, searching, pain, and hope as they concoct their potion. The fire of imagination transforms these elements into a brew that empowers those who dare to drink from the cauldron. The reader, having drunk this potion, sees herself and her world with new eyes, and takes her own place as creator of change.

1
Toil, Trouble ... and Joy: Feminism and Spiritual Reclaiming

What is the American feminist spirituality movement? Joel Kovel broadly defines spirituality as "the desire for being" (133), but goes on to say that spirituality "requires a sense of sin" and that "the modern person typically has too much invested in the self to let it go in a spiritual quest" (134–35). While feminist spirituality demonstrates a desire to experience "being" in the sense of a deeply felt relationship to and union with the universe, spiritual feminists reject the concept of sinfulness, and would argue that life in patriarchal society has given women too little a sense of self, rather than too much.[1]

In *Living in the Lap of the Goddess,* her recent ethnographic study of the beliefs and participants present in the feminist spirituality movement in America, Cynthia Eller notes that the term describes a wide variety of beliefs and practices, which despite their differences share an emphasis on empowerment as "both the goal and the reward of feminist spiritual practice" (3). Eller also observes a general interest in ritual, psychic skills, nature, and the validation of menstruation and childbirth.[2] In describing areas of tension and debate within the movement, Eller lists concerns about biological essentialism, the role of men, visions of matriarchies and patriarchies, the role of traditional religions, the nature of the Goddess, and concepts of leadership. What Eller finds "most significant about these agreements and disagreements is that dissension is so easily tolerated, and the urge to create dogma so readily suppressed" (4).

For this reason, a concise definition of the feminist spirituality movement is difficult, and must be broad enough to include the variety indicated by the preceding description. I use the term to describe the religious beliefs and practices of women who have turned from mainstream American religious traditions and created a woman-centered spiritual orientation which concentrates on immanent deity, often in the form of a Goddess, and on practices to facilitate female empowerment.

While I discuss the various projects of spiritual feminists later in this chapter, I first will comment on how the feminist spirituality movement began and spread, who its practitioners are, and who some of the leading women in the movement are.

The contemporary American feminist spirituality movement has its roots in questioning begun a century ago. For many early American feminists concerned with the issue of religion and patriarchy, the initial project was to expose the ways in which the Judeo-Christian religious tradition grounded and supported the oppression of women in the West.[3] The works of Matilda Joslyn Gage (*Woman, Church, and State* 1893) and Elizabeth Cady Stanton (*The Woman's Bible* 1895) are among the earliest examples of the critique of sexism within the Judeo-Christian tradition. This approach dominated the feminist critique of religion for some time. Summing up the results of her committee's examination of biblical thought about women, Stanton says flatly that "as long as woman accepts the position that [it] assign[s] her, her emancipation is impossible. Whatever the Bible may be made to do in Hebrew or Greek, in plain English it does not exalt and dignify woman" (12). Going beyond biblical analysis to a historical overview, Gage offers her work as "The Original Exposé of Male Collaboration Against the Female Sex." She introduces a number of ideas which recur in contemporary spiritual feminist thought: the postulation of ancient matriarchies; the analysis of the Judeo-Christian tradition as antisex, antibody, and antiwoman; and the witchhunts as an expression of the patriarchal fear of female knowledge and power. Charlene Spretnak refers to the approach typified by Gage and Stanton as "passing through a necessary stage of reacting to the sexism of patriarchal religion" (*The Politics of Women's Spirituality* xxi).

In 1968 Mary Daly's *The Church and the Second Sex* revived the concerns of Gage and Stanton by reintroducing a critique of Judeo-Christian religion as a cornerstone of women's oppression. The works of Rosemary Ruether (*Sexism and God-Talk: Towards a Feminist Theology* 1983) have also been highly influential. Along with the early works of Daly that typify an approach that I, like Christ and Plaskow, term "reformist" or revisionist, they advocate changing Christianity from within rather than abandoning it (*Womanspirit Rising* 10). *Sexism and God-Talk* examines the sexism historically displayed by the church while proposing that the symbol of Christ can serve as the foundation for an egalitarian social order and theological impetus. In *White Women's Christ and Black Women's Jesus: Feminist Christology and Womanist Response* (1989), Jacqueline Grant views African American women's relationship to the figure of Jesus as a force of liberation and resistance while she criticizes European American feminist analyses which dismiss Christianity. She sees them as limited by a focus which excludes the ways in which racial experience can be a modifying factor. Critics like Daly, Ruether, and Grant critique sexism and the perpetuation of patriarchy in traditional religions, while nonetheless finding either woman-affirming and redeeming aspects in those religions or in women's experience of such religions.

Some feminists, such as Daly herself in *Gyn/ecology: The Metaethics of Radical Feminism* (1978) and later works, rejected the reformist position, asking if there was, ever had been, or ever could be religious perspectives or practices outside of Judeo-Christianity which were not androcentric. The enterprise of researching and re-creating female-focused spirituality began as American women influenced by the women's liberation movement devoted their energies to answering these questions.

This phase of the feminist spirituality movement reflects the intersection and impact of several cultural forces during the 1960s–70s. Obviously, one force was the "second phase" of the women's liberation movement in America. Although many of the early articulators of this movement which received widespread attention were European American and middle-class, such as Betty Friedan, women from other cultural backgrounds and classes enlarged the scope of concerns of the women's liberation movement. This enlarged scope reflected the impact of the second force, the resurgence of ethnic pride, nationalism, and cultural heritage among Americans of non–European descent, such as African Americans and Native Americans. In fact, these struggles served as a basis and model for women's liberation, just as the suffragist movement had drawn its strategies from the abolitionist movement. Women from these groups challenged European racism as well as male sexism within and outside their cultures. The third force can be broadly described as "countercultural." The Vietnam War, changing gender and racial relations, and other factors combined to create an intense dissatisfaction with traditional societal roles and religions. They inspired many persons to experiment with alternative social practices, including alternative religions. What all three of these forces share is a desire for independence and liberation which served as the impetus for women to seek out religious practices which affirmed their identity as women, and often their specific cultural identity as well.

Many of the first women to publish material about feminist spirituality beyond the Judeo-Christian reformist position were European American women discovering European goddesses and witchcraft, the pre-Christian religion of Old Europe, and Jewish women uncovering the Goddess[4] heritage of the Middle East. As will be discussed in more detail below, works by African American and Native American women such as Luisah Teish and Brooke Medicine Eagle have been published by larger presses and in journals with a national readership. Since printed materials are one of the major means by which the movement has spread (Eller 33), the dominance of European American women's access to popular and academic avenues of publication has perpetuated the largely European American, middleclass composition of the movement. This problem is also true of the music and art of the feminist spirituality movement as agents of its dissemination. However, this situation may be more true in terms of nationally recognized examples, as opposed to more localized instances where marginalized women are gaining their voices.

Localized instances can include specific groups and gatherings, which have also contributed to the spread of the feminist spirituality movement. They may better represent the variety of women who have participated. A number of gatherings are lesbian in focus, such as the Michigan Womyn's Music Festival. As Eller has observed, the lesbian component of the feminist spirituality movement is significant, and is more racially and culturally inclusive than its heterosexual counterpart (20–21). Workshops and classes are offered in many cities across the country and, though some are costly, other teachers expand opportunities for attendance by offering "scholarships" or teaching for free.

Small groups are another means of transmission of spiritual feminist knowledge, and can be as secretive, specialized, open, closed, eclectic, or homogenous as their members wish them to be. While such groups are the hardest to document and quantify, they are where the popular movement becomes personalized, where women share with each other in the intimate and traditional fashion of oral networking. Undoubtedly, many ideas and traditions are circulated in this fashion which do not receive mainstream attention. Gael Baudino emphasizes this latter component in her recent novel, *Strands of Sunlight*. The Elvin protagonist, Natil, tries to find human witches, and is overwhelmed by the offerings of a New Age bookstore which offers "Wicca 101" for the beginner. Baudino's satirization of the commercialization of the movement culminates in Natil's turning away from the "gigantic cash register" and going to a human woman who feels a personal connection with the Goddess (56–60, 143–47).

Although feminist spirituality emphasizes the experience and empowerment of individual women, while retaining a "strong distrust of religious authority figures" (Eller 90), some women have achieved wide recognition for their work as priestesses, leaders, and teachers whose writings are well known by any woman with more than a passing exposure to the feminist spirituality movement. A brief description of several of these nationally known figures will help demonstrate the variety of practices they have popularized.

Zsuzsanna Budapest is often referred to as the "founder of the Women's Spirituality Movement in the United States." She claims to have received much of her knowledge from her mother, a Hungarian witch (*The Grandmother of Time* 37). Diane Stein claims that "many of today's Goddess movement leaders are [Budapest's] spiritual daughters, and all have been touched by her work, thought, and teaching" (*The Goddess Celebrates* 12). The author of a number of books, including *The Holy Book of Women's Mysteries I & II* (1980), *The Grandmother of Time* (1989), and *The Goddess in the Office* (1993), "Z" is also noteworthy for her outspokenness against patriarchal wrongs, and her belief that "a witch who cannot hex cannot heal" (*Holy Book I* 57). Budapest's practice is Dianic, or lesbian in nature.

In the anecdote I cited earlier of Natil's search for real witches, it is not surprising that the human, Sandy Joy, says of Starhawk's classic *The Spiral Dance*, "you've just got to have this one. This, an athame, and a little chutzpah, and you can put together your own coven" (145). *The Spiral Dance* (1979) has probably done more to popularize and inspire Goddess worship than any other recent text. In my personal experience, I have yet to meet a self-identified neo–Pagan/Wiccan who has not read the book. As Stein remarks, "There may have been a Women's Spirituality movement without Starhawk, but it could not have been as profound or fun" (*The Goddess Celebrates* 128). Starhawk's other works of feminist thealogy[5] are *Dreaming the Dark* (1982) and *Truth or Dare* (1987). She has also published two novels, *The Fifth Sacred Thing* (1993) and *Walking to Mercury* (1997). Her practice is eclectic in its sources and open to men as well as women, and continually emphasizes the importance of political action.

Stein herself has written a very accessible series of books which primarily focus on ritual, psychic powers, and healings. Two in particular, *The Women's Book of Healing* (1987) and *Stroking the Python: Women's Psychic Lives* (1988), are noteworthy for the emphasis Stein gives to personal anecdotes gathered from women across the country. The reader can almost feel that she is participating in a conversation with Stein playing the role of facilitator. Stein would probably agree with this analogy, for her goal is facilitating women's reclamation of their healing and psychic powers.

Luisah Teish is a Voodoo priestess from New Orleans who now practices in the San Francisco Bay area, and claims women like Starhawk as her "altar sisters." Her first book, *Jambalaya: The Natural Woman's Book of Personal Charms and Practical Rituals* (1985), approaches African diasporic religious practices from a feminist point of view, and is offered to all races of women as an effort to eradicate racism within the feminist spirituality movement (xii–xiii). Likewise, in *Carnival of the Spirit: Seasonal Celebrations and Rites of Passage* (1994), she writes that "This book is transcultural.... The nature of the land a people inhabit contributes more to ceremonial similarities and differences than skin color, hair texture, or buttock size" (xii).

Finally, Brooke Medicine Eagle draws on her mixed Native American and European American heritage to create her message of healing for the earth and all its inhabitants. She leads retreats and workshops, and has also released a number of cassettes, as well as written a book, *Buffalo Woman Comes Singing* (1991). Her teachings emphasize the immanent value of all creation, but do not purport to reveal the secret traditions of Native Americans. One Native practice which she feels is of great benefit to all women is the moon lodge, where a woman spends time alone and in meditation during her menstrual cycle. She emphasizes the importance of reclaiming this practice as much as possible in contemporary life (327–43).

What all these women share is a belief in the sacredness of women, the earth, and all its inhabitants. They teach their beliefs in a way that recognizes each woman's ability to create a meaningful spiritual practice for herself if only she will recognize that she can do so, and need not be told by a male religious figure or male-dominated religious institution what to believe and how to behave. The proliferation of feminist spiritual publications, music, art, gatherings, workshops, and groups makes it clear that an increasing number of women are eager to receive such a message. This marks the feminist spirituality movement as a serious site of contemporary feminist engagement.

Now, through a brief delineation of the scope and agenda of modern feminist spirituality in America, I will clarify the sources of my terminology. As noted earlier, the European American predominance in the movement has undoubtedly influenced the direction of much of the scholarship, with emphasis placed on European and Near Eastern subjects. While writers such as Starhawk do consider race in their works, as I do in this text, some European American spiritual feminists still exclude Africentric thought. For example, in *The Feminist Companion to Mythology*, Carolyne Harrington rationalizes her exclusion of African thought (the one exception is a piece on Egypt) by asserting that there simply was not room to include such works (5). Given that she gives ample space to Greco-Roman myth, a subject which has already received considerable attention by feminist scholars, Harrington's assertion seems questionable, and suggests the type of Eurocentric bias which needs to be eliminated.

Women from a variety of cultural backgrounds, including African American and Native American women, have also begun to recover and re-create woman-centered spiritual practices. In doing so certain trends are discernable. Through both research and the examination of personal and group experience, American feminists from the 1970s onward began exploring four major areas: 1) investigating the past through historical and anthropological work; 2) reexamining and tracing the evolution of myth and legend; 3) creating woman-centered ritual; and 4) redeeming the practice, often termed "womanspirit," of psychic skills denied or devalued by the western patriarchal scientific establishment.

While some women choose to explore the above issues through scholarship or practice, others choose art, especially the literary arts, as a means of encoding female-focused spirituality. My analysis illustrates how fiction writers are exploring the same or similar issues as the theorists/practitioners. As I will demonstrate, there are no distinct borders among these groups of women, as novelists may be practitioners, or practitioners may turn to fiction, or analysts begin performing rituals. This situation expands the idea expressed by Natalie Rosinsky, who in writing about feminist speculative fiction discusses the interaction between reader and writer as "feminist" and "nonhierarchical" (113). What the groups share is a need to articulate, through writing, the nature of their discoveries about women as powerful spiritual beings in the past, present, and future. My study focuses on the presence of spiritual feminist beliefs as they occur in contemporary fantastic fiction by European American, African American, and Jewish American authors. This focus reflects the preponderance of available materials, both fiction and nonfiction, while opening the way for similar in-depth studies of these ideas as voiced by writers of other ethnic or cultural backgrounds.

Investigating the Past

The unearthing of women's spiritual history and legacy has been a primary concern for many spiritual feminists. Even those spiritual feminists who do not do their own historical research have been strongly influenced by those women who have. In fact, the work of spiritual feminists in this area has created what Cynthia Eller refers to as a "sacred history" (151). Eller observes that spiritual feminists:

> have educated themselves in the niceties of archaeological research and have begun to interpret — and even to find — their own evidence. Others, equipped only with their imagination and desire, have filled in details where those were lacking and created a sacred history filled with poetry, grace, and numinous delight [152–53].

As this quotation suggests, science and poetry are combined in this history, serving as a unifying background against which individual women derive their personal experience of the feminist spirituality movement. Emphasis on the historical presence of Goddess worship and indications that societies could have existed where women were not subordinate to men is revolutionary in that it questions the image of patriarchy as an eternal presence. It further allows women to envision themselves as capable of creating a society which affirms the power and divinity of women. Unlike the majority of European American women, African American and Native American women are closer in time to recover the Goddess heritage of their peoples, and can readily find clear evidence of women acting as spiritual leaders within non–Christian tribal societies.

One of the pioneering works which claims the widespread existence of ancient Goddess worship in ancient Egypt, Mesopotamia, and Greece was Merlin Stone's *When God Was a Woman* (1976). Using a wide variety of archeological, historical, and mythological resources to find out what had been written or discovered about Goddess cultures, Stone argues that women enjoyed great freedom in ancient Mesopotamian cultures in which Goddess worship existed. The subjugation of those societies by Indo-European invaders brought about the patriarchal rule and [male] god worship which would characterize Judaism and Christianity. She notes that one of the greatest difficulties she encountered in her research was the androcentric cultural bias exhibited by previous scholars and historians, particularly in the dismissal of the Goddess religions as "fertility cults" and Goddess figurines as "fetishes":

> But archeological and mythological evidence of the veneration of the female deity as creator and lawmaker of the universe, prophetess, provider of human destinies, inventor, healer, hunter and valiant leader in battle suggests that the title "fertility cult" may be a gross oversimplification of a complex theological structure [xix–xx].

Marija Gimbutas, archaeologist and author of *The Goddesses and Gods of Old Europe: Myths and Cult Images* (1982) and *The Language of the Goddess* (1989), is a scholar who challenges androcentric analyses of Goddess imagery. She examines the art and artifacts of Goddess-worshiping cultures, investigating such images as the snake, the spiral, the vulva, the egg, and the earth mother, and their religious connotations of sacred life, death, and renewal. As symbols of the Goddess, these images emphasize the mysterious power of birth and the connections between the human world and the rest of nature. Elinor Gadon's *The Once and Future Goddess* (1989) builds upon the foundation laid by such women as Stone and Gimbutas by showing how Goddess symbology is being used by contemporary feminist ritualists and performance artists whose works challenge the dismissive notion of Goddess as fertility fetish. As with Gadon's work, understanding the significance of Goddess symbols in their original contexts allows critics such as myself to interpret their adoption by contemporary writers influenced by feminist spirituality, and to note that this "new" symbolic vocabulary would not exist for feminist artists if spiritual feminists were not also engaged in the process of recovery of women's spiritual history.

Just as Goddess imagery has frequently met with dismissal or diminishment, the investigation of and insistence on Goddess-worshiping cultures is often skeptically greeted as a nostalgic search for "a golden age of matriarchy in the past" (Binford, "Myths and Matriarchies" 544). While early postulations of matriarchal societies might now be seen as "visionary rather than scientific" (Carson, *Feminist Spirituality and the Feminine Divine* 38), the possibility of individual matriarchal societies, rather than a universal prepatriarchal matriarchy, awaits the judgment of unbiased anthropology and archaeology. Christ's *Rebirth of the Goddess* devotes a chapter to "Resistance to Goddess History" in order to help spiritual feminists understand and respond to this debate. Nonetheless, as Eller notes, for spiritual feminists the primary value of stories of a matriarchal past is as "a religiously and politically useful myth" (157) because imagining large scale female power is in itself empowering as it expands the realm of the possible. Writers of speculative fiction have found the matriarchal vision useful as a means of critiquing contemporary patriarchal culture, and also as a tool to depict powerful female figures and female-focused relationships. Critics such as Annette Van Dyke go further and claim the gynocentric nature of speculative fiction with a matriarchal component as specifically lesbian (2).

When spiritual feminists and fiction writers propose cultures in which women had power and in which a Goddess-focused religious perspective resulted in a world view which radically differs from those of patriarchal societies, the terminology used to describe those cultures can create confusion. "Matrilineal," for instance, refers to societies which traced descent (and usually property holding) through the mother. "Matrifocal" is sometimes used in this way, but refers more specifically to those cultures in which a form of mother Goddess worship existed. "Matristic" is offered in this sense as well, particularly in cases in which the power balance between the sexes is not clear, or in which females are known to have held roles of power, whether the gender-based delineation of those roles can be ascertained or not. Riane Eisler coins the term "gylanic" to describe a partnership model of society. The term comes from the Greek roots for man (*andros*) and woman (*gyne*) combined with a linking "l" (*The Chalice and the Blade* 105). Gloria Orenstein employs the term "feminist matristic" to describe the work of contemporary artists and thinkers who are influenced by "a holistic ethos ... associated with cultures whose cosmogonic myth features a Goddess, a female creator." She does so in order to differentiate such works from those by artists who have not undertaken "any feminist analysis of the social construction of gender" (*The Reflowering of the Goddess* xvi). Thus, we can see that the use of terminology to describe varying appearances of gynocentric power is still in an experimental, developmental stage.[6] I use the term "matrifocal" to indicate an emphasis on female lineage, Goddess worship, and interconnection. I have noted these other usages in order to clarify for readers the range of references.

Ancient civilizations are not the sole subject of feminist historical revision. The British and European witchhunts of the fourteenth through seventeenth centuries have suffered an almost complete erasure at the hands of patriarchal historians. Very few history textbooks cover this portion of the Inquisition with more than a few sentences, if that much. Barbara Ehrenreich and Deirdre English, authors of *Witches, Midwives and Nurses: A History of Women Healers* (1973), continued the work of Gage by noting the connections between the extermination of women as part of the witchhunts and the rise of a male medical establishment which had a stake in discrediting and eliminating the competition offered by midwives, herbal healers, and other female lay healers. Among their other skills, they provided means of contraception and abortion. During this period, in fact, the stereotype of the witch as a malevolent old hag is introduced into the popular culture. In her chapter "European Witchburnings: Purifying the Body of Christ" (*Gyn/ecology*), Mary Daly discusses how Christian doctrine represses sexuality, negating both sexual women and those who reject the role of marriage. Daly notes that the fear of women which motivated this repression and culminated in the witchhunts "masked a secret gynocidal fraternity, whose prime targets were women living outside the control of the patriarchal family, women who presented an option—an option of 'eccentricity,' and of 'indigestibility'" (186). Current estimates of the number of people killed in the witch craze range from the hundreds of thousands (Barstow 23) to the millions (Starhawk, *Dreaming the Dark* 187);

approximately 85 percent of the victims were female, many of those menopausal women (Stein, *Women's Spirituality Book* 12). In *The Curse,* the authors assert that the charge of "carnal abomination" leveled at accused witches barely masks a deep fear of women's menstrual cycles (Delaney, Upton, and Toth 42). From either perspective, the control of women's bodies was demonstrated in the most brutal ways by the church. How many of the women destroyed actually practiced some form of the pre–Christian nature religions of Europe, pejoratively termed witchcraft, is uncertain. What is certain is that feminist scholars such as Barstow and others are now shedding new light on the roles of sexism, ageism, religious intolerance, ruthless careerism, and classism as social forces at work during the witch-hunts.

The project of rewriting history allows women a new factual basis from which to reimagine themselves. In novels such as Kim Chernin's *The Flame Bearers,* Marion Zimmer Bradley's *The Firebrand,* Alice Walker's *The Temple of My Familiar* and Gael Baudino's *Strands of Starlight,* one can see the technique of historical revision at work. Feminist anthropological and archeological studies challenge the male-dominated construct of history and help inspire contemporary writers to depict an alternative vision of women's selves and their relation to the divine as a source of empowerment, as Mary Stange notes in "The Once and Future Heroine: Paleolithic Goddesses and Popular Imagination." Additionally, fiction writers can render the ways in which this alternative vision alters societal ethics and the structuring of male-female relationships. In doing so, both nonfiction and fiction writers give their readers a revisioning of the past which can create a new vision of women's future.

The Evolution of Myth and Legend

The second area of research developed by contemporary spiritual feminists has been reexamining and tracing the evolution of myth and legend. The rewriting of myth is also an enterprise for many contemporary women. Both strategies reflect the suspicion that patriarchal narratives are not the only or the earliest stories, and that androcentric myths and legends conceal gynocentric stories which may be "dis-covered": "finding the treasures of women's Memory, Knowledge, History that have been buried by the grave diggers of patriarchal re-search" (Daly, *Wickedary* 118). Charlene Spretnak, for example, was disgusted by the way in which the goddesses and heroines of the patriarchal Hellenic Greek myths, such as Persephone, Pandora, and Hera, were often depicted as helpless, evil, or jealous. She researched the pre–Hellenic nature of these figures and used the material to rewrite the myths in a form she felt created a reconstructed female legacy for her daughter. The result was *Lost Goddesses of Early Greece: a Collection of Pre-Hellenic Myths* (1978). Other authors do not rewrite myths so much as they rediscover and collect them, while still others also collect lore which may modify readings of extant myths, or allow new ones to be created. Merlin Stone's *Ancient Mirrors of Womanhood: a Treasury of Goddess and Heroine Lore from Around the World* (1979) and Barbara Walker's *The Woman's Encyclopedia of Myths and Secrets* (1983), a compilation of histories, symbolism, folklore, and mythology pertaining to Goddess religion, are two such collections. Stone likens the process of researching and assembling her material to a time when she glued together the pieces of a broken serving dish which had been her grandmother's:

> as with the dish, I would not allow myself to add any extra pieces, though I confess to using a small tube of glue. ... It was in much this same way, that I spent two years in piecing together the multitude of broken fragments of Goddess and heroine images, that are our heritage as women — with loving care, respect, and a deep concern for the integrity of using only what was truly a part of it [13].

Both Stone and Spretnak convey the hope of re-creating a female legacy stretching back into the past and forward into the future. In the same spirit, feminist literary scholars such as Elaine Showalter in *A Literature of Their Own* (1977) and *Sister's Choice* (1991) and Susan Koppelman in *Old Maids* (1984) have worked during the past few decades to recover "lost" writers and trace traditions and influences among female writers. *Cauldron of Changes* observes how writers of speculative fiction also work to create and strengthen this female literary and spiritual legacy.

   Collections of myths and legends inspire contemporary spiritual feminist scholars, artists, and practitioners exploring the relevance of the Goddess, either by carrying an ancient mythology into the present, or by creating an entirely new Goddess vision. Elinor Gadon's *The Once and Future Goddess* (1989) and Gloria Orenstein's *The Reflowering of the Goddess* (1990) document and analyze how both phenomena have occurred in the visual, performing, and literary arts. Karen Andes' *A Woman's Book of Power: Using Dance to Cultivate Energy and Health in Mind, Body, and Spirit* (1998) includes a matter of fact discussion of goddesses and feminine energy in relationship to dance and women reclaiming and accepting their bodies. Her easy presentation of Goddess material in an exercise book suggests the inroads feminist spirituality has made into the popular imagination.

Such studies and collections point out the need to understand the revisioning of mythology as it occurs in literary works, as will be demonstrated in my study of writings by Marion Zimmer Bradley and Alice Walker. By understanding that such literary revisions are related to the larger cultural backdrop of a uniquely feminist spiritual movement, one can recognize the interweaving of influence among practitioners, authors, and readers.

Ritual and Worship

The third area of feminist spiritual exploration, that of ritual and other acts of worship, allows contemporary spiritual feminists to imaginatively concretize their beliefs, experiences, and symbols. Eller observes that "[r]itual is the primary way in which spiritual feminists help each other to find a meaningful place in the world, to experiment with new and different social values, and to build a sense of community among themselves" (84). In creating rituals, contemporary women draw upon a wide variety of practices from cultures across the globe, and sometimes create new practices to suit their needs. Many strands of influence are present, including Celtic, Greek, Roman, Mesopotamian, African and African-diasporic, and Native American.

While some women may be fortunate enough to have inherited a ritual tradition from their foremothers, more often spiritual feminists are inspired by research into traditions and customs, which they then modify by liberal doses of invention. Such borrowing is not without its problems. European American women in particular have been criticized for not respecting cultural boundaries. However, in my experience of the neo–Pagan movement, I have seen African Americans following Celtic and Norse traditions, and European Americans trained in Santerian and Native American traditions. The debate over who "owns" spiritual practices and the role of genetics and culture in choosing a "correct" spiritual practice is an ongoing one. Although these rituals range from those enacted by and for the self to performance art pieces which enact planetary healing, my research and practice allows me to discern three overlapping but individual categories of ritual: woman-centered rituals, Goddess rituals, and earth-centered traditional rituals. Contemporary women draw on ritual, whether performed alone or with others, to affirm themselves as participants in a nonpatriarchal tradition while also affirming power and divinity inherent in themselves and the world. These contemporary feminist rituals provide concrete experience of the theological tenets of the feminist spirituality movement.

Paradoxically, women who publicize and publish Goddess rituals have no desire to set up any normative structures for ritual. Instead women ritualists wish to spark the imaginations of other women, urging them to use published rituals only as starting points, if at all. Most patriarchal religions, such as Catholicism, are concerned with setting up dogma and doctrine. In contrast, women who are recognized for their work in the feminist spirituality movement encourage grassroots adaptation and reformulation of any ideas they contribute. For example, in the "Freedom with Lady Liberty" ritual, nationally recognized Pagan rights activist Selena Fox encourages those engaged in various battles for freedom to incorporate, as they see fit, the image of Lady Liberty as a modern Goddess figure (*Goddess Communion* 9–10). As Kay Turner affirms:

> Successful and enduring change in the status of women will come only through the parallel transformation of symbols and realities. Feminist ritual practice is currently the most important model for symbolic and, therefore, psychic and spiritual change in women [21].

Here Turner, like Christ, stresses ritual as important in changing women's perceptions of themselves and their power. Also, a multiarticle discussion between Gloria Orenstein and Christine Downing in *Women's Studies Quarterly* attests to the use of ritual as a powerful, and perhaps even risky, pedagogical tool.

In short, Goddess rituals, whether as performance art or as personal art, constitute a major part of feminist ritual exploration, and reveal a reclamation of history, the future, and the female imagination. Therefore, understanding their contemporary relevance helps the reader contextualize the depiction in fiction of goddesses and Goddess rituals by such novelists as Kim Chernin, Marion Zimmer Bradley, Lynn Abbey, Gael Baudino, Alice Walker, and Starhawk as acknowledgments of a living spiritual practice and as an encoding of spiritual practices denoting female strength and value.

The first type of feminist ritual practice has to do with rites of passage and situations specific to women's experience. Woman-centered rituals vary widely and are usually performed by a number of women who either come together for one ritual occasion or who meet in an ongoing group. As Carol Christ discusses in "Why Women Need the Goddess," rituals for rites of passage have arisen in response to the feminist understanding that the rituals of patriarchal religion and society do not value women's power, bodies, or lived experience (*Laughter of Aphrodite* 117–22). Weddings and births are the only ritual occasions involving women which receive much notice in modern American society. Those events grant a woman worth only in relationship to a man or a child. In contrast, modern feminist rites generally celebrate stages in the woman's own development or awareness, thus reflecting the feminist motto that "the personal is political" (Collins 362–63).

In other words, for women to consciously choose to celebrate aspects of their personal lives is a political action in that it challenges prevailing societal assumptions of what is valuable and holy. For example, an increasingly popular ritual is the coming of age ceremony for a young woman upon her first menses. Desiring a more positive response to the natural processes of their daughters' bodies than most women received upon beginning menstruation, women hope to remove "the curse" of shame and guilt which patriarchal society imposes on women's bodies.

In a moving passage, Carol Christ tells us of a ritual she performed with a young woman, Claire, and her mother on the isle of Lesbos:

> I show Claire a beautiful carved image of a flower within a vaginalike oval shape. I tell her that she must understand that her vagina, her sexuality, is her own, that she may share it when she chooses, but she must never give her power to anyone. We pour honey for our sexual juices, and red wine for our blood onto the flower. It glistens in the sun. "Nothing about our sexuality is dirty," we say. "Remember this image. Hold it in your mind all your life" [*Laughter of Aphrodite* 193].

Another ritual which notes women's bodily changes is the menopausal or "croning" ritual; this can also occur when a woman's uterus is removed. The croning ritual celebrates the wisdom which comes with age and the creativity of the mind; Z. Budapest calls it "the last stage of [a woman's] Queenhood," by which she means existence as an "individualized independent strong woman" (*The Holy Book of Women's Mysteries II* 55). Not all woman-centered rituals serve a celebratory function: rituals for cleansing and purification after rape or abortion are now a staple of contemporary women's religious mysteries and appear in works like Luisah Teish's *Jambalaya* and Z. Budapest's *Holy Book of Women's Mysteries I & II*.

Such rituals demonstrate that rather than being escapist, as some critics charge, the range of women's rituals reveals the depth of the psychic damage women incur from living in contemporary patriarchy, and the resilience women display in reclaiming their souls, minds, and bodies. In commenting on women's rituals, Hallie Iglehart mentions the interconnection of ritual's psychic and psychological underpinnings, which "acknowledg[e] the political, economic, and social realms, and emphasizes our total power, rather than our helplessness, by offering concrete, effective tools for changing our old patterns" (124). Thus, women's rituals stress empowerment rather than victimization.

In addition to women's rituals are Goddess rituals, which are created by spiritual feminists to focus on either specific goddesses or the Great Goddess. The reasons why women perform Goddess rituals are as varied as the women who perform them, and as the definitions of "Goddess." While there are variations in the use of the terms goddess and Goddess among individual authors, most use Goddess (with a capital G) to refer to the original principle of immanent divinity which affirms the natural processes of life, death, and change, as well as the inherent worth of each person. Some also use the uppercase form when referring to specific goddesses which embody these same qualities. References to the Goddess are meant to convey primacy—the capital "G" paralleling the capital "G" of the god names of Judaism, Islam, and Christianity. In both instances, the capital conveys the awe of the sacred.[7] However, "she" will remain lowercase, which I feel more appropriate for the scholarly tone of this text. In *Feminist Spirituality and the Feminine Divine,* Anne Carson notes that for spiritual feminists "[t]he deity is female, spoken of as the Great Mother, the Great Goddess, and thought of as either a single entity, a polytheistic many-persons-in-one Goddess, or as a symbolic Great Presence, Prime Mover of the Universe, Spark of Creation" (5). This stance emphasizes the transcendent view of the Goddess; however, she is also viewed as immanent. Wiccan priestess Starhawk writes that when people ask her if she really believes in a Goddess, she replies "'Do you believe in rocks?'" She observes that "[t]he phrase 'believe in' itself implies that we cannot *know* the Goddess.... But we do not *believe* in rocks.... We know them; we connect with them ... we do not believe in the Goddess—we connect with Her" (*The Spiral Dance* 91). These statements exemplify the emphasis many women place on the Goddess as deity which is located internally as well as in the external world.

Though we do not yet know the full story of the evolution of Goddess worship, the appearance of gods, and the eventual erasure or subordination of Goddess worship, what we do know is that women who explore some facet of Goddess spirituality today do so because they see in Goddess symbology an affirmation of life and female identity which they perceive as lacking in the currently dominant world religions. Many women who turn to feminist spirituality do so because they question the perception that these religions were started by "great men" who had received a "great truth." Feminist skeptics such as Mary Daly note how the "great truths" often involved the devaluation of the natural world and of women.

Perhaps the revolutionary potential of the Goddess movement lies not in creating a definitive definition or image of the Goddess, but rather in the freedom she grants to women by inspiring them to take charge of their own religious imaginations and lives. Naomi Goldenberg describes this freeing of the imaginal process as a type of "psychological polytheism" (129). Yet another relationship to goddesses, though sometimes evoked through ritual, does not involve worship per se; rather, feminists investigate goddesses as archetypes of women's self-experience. Jean Bolen's *Goddesses in Everywoman* (1984) and Nor Hall's *The Moon and the Virgin* (1980) are two examples of this approach. Christine Downing's *The Goddess* (1981) is another; she explores her own life in relation to the various Hellenic myths of the Greek goddesses, seeing them as patterns in women's lives which each woman experiences at one time or another. Thus, a woman in academia might easily relate to Athene, while a young girl could see in her own life the story of Artemis.

Like others, I recognize western, androcentric bias in Jungian analysis in general and archetypes in particular. Something which claims to be universal, yet is so blatantly biased in favor of the classical tradition of the West, is immediately suspect. Thus, Bolen and Downing's reliance on the Greek goddesses reflects the very influence of the patriarchal tradition which should be challenged by these works. It also exhibits cultural ahistoricity and nonspecificity. Although these authors do have some valuable insights, their work is narrow in this sense. On archetypal theory, Orenstein notes that it reduces "women artists to the problematic status of unconscious or mad visionaries, a myth from which they [have] every desire to be liberated." To emphasize women as conscious creators, we must "underscore the importance of the actual, lived experiences as well as of the impact of feminist scholarship on the creative works of women artists" (*The Reflowering of the Goddess* 11). As Christ has observed, uncritical acceptance of archetypal theory "has led critics to view the Goddess movement as restricting women to stereotyped roles" (*Rebirth* 88).

Contemporary Goddess rituals typically reflect a variety of approaches which I have chosen to categorize. The accounts in Sherry Mestel's *Earth Rites* (1978) demonstrate this variety. The "historical" approach is exemplified by two rituals led by Mary Beth Edelson. "Memorials to the 9,000,000 Women Burned as Witches in the Christian Era" and "Mourning Our Lost Herstory: Remembering Ritual" both invoke the presence of the Goddess in the present and mourn her patriarchal suppression (48–55). Another, Nancy Black's "In Celebration of the Journey Thru Space: a dance of life with four women" demonstrates the "natural/elemental" approach as well as what we might term the "experiential approach." The experiential approach explores stages or aspects of women's lives. Black's ritual ties together the four seasons and the four ancient elements (earth, air, fire, and water) with four of the aspects of the Goddess she finds in women's lives: the young virgin, the lover, the mother, and the wisewoman (71–79). The vision of four aspects is less common than the idea of the Triple Goddess, celebrated in Donna Persons and Louise Udaykee's "Ritual to the Moon Goddess in Her Three States: Virgin, Mother, Old Woman" (83–86). Finally, Donna Henes provides a ritual for "The Coming Out of Spider Woman" (98), which demonstrates the "mythological approach," where distinct mythologies are drawn upon by ritualists.

Another area of feminist ritual which remains closely linked to more general Goddess rituals, but differs from them in important ways, is that of earth-centered traditional rituals. Such rituals center around deities connected with the earth, and can be traced to place as well — to Europe in the case of Wicca, Africa in the case of Voudoo, or the Americas in the case of Native American traditions. For a discussion of Voudoo ritual in a feminist context, see Luisah Teish's *Jambalaya* (239–63). Jamie Sam's *The Thirteen Original Clan Mothers* (1993) and Paula Gunn Allen's *Grandmothers of the Light: A Medicine Woman's Sourcebook* (1991) offer rituals based on Native American practices. These varieties of earth-centered ritual share an emphasis on the creation of sacred space, the invocation of the directions, and egalitarian leadership which also recognizes commitment and skill. Because my own area of expertise is Wicca, or neo–Pagan witchcraft, and Wiccan elements play a role in a number of the novels I discuss, I will concentrate on a description of Wiccan rituals.

While some women have drawn on the figure of the witch as persecuted during the witchhunts for an ideal of female rebellion in a patriarchal society, as in the New York Radical Women's WITCH ("Women's International Terrorist Conspiracy from Hell," *Going Too Far* 72), contemporary neo–pagan witchcraft as defined and practiced by women such as Starhawk actually traces its roots to the pre-Christian nature religions of Old Europe.[8] One of the clearest evidences of this lineage is witchcraft's celebration of eight seasonal festivals, the four Celtic fire festivals plus the equinoxes and solstices. The other is the Pagan reverence of deity as female. Contemporary women have been drawn in increasing numbers to witchcraft's acceptance and reverence of the female and the natural world. As a result, many experience a desire to bring about change in the outer world through political action. Sylvia Bovenschen, in analyzing the figure of the witch in women's protests, is pessimistic in her evaluation, largely because she fails to connect the reemergence of the witch with a spiritual practice which is feminist in its politics (83–87). In contrast, in her landmark study of contemporary neo–Paganism, *Drawing Down the Moon* (1986) Margot Adler notes that "feminist Witches have stated that Witchcraft is not incompatible with politics, and further that the Craft is a religion historically conceived in rebellion and can therefore be true to its nature only when it continues its ancient fight against oppression" (173).

The varieties of witchcraft practiced today allow women to explore their spirituality alone (solitary practice), with both men and women (many branches), or only with other women (Dianic), as they wish. Thus, witchcraft and its rituals may be seen as either a grassroots means of creating the spiritual basis of egalitarian community between the sexes or as reclaiming and reinventing women's mysteries. Earlier "how to" introductions to witchcraft, such as Starhawk's *The Spiral Dance,* Janet and Stewart Farrar's *The Witches' Goddess* (1987), Z. Budapest's *The Holy Book of Women's Mysteries,* Doreen Valiente's *Witchcraft for Tomorrow* (1978), and Marion Weinstein's *Earth Magic* (1986) are now accompanied on bookstore shelves by a plethora of new introductory texts which testify to the growing interest in neo–Pagan witchcraft as a grassroots movement. The varieties of contemporary witchcraft differ from the more "generic" Goddess worship and ritual discussed above in that there is an identification with a specific locale, Europe, and in that there are historical connections which predate the modern women's liberation movement. The spread of Wicca as part of European beliefs corresponds to the overwhelmingly European American makeup of both the feminist spirituality and neo–Pagan movements (Eller 18–19, Adler 253). On a positive note, this situation reflects the desire of European Americans to connect with an aspect of their heritage which does not promote exploitation and oppression, rather than borrowing from other traditions, a practice which has drawn sharp criticism, especially from Native Americans (Smith 169).

Wiccan rituals, like many Goddess rituals, involve the creation of sacred space as symbolized by the circle; attunement with the four elements of earth, air, fire, and water; and invocation of the Goddess in one or more of her aspects. In some forms of Wicca, the God may also be invoked, but he is the Goddess' complement and consort, not her lord and master.[9] As I have noted, the major festivals of witchcraft are solar and fire oriented celebrations; the other major ritual, the esbat, is lunar oriented, celebrating the times of the dark and full moons. Also, personal rites, such as dedications of a child, handfastings (marriage), and initiations are performed. While some witches practice alone, either by choice or necessity, the coven is the term by which the worshiping group is usually known. While patriarchal media have done its best to depict the coven as a collection of diabolical, power-hungry Satanists, members of covens see their groups quite differently. As Starhawk puts it:

> The coven is a Witch's support group, consciousness-raising group, psychic study center, clergy-training program, College of Mysteries, surrogate clan, and religious congregation all rolled into one. In a strong coven, the bond is, by tradition, "closer than family": a sharing of spirits, emotions, imaginations. "Perfect love and perfect trust" are the goal [*Spiral Dance* 49].

The coven, then, provides an opportunity for people to explore knowledge and share spirituality in a system other than one defined by a patriarchal, hierarchical structure. The size, usually anywhere from three to twenty members, also encourages independence, autonomy, and diversity among groups.

A number of the novels I discuss openly introduce the figure of the witch, suggest her presence, or depict groups operating on the ideals of the coven structure discussed above. The critic who reads such texts as Gael Baudino's *Strands of Starlight*, Lynn Abbey's *Daughter of the Bright Moon*, Gloria Naylor's *Mama Day*, or Marion Zimmer Bradley's *City of Sorcery* with only the image of the Satanic hag in mind will fail to understand the witch as a figure of female power and spiritual leadership.

Spiritual feminists combine woman-centered, Goddess, and earth-centered approaches when creating rituals in order to dissolve false binaries such as nature/culture and spiritual/political. Through ritual, they first seek changes in their own consciousnesses as a necessary part of making broader changes in social consciousness. For example, rituals can help dissolve the barriers between women, especially women of different cultures. Luisah Teish, who calls her own altar circle, or ritual group, a "rainbow" due to its racial variety, notes that unity requires effort, but asserts that "[a] demonstrated effort to respect the ancestral culture of your altar sisters will de-fang the demon racism and inspire a level of trust. Let us enrich our individual lives by celebrating our collective diversity. All flowers are not roses" (*Jambalaya* 254). I observe spiritual feminists as using ritual as a spiritual tool to "exorcise" the patriarchal demon of an internalized sense of inferiority, whether based on gender, race, class, or sexual preference, from the deepest areas of consciousness. In order truly to overcome the false dichotomy between the spiritual and material, action in the material world can be seen as spiritual action (Starhawk, *Dreaming the Dark* 169). This viewpoint enables many groups to combine public ritual with group action.

One of the better known groups which typifies this approach is the Reclaiming Collective, with Starhawk as one of its most recognized members. For those demonstrators who care to participate, the Reclaiming Collective has offered creative ritual at protest actions such as ones held at the Diablo Canyon Nuclear Power Plant. Starhawk comments: "In planning a magicopolitical event, the importance of having a clear focus cannot be over-stressed. If the purpose of an action is vague or the target is obscure, no spark is kindled in potential participants" (171). But with focus comes action, the power of which is at work on many levels. As Starhawk notes, "Changing anger to will is one useful magic trick I have learned in all these years of training and practice" (*Dreaming* 177). Feminist ritual connects individual empowerment with social change.

The role of ritual in the feminist spirituality movement must be contextualized for two important reasons. First, one must understand the influences which allow for the current literary representations of these types of rituals. Second, one must understand what authors who are influenced by ritual are bringing to their works. For instance, just as a knowledge of Flannery O'Connor's Catholicism is crucial to an interpretation of her work, so too is an awareness of Gael Baudino's role as a minister of Dianic Wicca important for interpretation of her theological stance. Just because one religion is less well known or accepted by the dominant culture, does not reduce its presence as a component of a text's meaning. Many of the novels I discuss include ritual without focusing on it entirely. A critic who is unaware that contemporary ritual practices are being drawn upon risks missing important spiritual aspects of the texts, aspects which I believe many readers recognize and relate to, allowing them to understand the larger thematic concerns of the author.

Womanspirit

Finally, the fourth area investigated anew by spiritual feminists is that of psychic phenomenon, or "womanspirit." In her *Dictionary of Feminist Theory,* Maggie Humm defines womanspirit as "[a] feminist spiritual philosophy which weaves together strands of women's history and mythology. Womanspirit is based on a belief in the Great Goddess and it advocates study of astrology, dreams, the I Ching, Tarot, and Yoga" (241). In my discussion I use the term "womanspirit" to refer more specifically to the alternative studies of healing, divination, meditation, and other psychic exploration to which Humm alludes. While some men have used these techniques at various times throughout history, contemporary women's use of them differs in serving both a spiritual and political feminist purpose. This double purpose also differentiates these arts from their other reappearance in popular culture under the nomenclature of "New Age" metaphysics, which focuses on the individual in a nonpoliticized context. As Starhawk comments in *Truth or Dare*, at its worst, New Age philosophy dismisses the fact that "reality is a collective event and can only be shaped by collective action" (24).

The New Age concept of creating one's own reality can be positive, however, when it informs women's appropriation of tools not recognized by a narrow, male-dominated scientific view of the universe which chooses to validate only those perceptions which can be observed in the laboratory. Spiritual feminists are concerned with healing women and the planet, and they use whatever works. In "The Healing Powers of Women," Chellis Glendinning asserts that "for women to heal ourselves is a political act. To reclaim ourselves as whole and strong beings is to say 'No' to the patriarchal view of women as weak and 'misbegotten'" (*The Politics of Women's Spirituality* 291). Unlike therapies or drugs which purport to heal women while failing to identify sexist and racist oppression as the primary threat to women's spiritual, mental, emotional, and physical health, the spiritual feminist works to heal the social organism. Since feminist spirituality recognizes organisms as interdependent, healing must take place not only within the individual woman, but within the community and the globe, in all areas of relationship among all life forms. The creation of a life-affirming value system and praxis is the healing goal of the feminist spirituality movement.

In addition to healing, many women choose to develop psychic skills, viewing them as additional ways of knowing which must be exercised in order to keep a balance between the various qualities or faculties of the mind. Following Jung, these qualities have traditionally been described as "masculine" and "feminine" traits, or at times, "the" masculine and "the" feminine. While these usages are problematic in that they convey a type of essentialism, a number of feminists have found Jung's terminology useful, and write about the human need to connect with our psychic, intuitive side, the feminine qualities suppressed by patriarchy (Mariechild xii–xiv). Many spiritual feminists hope that as these faculties once again gain broader acceptance, such gender-restrictive terminology will change, since the language is often interpreted as indicating that females are naturally psychically gifted while men are not. Most writers on womanspirit, including Mariechild, claim that everyone is psychic in some way, that psychic power is only awaiting development, and that this exploration provides new sources of energy with which to fuel the struggle to enact change and live full lives (xiii). These authors assert that if women are to reclaim power, they should not limit themselves to the narrow definition of power as the ability to control and dominate the material world.

The concept of psychic phenomena as displayed in contemporary speculative literature raises two issues. First, the acceptance of the psychic realm as real begins to blur the lines between typical definitions of fantasy, magical realism, and realism. Second, such presentation serves as an exploration of what it could be like to have these abilities fostered culturally. All the novels which I discuss in my study include psychic phenomena as integral to the human experience. The continuing interest among spiritual feminists and numerous other groups and movements in psychic exploration strongly indicates that the realm of the psychic not be viewed merely as a generic set piece when represented in literature, but instead as an indicator of the ongoing search for a mental balance upset by the dominance of the patriarchal scientific worldview.

Womanspirit techniques, like rituals, the Goddess, and historical/mythological revision, serve to empower women by helping women to see themselves as powerful, creative beings who do not have to accept or perpetuate patriarchal reality for themselves. Eller notes that the goal of feminist spirituality is the empowerment of women as women, to "creat[e] a new kind of womanhood, one that is not oppressive ... and does not require that [women] be disempowered" (217). The purpose of feminist spirituality is not to escape political challenge, but to offer women the tools to change themselves and the culture. As Judith Martin declares, feminist spirituality helps women to "find their true selves and, thereby, be empowered to contribute as equals to the construction of a more just, egalitarian and peaceful world order" (118).

2
Rewriting History and Legend

Lacking feminist narratives to compete with those of the Bible, classics, and legends, women have had to create the stories which otherwise might have been handed down to us by our foremothers. Although some might argue that exceptions exist in the realm of personal or familial storytelling, feminists criticize the dominant texts which form the foundation of western culture as androcentric, perpetuating the interests of patriarchy by serving as authorities and prescribing role models.[1] Since androcentric narratives have so strongly shaped the world in which women find themselves, many women writers have felt a need to counteract the stories of patriarchy with female-focused narratives of their own. Women who write against patriarchal narratives frequently change form as well as content. Critics such as Annis Pratt and Ellen Moers have found that one change in content is usually achieved through a focus on female characters and subjects traditionally considered feminine, such as relationships; formal changes include the adoption of circular rather than linear narrative.

Four novels which exemplify the feminist retelling of myth or legend are Kim Chernin's *The Flame Bearers,* Marion Zimmer Bradley's *The Mists of Avalon* and *Firebrand*, and Alice Walker's *The Temple of My Familiar*.[2] Bradley and Chernin rewrite texts which reflect the Jewish, Christian, and classical foundations of western patriarchal culture, foundations whose premises are seriously questioned by feminist reinterpretation. Walker's text adds the lens of race to gender, challenging the androcentric white supremacy inherent in western stories by connecting Goddess history to Africa. Each novel attempts to portray the previously unvoiced female side of these narratives, and in doing so provides a critique of various aspects of patriarchal history and values. Such critiques can also have the effect of producing a change in the reader's consciousness by awakening her to a new perspective on both past and present. I refer to this concept as "magical storytelling." After first examining the concept of magical storytelling as it appears in *The Flame Bearers*, I compare Bradley's uses of this technique in *The Mists of Avalon* and *The Firebrand*, followed by a reading of *The Temple of My Familiar*.

Although these aforementioned feminist narratives do create "herstory," I have chosen to title this section "Rewriting History and Legend" to emphasize that these feminist texts demonstrate a desire to revise, and thus challenge, the dominant male narratives of western culture. While some critics might read these disruptions of tradition as nonetheless perpetuating the narratives they challenge, I argue that when women writers shift the focus of these texts to female subjects, the change effected is so great as to create a new kind of text. As Gloria Orenstein points out:

> Today's feminist matristic literature has the awesome task of dismantling those patriarchal cultural constructs which have masked the historical verities of female empowerment over eons of time, and which also have denied and degraded the human connection to the spiritual and natural world [*The Reflowering of the Goddess* 130].

In depicting female empowerment, these female writers do not seek to create a final feminist redaction, but rather a tapestry of different feminist voices responding to patriarchal exclusion. Orenstein observes that "what is most important is the dynamic by which one version sparks another, rather than the dynamic by which one version supersedes or dominates all others" (139). However, it must be noted that Bradley and Chernin are writing as European American women, an identity reflected in their primary concentration on gender to the exclusion of racial oppression. Walker, as an African American, emphasizes the role of race and class to a greater degree in the re-creation of history through fiction.

In revising the male monomyths of western literature, women writers often give priority to the female figures which in androcentric works lack authenticity for female readers. Women writers challenge the portrayal of women as either virgins or whores, as with the Old Testament's two Marys; "mad" prophetesses, such as Aeschylus' Cassandra; or evil witches, like Mallory's Morgan le Fay or the classical Medusa. Like the feminist historians and archaeologists who are discovering new materials about women's lives, and reevaluating old ones, feminist writers suspect that patriarchal interests have given us biased versions of history and legend, versions fostered by the attitude "history books are written by the winners."

While Gayle Green argues that the "search for women's cultures and communities, for lost matriarchies and goddesses" is "nostalgic" (292), I find that these texts are, in fact, efforts to remember the "more productive [form] of memory" based on a desire "to bring to mind" or "think of again," "to be mindful of," "to recollect" (297). Having struggled against such discursive erasure for millennia, women are articulating their present experiences, and are now imagining what the alternative histories might be. The writers in my study have chosen to try to answer the question, "What would these women say if they could share their side of the story, if they could comment on the actions of the men highlighted in these texts or mythologies?"

The work of feminist archaeologists, anthropologists, and historians has created a factual grounding, a rough sketch of women's history that fosters imaginative production and speculation concerning the missing pieces of the puzzle, as Christ discusses in "Reclaiming Goddess History" (*Laughter of Aphrodite* 161–78).[3] Equally important are the ways in which feminist use of factual research has furthered feminist artistic creation, notably so in the realm of speculative fiction, under which I would include magical realism. Because fiction writers are not bound by the need to adhere to known facts and educated hypotheses, they are free to fill in the thoughts and motives of women who struggled against patriarchy in its various manifestations, while simultaneously "project[ing] ... feminist goals from the critical to the fictional plane" (Murphy 84). They may also give fictional flesh to hypotheses about matriarchal and matrifocal cultures. Orenstein comments that "they must give consensus reality to their interpretations of the scant evidence we have. In this sense, historians may act as creators, and creators may act as historians" (*Reflowering* 131).

At the center of these creative histories is the story of the change from Goddess worship to God worship, an area of study about which Orenstein charges that we are suffering from "matristic, historical amnesia" (23).[4] Chernin, Bradley, and Walker tell stories designed to help women remember their lost history. *The Flame Bearers* tells the story of a sect of women who have continued Canaanite Goddess worship among the Jews. *The Firebrand* focuses on Kassandra's struggle to choose between serving the male gods of her culture, and the older goddesses whom she discovers, and *The Mists of Avalon* details the efforts of Morgaine to preserve Goddess worship in the face of the Christianization of Britain. *The Temple of My Familiar*, with its interwoven stories and focal characters, has Lissie present the rise of Goddess religion and the obscuring of black female power. Of these four novels, *The Firebrand* and *Temple* go the furthest in portraying the effects of feminist reevaluation on men's and women's lives by speculating on the possibilities for an egalitarian society.

As depicted in these novels, the conflict between Goddess culture and God culture goes far beyond the gendered depiction of deity. The conflict is between life-affirming value and symbol systems, and those which celebrate death and transcendence of the material world. Some spiritual feminists describe this conflict as "earth religion" versus "sky religion," referring to the patriarchal Indo-European tribes which forced worship of their violent sky Gods onto the Goddess-focused peoples they conquered.[5] Chernin, Bradley, and Walker explore the implications of this change in religious focus for the earth and its peoples, especially women. Their texts argue that this paradigm shift lies behind the societal glorification of war; the domination, destruction, and poisoning of the earth; and the exploitation and subjugation of women and people of color.

While Walker's Lissie is comfortable with her female power and the information gained from her past lives, Chernin and Bradley's female protagonists are often unwilling to engage in the religious conflict in which they find themselves. But this larger religious struggle becomes interwoven with their personal efforts to discover their voices, identities, and power. Therefore, before they can champion the Goddess, they must define her for themselves. Thus, these retellings go further than recovering female stories and perspectives. Like contemporary women, these protagonists must strive to describe their spiritual longings and name the object of those longings. Therefore, in my discussion of each novel I also note details of the protagonists' spiritual stories.

Carol Christ describes these writings as "ritual events," observing that "as women writers share their naming of experience, they forge connections to other women who hear their own unnamed longings voiced, their perceptions of the world and its powers given form" (*Diving Deep and Surfacing* 7). Although Gill Frith argues that myth criticism "offers a romantic, celebratory vision of a lost tradition of female goddesses [are there any other kind?] and woman-bonding ... and depends upon the assumption that women are naturally and uniformly *good*," the stories of the protagonists I discuss here and in the following chapters do not reinforce this idea. These characters struggle with themselves as well as with other forces, and when they fail, they often fail spectacularly.

The connection between the mythic and the personal is also linked to the recovery of the past through the enterprise of fiction, resulting in an emphasis on storytelling as a type of magic. If magic can be viewed as an action bringing about a change in consciousness which results in a change in one's world or reality, then storytelling which aims to alter consciousness, and thereby one's reality, can be termed magical.[6] When the story concerns deity and the life of the spirit, then that story is sacred as well as magical. Each of these novels, to some degree, reflects a concern with sacred, magical storytelling. In this sense, fantastic/speculative fiction not only depicts magic, it also works "magically." The female reader is taken into a past which has been hidden from her; she follows the journey of the protagonist to an understanding of the Goddess, and she may come away from the novel inspired to put the perspectives she has gained to work in her own life and world.

Rather than prescribing female behavior, feminist authors produce texts which aid the reimagining of one's past and allow a woman to write the script of her own future in a manner which challenges the typical plot structures which patriarchy outlines for women. Thus, these authors combine "the feminist politic of 'grass-roots activism' with the original meanings of text as a 'woven' fabric or structure" (Rosinsky 107). Commenting on the integration of women's spiritual and social quests, Christ remarks that one result is that "women will be eager to point out the false naming of power and value within patriarchy and to begin to name self, power, and value anew based on their experiences. They will be eager to create new ways of being for women in a new social world" (*Diving Deep and Surfacing* 130–31). When a woman does so, she becomes a magician, actively shaping her identity and her actions, rather than passively accepting the roles dictated for her by patriarchal culture.

Kim Chernin: The Transformative Word

The Flame Bearers has two interrelated subjects: first, the Goddess-focused teachings of the Flame Bearers as transmitted by the Shadmi women; and second, the resistance of Rae, the protagonist, to the responsibility implied by her role in this female spiritual tradition. Together, these concerns can be read as a parallel to the struggle of many contemporary women who try to maintain or recreate Goddess spirituality in a patriarchal world inimical not only to such efforts, but to the very idea of independent female existence. Although such women may be convinced of the worthiness of the task, the weight of the responsibility and the resistance encountered can cause them to want to pass the burden to some hypothetical others who can take their place.

Did the religion of the goddess die out or, as Chernin proposes, did it simply go underground, viewed by men as "women's nonsense — tolerated, when it was noticed at all, because it seemed so silly" (*FB* 51)? By proposing this scenario, Chernin writes a female-focused alternative history to the narrative of the Old Testament, creating a voice for the lost stories of the women of Canaan, the ancestresses of today's Jewish women. In turn, this storytelling may create a change in the consciousness of Chernin's present-day readers, Jewish and non–Jewish, by recognizing the existence of female-focused religious practices destroyed by the followers of Yahweh. Thus, belief in the Judeo-Christian tradition as primary is questioned.

The idea of sacred storytelling is particularly crucial to *The Flame Bearers*. Sarah Rachel's storytelling to Rae and the other Shadmi girls, and the lessons she tries to convey to them, are paralleled by the reader's position as audience to Kim Chernin's story of the Goddess worshipers of Canaan and of present-day worship, ritual, and magic. Like Rae, part of a listening audience, Chernin's reading audience must wrestle with the question of whether or not to become "Flame Bearers," carriers of true stories and healing into a world in desperate need of such knowledge and power.

The fictional creation of the Flam Trogers, or Flame Bearers, is Chernin's attempt to answer the question, "What became of the goddess worshipers of Canaan after Yahweh 'delivered' the Promised Land to the Hebrews?" The Old Testament tells us that during the conquest of Canaanite cities, many of the unmarried women were chosen as "brides" for their captors (Num. 31:17), and that the prophet Jeremiah railed against the followers of the goddess Ashera [also known as Astarte or Ashtoreth, depending upon locale] (Jeremiah 44). Clearly, the women of Canaan tried to keep their native religion alive even in the face of conquest. In fact, they had a great deal of success doing so, perhaps because many of the Hebrews remembered the Goddess worship of their ancestors.

However, Chernin's promotion of a Goddess tradition within the realms of organized Judaism is not depicted as anti–Jewish, regardless of the criticisms the novel expresses toward "el Shaddai," for example, by Sarah Rachel's mother: "Hach," she would snort, "and which of these father-worshipers didn't kill The Mother? Only the Hebiru were guilty? This nonsense is what you believe?" (110). Chernin indicates both the responsibility of the Hebrews for the destruction of Goddess worship in the Middle East and the possibilities for redemption to be found in an acknowledgment of history. Thus, the reader is warned away from anti–Semitism. As Carol Christ points out, we must "understand the role of biblical religions in the suppression of Goddess religion and female power in the West without 'blaming Jews'" (*Laughter of Aphrodite* 85).[7] This is an important caution which enables the reader to focus on Chernin's major concern, which is the value of female-focused religious tradition for the contemporary woman.

Through the Shadmi line of women, Chernin creates a believable model of historical Goddess worship and feminist resistance to patriarchal restrictions. The Shadmi line of Flame Bearers has a special distinction, as Sarah Rachel notes: "In our village it was said that one Shadmi, from every generation, became one of the Hovrodnikim. You know what it means? Lovers of the people. They are the seven sacred women to rise up in every generation" (60). Raisa, Sarah Rachel's mother and Rae's great-grandmother, is described as displaying typical Shadmi independence which does not conform to orthodox Jewish culture; she refuses to shave her head and wear the *shaytl*, or orthodox wig, and she also defies patrilocality by refusing to live at her husband's father's home.

Chernin uses the story of Raisa to emphasize the importance of women as teachers of female tradition; in this case, an intellectual and spiritual tradition, not a domestic one. By doing so, she also places herself within this tradition through the spiritual teachings present in her writing. In Raisa's time, Flam-Troger women would often dress as men so that they could move freely among the Jewish villages and spread the sacred teachings and rituals to other women (61–62). They would also open up schools, as did Raisa, to teach the girl children, and to search for successors who carried "the heylige ikra ... the sacred spark" (63). This searching and teaching can also be interpreted to apply to the present-day work of spiritual feminists within the academy. In one sense, Rae is carrying on a spiritual tradition within the academy, as exhibited in her research. On the other hand, she is not consciously emulating her lineage, but passively transmitting it. In *The Flame Bearers*, Chernin creates a history of female resistance to patriarchal religion, language, and history, a resistance transmitted from mother to daughter so that women would not suffer what Gloria Orenstein terms "amnesia" in regards to their history, their powers, and their interconnection with other life forms (*Reflowering* 23).

Given that Chernin creates for Rae an empowering female heritage, which many women would find enviable, one must ask why Rae wishes to run from it. She does so for several reasons: she questions whether her heritage is relevant for modern times; she fears the responsibility that being one of the Hovrodnikim would entail. And she worries that accepting the life of a Flame Bearer will overwhelm her hard-won individual identity. Through her characterization of Rae's struggle, Chernin addresses some of the questions feminists have about the role of spirituality, especially Goddess spirituality, in their lives.

How "Old World" powers and stories can function for the twentieth–century American mind, raised on the worship of things scientific and technological, is a valid question. Are mysteries only awaiting the proper scientific tools to investigate them? Jacob, the husband of Rae's cousin Naamah, is often used in the novel as a sounding board for Rae's questioning of the relevance of being a Flame Bearer. In voicing her doubts about the relevance of her grandmother's teachings, she tells him, "It can't be transplanted. Here, it's a grotesque" (40). When Jacob warns Rae not to divulge any teachings which would not be permitted to him, she responds scornfully. But Jacob warns her: "'You think you have solved the mystery by calling the mystery "psychic phenomena"? ...You think you can cast it off like that and run away and leave it behind? You cannot'" (44–45).

Like some modern spiritual feminists in the academy, Rae is torn between these two perspectives; university trained, she can rationally dissect the idea of a living mystery tradition:

> To me it all seems a remarkable concoction of self-inflation and fantasy woven about with fragments from an undoubtedly genuine folk tradition. ...I spent, after all, more than four years on a thesis to demonstrate the presence of Asherah worship in the Old Testament. ... My grandmother took literally what was in reality a great and beautiful fable, the compensation no doubt on the part of generations of women for their exclusion from intellectual and spiritual Jewish life [158–59].

Here, Chernin mocks the way in which scholars, even feminist ones, can be so bound by the patriarchal emphasis on rationality and categorization that they drain the lifeblood and vitality from their object of study.[8] This critique also points to fantastic fiction as more amenable to the depiction of spiritual matters.

Further, Rae's arguments reflect the fears that some feminists have about the pursuit of Goddess studies and ritual practice: that such pursuits only serve the patriarchal labeling of women as emotional and intuitive beings, incapable of logic and out of touch with the "real" world. Readers, especially female ones, are not to take stories of magic and power "too literally," lest, like Rae's grandmother, we wish to be mocked as over credulous and gullible. If, like Rae, we are confronted with evidence that what some would call magic does exist, then we too must face the battle between what our experience tells us is real, and what our culture tells us can be real. Feminist spiritualists, especially those in the academy, are frequently marginalized and their work discounted because their subject matter lies outside standard patriarchal academic notions of the possible or acceptable.[9]

Rae's fear of the responsibility of being a holy woman, a Hovrodnikim, is also common to modern women on a spiritual quest. The Flame Bearers are said to gather "when the world trembles and shakes, knowing it stands at the edge to lose itself; into the voids, the Flame Bearers gather. From the four corners they are called back to the place where the four corners meet" (46–47). Our world, which faces the possibility of ecological ruin, nuclear and biological warfare, and social unrest and upheaval, can be seen as ready to fall "into the voids." Many feminists assert that a feminist perspective is necessary to avert these disasters, the logical results of the destructive patriarchal drive to control.[10] Yet knowing the rightness of the struggle does not lessen the burden of waging it. If, like the Flame Bearers, women are joining across the globe to save themselves and the planet (as in the ecofeminist movement), they might, as Rae does, question why this responsibility has fallen to them, and if anyone else can do it.

The weight of the responsibility of acting as a "holy woman" has two other components: a sense of separation, and a need to continually question what constitutes reality and truth. Sacred stories can help women with both issues. Like Rae, feminist spiritualists may feel separated from those who do not choose such a path. Moving outside the pale of what much of society calls reality, women redefining their spirituality must continually question for themselves what is belief and what is madness. As Jacob says concerning Rae's confusion over how to interpret her grandmother's legacy, they must "[suffer] in the ambiguity"(45). Maya, Rae's jealous cousin, also serves to warn the reader of the dangers of fanaticism and competition, for in her desire to prove herself more worthy than Rae, she becomes unbalanced and goes mad. For those who have no teachers to direct them, as Naamah notes, "the initiation comes up out of itself, crude and terrifying" (205). Women undergoing an initiatory process may feel lost until they connect with others who "dig up what science and reason have buried," which is why matristic storytelling and the reclamation of female tradition is so important (164). Carol Christ observes that this "new naming," as she terms it, allows "new possibilities of being and living for … all women. With the creation of a new language, the possibility that women will forget what they know is lessened" (*Diving Deep* 23).

Rae's dilemma speaks to the risks and rewards which result when women begin to write/tell/live their own stories. Sacred stories of women's spiritual history remind women of the larger context of their personal stories. To try to heal the world is an uncertain enterprise, yet there are rewards: "In the eyes of the people a Flame Bearer sees herself" (126). A Flame Bearer gains her identity through her holy work, not through the traditional integers of spouse or children. Sarah Rachel, for example, is revered for her spiritual position and abilities by the group of women with whom she regularly meets (22). This calling both frightens and intrigues Rae: the chance to create her own subjectivity in ways most women do not realize or attempt. While some may view a life of service as a traditional female role, in *The Flame Bearers* service is depicted as powerful and invested with authority earned by respect for one's abilities.

Through Rae, Chernin emphasizes that the spiritual woman cannot deny her nature. Rae's struggle to create her own identity brings her into conflict with her role in the succession of Flame Bearers. "Rae" is the shortened form of Isarael, "'she who wrestles with God and prevails'" (35). Clearly the male God of the Jews is the one against whom Isarael is expected to wrestle and prevail. Also, while the biblical Jacob wrestles with God and prevails, Rae's verbal wrestling with the character Jacob is essential to her acceptance of her existence as a Flame Bearer who must prevail as successor. Rae's appearance also underscores her essence and existence as a Flame Bearer; she is described as having "slanting, yellow eyes" and red hair, and even wears red boots on her return home (34). Still, her formation of an east coast academic life demonstrates her strong desire to escape the destiny expected from her since birth, no matter how many family ties she must destroy in the process.

Near death, Sarah Rachel, believing herself to be the last of the Shadmi line (a belief the reader later finds is mistaken), misuses her power by attempting to force Rae's choice, rather than having her make it freely. Sarah Rachel, who is Rae's surrogate mother as well as grandmother, has expectations for Rae which are as confining in their own way as those a traditional mother in a patriarchal family might have for her daughter, which shows that women can also be oppressive. The spiritual life must be acknowledged and chosen, not forced by another. Thus, Rae's temporary embracing of life in a patriarchal institution, the academy, serves as an understandable act of individuation. Chernin's plot, which indicates that this period of rebellion must be followed by a period of reexamination of identity, asserts that both phases are an understandable part of women's struggle to understand and accept their spiritual natures.

When a woman chooses the spiritual path, her life story may seem to write itself, as though scripted by an overwhelming, transformative force. As Rae approaches the corpse of her grandmother, she is transfigured: "Her hair turned white before she reached the gray chair near the window. A scar, which no one had seen for a long time, appeared on her forehead. It looked something like a sickle moon and something like a small flame" (142). The ashlike nature of Rae's appearance at this point is suggestive of the crucible, the process by which the extraneous desires of the ego are burned away in order for the soul's purpose to be revealed and acted upon. Rae's destiny finds her in the form of "Kovahl. The story the way it must be written. Not the way we want it should be" (93). The need for Rae to fulfill her identity as a Flame Bearer wrestles with, and overcomes, her desire to be an ordinary woman with the usual worldly concerns. When the reader applies the implications of Rae's transformation to other women involved in the struggle to identify themselves as spiritual questers, she finds that Chernin is validating the primacy of the spiritual life, affirming its need to be at the center of the mental and physical manifestations of identity and life, rather than a tangential concern.

At other times, the spiritual woman uses other women's stories as guides, but in doing so makes them her own as well. When Rae makes her decision, she is unsure of what she must do as the successor. The remainder of the novel details this portion of her search, and here, Chernin's ideas concerning magical storytelling coalesce. As I have noted before, the Flame Bearers rely on both oral and written transmission of their teachings. Their oral tradition is designed to do more than impart information:

> this storytelling — with its repetitions, incantatory style of delivery, the rhetorical flourishes, the slight swaying forward and back in the old woman's body, the stylized gestures and self-answering questions — had as its central purpose the induction of a trance state in which the girls would relive the scenes she was describing [66].

As Orenstein notes, "storytelling in the oral tradition, as Chernin conceives it, induces gnosis and is a sacred, magical art giving access to secret knowledge, both of women's histories and of their mysteries" (*Reflowering* 155). Such storytelling may free one not only to imagine the subject but also to enter into the story. Sarah Rachel, noting that the stories of men are preserved in books and libraries, comments: "But our stories, the women's stories, what becomes of them? And what became of Kiryat Sefer, our City of the Book, and the libraries we had there and the houses of study? In the heart they live, where else? And in the memory" (90). She indicates that while the stories of women may not be as widely circulated as they should be, they are all the more valuable because they must be sought after. This statement is not only a commentary on the importance of feminist magical storytelling, but also a rationale and defense of Chernin's own techniques in the creation of her "sacred" text.

Through Rae and Naamah's investigation of Rocha Castel, Chernin creates a more explicit connection between oral tradition and the written text. The key to Kiryat Sefer, the mystical City of the Book, is held by

Rocha Castel, the great scribe of the Flame Bearers, to give to "Ha Melamed Gadol, for the Great Teacher the next time she walks upon this earth" (65). Rae is given the key but gives it to Maya in the mistaken belief that by her act she can help pull Maya out of her madness. Instead, the key accentuates her imbalance, and in a scene where Maya nearly dies after dancing with the fiery vision of Hannah Leah, the key disappears, leaving only burning logs, and a scar on Maya (215–17). One cannot live another's life, or write another's story for her, as Naamah realizes, and Rae's misconception that she can do so provides another setback on her search, forcing her to work with Naamah's efforts in the written realm. Again, "kovahl," the story as it must be written, is at work in Rae's life. The spiritual journey requires that each woman achieve her understanding on an individual basis; authors and teachers can help by pointing out "key" texts and stories, but the burden of incorporating that knowledge as part of one's life ultimately rests on the woman's openness to intuition and inspiration.

Chernin implies that the story of women's spiritual history and future must be written through a process of magical incantation, a calling into being which makes the story of the past visible in its telling in the eternal present. When Rae muses about whether Naamah's dictation, or automatic writing, should be accepted, she notes that no one is bothered when men claim to have received inspiration for their writing, but that when women do it people dismiss their work (243–44). This comment serves as a defense of Chernin's method and storytelling purpose. Orenstein, following through on Chernin's hints that *The Flame Bearers* is a treatise on feminist literary and mythic production, makes this observation:

> it dawns upon the reader of this genre of feminist matristic fiction that there may be a level of truth in the fiction that is of the order of a mystical revelation rather than of a purely imaginary invention. In any case, where the line between imagination and the Gnostic accessing of past-life recall is to be drawn certainly becomes blurred in feminist matristic literature. The teaching transmitted by this novel is that the act of creation is one means to accessing a kind of truth that our written records deny [*Reflowering* 156].

While stopping short of saying that inspiration equals factuality, Orenstein asserts that women's fictional texts may often be read as glosses on a process which creates works which are more than "fictional." In effect, the purpose of storytelling is not to set out the facts, but to create a story through sound and meaning that creates in the hearer a state of consciousness that brings about transformation. Orenstein notes that "Storytelling ... becomes the dominant metaphor for the magical art that literally creates a new feminist matristic reality in which we, too, can participate" (150). As if to respond to those who find such a notion implausible, Sarah Rachel says: "What was for us the world of ourself would be for the others, who came after, only a story. Words in the air ... smoke with no fire" (135). But this is not the reality of the situation. As Naamah works through the letters of Rebekah, Sarah Rachel's forgotten sister who was called to work with the Falashas, or Ethiopian Jews, she finds that the Falashas' name for the Flame Bearer tradition is "Nappeh, a user of the bellows, charash, a smith who works magic" (269); clearly, where there is smoke there is also fire, and magic.

The writer, or smith, is seen as forging a magical product — the story. For one to understand these texts, however, one must understand that the style employed is "a Flame Bearer way of communicating on many levels at one time." Just as Naamah and Rae must read Rebekah's letters on many levels if the way to Kiryat Sefer is to be found, so also must we read the levels of Chernin's text which convey her desire to create a history which may enable women to help end "the age of el Shaddai." Chernin, figuratively a "great scribe" like Rocha Castel, offers her readers a key to help them find their way back to the lost city of women's history.

For the reader, as for Rae, the stakes are a return to Chochma, the Mother. But what does that mean? To return to the Mother is to leave the reign of Shaddai, "the Lord of Fear"(83). It charges one to work for the day when the peoples of the world are unified and at one with the land (73). Here, Chernin articulates a vision which is based on interconnection while it acknowledges diversity, and is ecofeminist in its concern for the land. Finally, it signifies working the magic needed to heal a world which on the brink of collapse (46). And part of the work, part of that magic, is telling the stories which help us change our consciousness, as Chernin does within and through *The Flame Bearers*. In a comment likely aimed at feminists who dismiss the importance of spirituality, Chernin seems to be saying:

> You think I am foolish sitting here with my old papers? But how do you know what matters in the world? You are so certain marching about in a picket line with a sign, and writing a petition and walking in Washington is more effective than telling an old story? ...Why are you so sure? [203].

By rewriting ancient Jewish history, Chernin urges all women to remember a time when we were free, and to bring the life-affirming, matristic qualities of that era's Goddess worship into our present as a basis for action and social change. Change fostered by spiritual renewal begins at the individual level, but does not end there; it moves outwardly to affect others. As Nancy Passmore charges, "[e]very thought you have directly affects every event in all the universes. Awareness means participating in your own evolution" (171). When women revise history, they literally see it from a different stance: one which places them at the center. By carrying this centrality forward to the present, women are empowered to create the future as well.

Marion Zimmer Bradley: The Priestesses Speak

Like Chernin's *The Flame Bearers*, Marion Zimmer Bradley's *The Mists of Avalon* and *The Firebrand* are excellent examples of the rewriting of androcentric narratives from a feminist perspective of magical storytelling. In the same way that Bradley's Darkover ouvre revises many of the conventions of traditional male science fiction texts, *The Mists of Avalon* and *The Firebrand* revise specific Christian and classical narratives, as opposed to generic conventions. In a similar fashion to Chernin, Bradley not only retells each legend from the point of view of a female character, but also situates the legend within the historical conflict between God and Goddess worship, thus drawing on a perspective made possible by feminist scholarship.

One can view *The Mists of Avalon* as accomplishing three purposes: first, the novel retells the Arthurian legend from the point of view of a female character who sees the primary conflict as one between Goddess religion and Christianity; second, the novel asserts the desire for the Goddess as a continuing human need; and last, the novel serves to define power by contrasting power over others with inner power, or power over one's self. Bradley personalizes the conflict between Goddess worship and Christianity through Morgaine's struggle to understand her role as a priestess and to claim her own power.

As a retelling of Arthurian legend, *The Mists of Avalon* also points to the grail legend as a symbol of the Goddess, the loss of whom is sensed by the human psyche even as Christianity "won." Orenstein describes the novel as "concerned with wresting the Grail from the hands of patriarchy, and returning it to the Goddess in order for life on Earth to flourish again" (*Reflowering* 182). This focus on the grail encompasses the realization that it does matter what names we call deity, even if, ostensibly, we refer to the same reality or source. As Carol Christ argues, when we view deity as an omnipotent, judgmental father figure, we grant that authority to men and patriarchal institutions (*Laughter of Aphrodite* 138). In addition, Bradley's sources for her rewriting (discussed in detail later) point out that our relationship to the past is a circular, as opposed to linear, process. Our present existence colors our perception of the past, and the past continually reaches forth to shape the present and future. Thus, the feminist revisioning of history and legend details the different effects of patriarchal religions and matrifocal religions on women's lives, thereby questioning contemporary patriarchal religions and positing the value of Goddess religions for contemporary culture.

The positive treatment of women in Goddess religions and their negative treatment under Christianity come under close examination in *The Mists of Avalon*. Much like Chernin, in Bradley's fictive world the loss of the Goddess is much more than the loss of a symbol. It also signals the loss of entire cultural supports for female autonomy and power. In the Goddess-focused religion of the British Tribes, women are seen as the Goddess' representatives. Whether or not they are her priestesses, all women relate to her aspects as Maiden, Mother, and Crone at various points in their lives.[11] In Christianity, however, all women are symbolically linked with Eve; they share her willfulness and sinfulness, should be subservient to males, and certainly are not fit to create doctrine or perform holy rites. Bradley emphasizes this conflict over women's proper roles in an exchange between Gorlois and Morgaine's mother, Igraine, concerning Morgaine's future. Igraine, whose mother is the Lady of Avalon, takes pride in her royal and magical heritage, while her husband Gorlois, following the Roman fashion, adheres to patriarchal Christian beliefs:

> Morgaine perhaps should be brought up in a convent of holy women, so that the great evil she has inherited from your old blood will never taint her. ... A holy man told me once that women bear the blood of their mothers, and so it has been since the days of Eve, that what is within women, who are filled with sin, cannot be overcome by a woman-child; but that a son will bear his father's blood even as Christ was made in the image of God his father [86].

Clearly, a woman would have difficulty approaching the Christian God, and representing God would be totally out of the question. Later, on her deathbed, Igraine dismays Gwenhwyfar by telling her she sent Morgaine to Viviane to keep her out of "'the hands of the black priests who would teach her to think that she was evil because she was a woman'" (359). That Bradley's sympathies lie with Igraine's sentiment can be seen from the fact that she not only uses Morgaine as the controlling consciousness of the novel, but also radically revises her traditional depiction, as Lee Tobin and Jeanette Smith have observed. Charlotte Spivack also asserts that

> This complex and largely sympathetic character is a far cry from the evil manipulator portrayed in such tales as Sir Gawain and the Green Knight. Here she is both fate and the fated (Morgana Fata), both the fairy enchantress (Morgan le Fay) and the embattled human, subject to pressures from within her own nature and from the world without [153].

Whereas previous redactors of the legend have seen Morgaine as wicked and malevolently sorcerous, the precipitator of Arthur's downfall, Bradley creates a Morgaine who is a devoted priestess trying to preserve a heritage threatened by Christian intolerance.

This heritage includes a reverence for the natural world and for physical processes. Like Chernin's view of Chochma, Bradley depicts the Goddess as the earth mother with her cycles of death and rebirth. Her constant is change. The God of the Christians, however, is viewed as transcendent, with death and change the marks of a separate and "fallen" world. In the religion of the Tribes, sex is celebrated both for pleasure and as the act of human fertility. In ritual coupling, the female and male are considered to be the Goddess and the God, whose intercourse promotes fertility for humans, animals, and plants. In early British theology, the king first "wed" the land through hieros gamos, or sacred marriage, with the priestess.[12] Thus, Viviane chooses Morgaine as the priestess who mates with her half brother Arthur, the "King Stag," not out of a perverse desire for incest, but out of hopes that Morgaine will use the relationship to shape Arthur's rule with the power of Avalon.

Unfortunately, Viviane does not count on the influence of Morgaine's early Christian upbringing. Morgaine does not consider the ritual coupling as incestuous, but feels that the subsequent lovemaking for pleasure (as opposed to ritual) was incestuous, even though she did not realize Arthur's identity (181). The preaching of the priests of her childhood causes Morgaine to flee Avalon and Viviane, forsaking her priestesshood, ruining Viviane's plans for her, and setting into motion the series of events which ultimately lead to Arthur's ruin. Though Arthur seeks salvation in the Christian faith, Bradley depicts Christianity as being sterile and puritanical, and at the root of the causal chain which ends in his downfall.

Bradley also depicts the historically verified hostility of the Christian priests toward the celebration of sex and nature, which led them and their followers to try to exterminate the folk festivals of the land.[13] Morgaine and Gwenhwyfar represent opposite positions on this process, thus highlighting the difference in the deities each woman serves. In one example, as queen of Wales, Morgaine goes with her husband Uriens to observe the blessing of the crops, a festival of pagan origin now attended by the priests. She thinks to herself, "these priests hate fertility and life so much, it is a miracle their so-called blessing does not blast the fields sterile" (583).

Further, when Uriens, at the instigation of his priests, threatens to cut down the sacred groves, she thinks "if you do, I shall do murder" (657). With the encouragement of her priests, Gwenhwyfar makes it her personal mission to Christianize Arthur's court and land. She sets up Pentecost as the day of highest court celebration, not one of the days of Pagan celebration, such as Beltane. She also works to encourage Arthur to outlaw the celebrations of the folk and to cut down the sacred groves. Commenting on Gwenhwyfar's puritanical nature, Tobin notes that "[e]ven though Gwenhwyfar plays more by the rules than the other women, she is the one who is raped" (153). This fact, combined with her inability to bear children, suggests that it is literally fruitless for women to follow Christianity. Although Gwenhwyfar finally convinces Arthur to fight under the banner of the Virgin and the cross, thus forsaking the Pendragon, this nearly causes the revolt of the Tribes, for they accurately see this act as an abandonment of his vows to Avalon and the faith of the Goddess (395–97). By implication, the abandonment of Goddess religion and principle is the root of our world's ecological and other crises.

Another area where conflict arises between the religion of the Goddess and Christianity is that of psychic powers. The powers of telepathy, precognition ("the Sight"), and divination are seen by many of the Christians in the novel as evil and sorcerous. This perspective stands in contrast to *The Flame Bearers*, where these powers are dismissed as irrational in the modern world. For example, Elaine approaches Morgaine for her knowledge and help, only to call Morgaine's wisdom and workings "sorcerous" later. Annette Van Dyke also notes that in *The Mists of Avalon*, Morgaine's sister Morgause also develops psychic powers, but uses them for selfish purposes, suggesting that "without the ethical standards imparted by the Goddess Religion — the training — the sight may be misunderstood and misused" (98).

While the differing treatments of women, nature, and psychic life characterize the struggle between Paganism and Christianity in the novel, the symbol of the Grail reveals how the Goddess, though outwardly denied by Christianity except in the sanitized form of the Virgin Mary, represents an enduring need of the human psyche for the unity, abundance, and interconnection denigrated in patriarchal Christian theology. In a move which underscores the drastic revision she has taken with the Arthurian tradition,

Bradley depicts Morgaine as the bearer of the Holy Chalice of the sacred Regalia of Avalon, which becomes the Grail of legend. Kevin, the traitorous Druid, had stolen the Regalia to be used by the priests of Arthur's court. As Bishop Patricius puts it, to be "newly dedicated in service to the True God" (770). Enraged, Morgaine invokes the presence of the Goddess, and in a moment of vision realizes the purpose her life has prepared her for: "She knew with certainty that all her life had been in preparation for this moment when, as the Goddess herself, she raised the cup between her hands."

As the force of the Goddess moves through her, Morgaine bears the Chalice around the room. As each person drinks of it, he or she receives a particular vision, and each finds "his plate filled with such things as he liked best to eat ... again and again she heard that tale, and by that token she knew that what she had borne was the cauldron of Ceridwen" (771). Ceridwen, Goddess of the cauldron from which all life flows and to which it returns only to be born again, appears to the Pentecostal crowd to remind them of the true meaning of the Chalice. It symbolizes the womb of the Goddess, and of woman, who manifests the changes which lead to birth, and then to death, in the cycles of her body.

The threatened co-optation of the Chalice is blasphemous for it would have been used to serve those who molded the teachings of Christ into a denial of the changing nature of earthly life. The disappearance of the Chalice inspires a quest to obtain it, a quest which scatters the Companions in the name of the God in whom Arthur has placed all his hopes for the unity of Britain. If the Grail is the symbol of the Goddess, then any quest made for it in the name of a male god is doomed to failure. A system conceived in duality, as the Christian one ultimately is in practice, can never achieve wholeness when it exists in a state of denial of the feminine.

Yet the psychic wholeness brought by the feminine will be sought in one form or another, and since it is never absent, only repudiated, those who are willing to forgo the system will begin to approach wholeness. At the close of the novel, Morgaine visits the convent at Glastonbury. There she discovers that the young nuns, finding their God "so great and terrible," worship Mary as their mother, and adopt such female "saints" as Brigid. Morgaine looks at the statue of Brigid which Patricius has brought from Ireland:

> But Brigid is not a Christian saint, she thought, even if Patricius thinks so. That is the Goddess as she is worshipped in Ireland. ... Exile her as they may, she will prevail. The Goddess will never withdraw herself from mankind [875].

This scene encapsulates and forecasts women's ability and need to search for the Goddess as exhibited in contemporary Goddess spirituality, and their willingness to forego male-centered religious systems in their search for wholeness. Even though Morgaine finds some comfort with her realization, the novel continually asserts that it does matter what one calls Deity.

The conflict concerning the naming of Deity hinges on the knowledge that names have power: for humans, the power to shape and create our reality. This belief in the power of naming is similar to the distinction Chernin places on the realities created by el Shaddai and Chochma. As Bradley's Taliesin says in speaking of "God" and "the Gods," "The older I grow, the more I become certain that it makes no difference what words we use to tell the same truths" (279). At an abstract level this sentiment may be true, at least for the ultimate Source one is addressing, but Kevin's treachery lies in going beyond Taliesin's position, for he aids the priests who would dictate how others call upon Deity and who term one version truth and the other sin.

Women's sacred histories emphasize how the naming of Deity can make a great deal of difference for women. Thus Morgaine, who realizes that "the Presence ... is One," recognizes that the priests' refusal to tolerate or speak of the Goddess is motivated by a lust for power and control, which bodes ill, especially for the earth and women. Carol Christ notes in *The Laughter of Aphrodite* that symbols "lead people to feel comfortable with or to accept social or political arrangements that correspond to the symbol system" (118). When the symbol of a male God is the only one available, the religion functions to "keep women in a state of psychological dependence on men and male authority, while at the same time legitimating the political and social authority of fathers and sons in the institutions of society" (118). Morgaine understands that Avalon, which represents the sacred feminine, will not be allowed to exist in such a society, and that Arthur's abandonment of Avalon for the Christian faith will cause Avalon to recede further and further into the mists, becoming a legend which can only be reached through the routes of the imagination. Searching through the obfuscating mists of patriarchy, Bradley has found the history and land of the Goddess with her imagination. Speaking her "words of power," Bradley parts the veil between the patriarchal and matrifocal worlds, allowing her readers to enter Avalon, the Isle of Apples, and eat of their wisdom, the wisdom of the fivefold star of the Goddess.[14] As with Chernin's effort to bring her readers to the lost city of Kiryat Sefer through magical storytelling, Bradley's text allows a reimagining of female history and power which the reader can carry back into consensus reality as a source of empowerment. However, Bradley's novel relies more on the idea of a reimagining, rather than the proposal of a tenuous tradition, as exhibited in *The Flame Bearers.*

That Bradley's novel should be interpreted within the larger context of feminist spirituality is indicated by a review of her sources. Her indebtedness to other efforts by feminist spiritualists is evident in the "acknowledgments" section of the work. She mentions at least a reading knowledge of Gardnerian Wicca, and personally thanks several prominent neo–pagan groups for helping her to understand "the feel of the ceremonies" (vi).[15] Bradley also credits Starhawk's *The Spiral Dance,* a neo–Pagan classic, for helping her to re-create the "training of a priestess." Finally, she gives her thanks "for much personal and emotional support (including comforting and backrubs) during actual writing of this book, to Diana Paxson, Tracy Blackstone, Elisabeth Waters, and Anodea Judith, of the Darkmoon Circle." Considering that Paxson has written several novels from a feminist pagan perspective (*Brisingamine, The White Raven,* and *The Serpent's Tooth*), and that Judith has authored a book on chakras [energy centers of the human body] (*Wheels of Life*), one might reasonably conclude that the members of the Darkmoon Circle share an interest in feminist spirituality which is more than passing curiosity (Fry, "The Goddess Ascending" 76–77).[16] Such clues, as well as the plot, indicate the importance of the cultural context of the reawakening of Goddess consciousness and spiritual practice. However, the effects of texts and practices can be circular, as this anecdote of Cynthia Eller's demonstrates: "In one workshop I attended on feminist wicca, the leader asked if anyone among the approximately twenty women present had read *The Mists of Avalon.* At least eighteen women raised their hands" (34).

The third major idea explored in *The Mists of Avalon* is the struggle women experience in trying to free themselves of patriarchal views of power as control over others. Through the characters of Viviane and Morgaine, Bradley differentiates between the idea of power over others and the idea of inner power, or power within.[17] While Viviane, as Lady of the Lake, is supposed to be the most visible human embodiment of the Goddess, whose power lies in interconnection, her actions show the degree to which patriarchal ideas of rulership and power have influenced her. In reaction to the effects of Viviane's power-mongering over her, Morgaine rejects both forms of power, and must eventually journey back to the source of her inner power and learn to use it. Here we find a similar generational struggle to that between Rae and Sarah Rachel, one where conflict occurs between women even as a female-focused tradition is being passed on.

Ideally, Viviane, as representative of the Goddess, should exhibit the qualities of that Deity: generosity, fertility, compassion, growth, fruitfulness, change, destruction, and death. The latter qualities are not negative or evil, but occur in a cyclical manner in order to maintain balance in the natural world. Unfortunately, Viviane has difficulty representing many of these qualities. She gives birth, but remains emotionally and physically distant from her offspring. Viviane also sees compassion as a weakness, causing her to distance herself from the people she comes close to loving, so that she may use them for her own plans and purposes (122). Rather than allowing events to happen "as the Goddess wills," Morgaine notes that Viviane "is all too sure that she knows the will of the Goddess" (147). The patriarchal ideas of control, fostered by an all-powerful patriarchal God, are what Viviane believes she is saving Britain from. In fact, she has already become corrupted by her "enemy." This view of power is part of the spiritual legacy she passes on to Morgaine, who moves through several stages of struggle with the issue of power before she finds the resolution which Viviane cannot.

The first stage of this struggle is one in which Morgaine rejects power-over, as exemplified by Viviane, but in doing so also rejects the aspects of the tradition of Avalon which have strengthened and sustained her. Here, Bradley's portrayal of Morgaine resembles Chernin's depiction of Rae, in that both characters rebel against individuals, and are unable to differentiate between those individuals and the teachings/sects they represent. In this sense, Bradley's portrayal of Morgaine differs greatly from that of Mallory's avaricious and power-hungry Morgan le Fay; Morgaine is the victim rather than the victimizer. In her despair over the incest and pregnancy, Morgaine abandons her position as priestess and future Lady of Avalon. Morgaine not only escapes Viviane's manipulation, but also unthinkingly abandons the entire support system she has relied upon as a priestess in training.

The second stage Morgaine goes through in her exploration of types of power is the abandonment of her personal power. As with Rae, this psychological and emotional distance/avoidance is paralleled by physical separation and movement. Morgaine drifts from Orkney, to Caerleon, to the world of the Faery, and back to Camelot, where she and Viviane are reunited, which results in Morgaine's willingness to return to Avalon. Again in an interesting parallel with Rae, there is a loss of the elder/ leader, causing the mantle of leadership to be passed to the mentee, who then experiences doubt and loss of direction. Viviane is murdered, and all of Morgaine's doubts return. Feeling that she is unworthy to return to Avalon in Viviane's place, Morgaine again abandons conscious control of her life, lost in a state of numbness and suspension. She marries Uriens and lives in Wales as queen until her stepson Accolon, a Druid, reawakens her sexuality, and thus her perception of the cycles of life and corresponding desire to serve as a priestess.

Morgaine then begins the struggle to reclaim her identity and her personal power, thus entering the third stage. Her identity is both secular and place-oriented, as well as tied to a female spiritual heritage: "I am queen in North Wales, and I am duchess in Cornwall, where Gorlois's name still means something, and I am of the royal line of Avalon" (579). As noted above, her awakening is tied in with her sexuality. Like Rae, Morgaine begins relearning all that had once been second nature to her as a priestess: not just rituals and salutations, but the movements of the lunar and solar tides, connection with the forces of the earth, and the Sight. Morgaine decides to take up the work which Viviane left unfinished: holding Arthur to the vows he made to Avalon. Importantly, her reawakening is characterized by a combination of sexuality, union with nature, and visionary capabilities, characteristics which Carol Christ sees as integral components of women's mystical experiences (*Diving Deep and Surfacing* 20–23).

In the fourth stage she must learn to differentiate between types of power. To a large degree, this problem arises from a difficulty in distinguishing between the Goddess' power and her own, the same difficulty Viviane experienced. Truly, if all life constitutes the Goddess, then the individual will of the soul is linked with that larger entity. However, one must not confuse the ego's desire for power with the will of the soul, nor mistake the part for the whole. Morgaine, who recognizes the power of the Goddess within herself, correctly perceives that the Christian denial of the Goddess is a threat to women and other forms of earthly life. This is why Arthur's vow, the last stronghold against the power of the priests, is so important. However, like Sarah Rachel, she is mistaken in her belief that only she can preserve the worship of the Goddess. Yes, she may be the only one who can preserve the worship of the Goddess as practiced in Avalon, but, as the actions of the nuns at the close of the novel show, the desire for that which is symbolized by the Goddess will bring about her worship, even if under another guise.

The Goddess represents balance, not omnipotence, even in her death-dealing aspects, and women must understand this idea of power. Before Morgaine comes to this realization, she must live in her own life the role of the Goddess as the Crone: destroyer, death-bringer, and dispenser of justice. Having already served in the roles of Maiden and Mother, Morgaine must test herself in the role of that last side of the Goddess before she can fully reclaim a balanced sense of power. First, when Avalloch, another of Uriens' sons, threatens to reveal the affair between Morgaine and Accolon unless Morgaine sleeps with him as well, she plans his death, not only to protect herself, but also to protect the Pagan worship in Wales (667). Next, when Arthur refuses to return Excalibur, she resolves to pit Accolon against him, in the mistaken belief that "Accolon should rule for Avalon" (720). Like Viviane, she could hardly have been more wrong in her assumptions.

Shortly after Morgaine miscarries/aborts the child fathered by Accolon (this is an ambiguity present in the novel), she finds that Accolon has failed against Arthur and lies dead as a traitor (743). Because she has wrongly attempted to use these destructive powers against others, and force them to her will, Morgaine fails, destroying all she has valued or worked for.

In stories of the female spiritual journey, one finds that the protagonist must experience a nadir in her life before a proper spiritual reorientation toward power can be achieved. Murdock terms this the descent aspect of the heroine's journey, which "may involve a time of voluntary isolation—a period of darkness and silence and of learning the art of deeply listening once again to self: of being instead of doing" (8). These qualities are evident when Morgaine abandons her life as royalty and then reaches her physical and spiritual nadir at Tintagel, her literal birthplace which becomes a place of figurative rebirth (751). Yet Kevin, aided by intuition, comes to her as a guide and helper, and in one of the novel's most moving passages, uses his music to invoke the presence of the Horned God, calling Morgaine, as the Goddess, back to life (755–56). She leaves Avalon only once more, to bear the Holy Chalice as the grail, secure in the knowledge that "I have called on the Goddess and found her within myself" (803). Her statement echoes the words of the "Charge of the Goddess": "... your seeking and yearning will avail you not, unless you know the Mystery: for if that you seek, you find not within yourself, you will never find it without" (quoted in Starhawk, *Spiral Dance* 91).

Because this action is not an attempt to manipulate others, but is in fact the Goddess' own statement of her presence, the carrying of the Chalice marks a pinnacle of Morgaine's attunement with the source of her own power. By being, rather than doing, Morgaine becomes one with life, and thus one with the Goddess. With this knowledge comes balance: she can act from a position of strength, yet it is a position which acknowledges interconnection. This depiction of her "resurrection" is evocative of many goddesses with chthonic aspects, such as Persephone and Inanna. Like Morgaine, they gain their greatest powers after losing the outer trappings of power and undergoing a type of death, then emerging into a new life, a pattern Annis Pratt refers to as the "rebirth journey" (*Archetypal Patterns* 136–37). For many spiritual feminists, this death is the rejection of life as defined by patriarchal judgments about women, which then frees them to create their lives outside those prescriptions.

The stages which Morgaine experiences, the rejection of power-over, the abandonment of her personal power, the rediscovery of her power-within, and her learning to differentiate between it and power-over are important in contemporary women's lives as well, and will be explored more thoroughly in the following chapter. For now it is sufficient to emphasize that spirituality based on interconnection allows a woman to break away from the "dominator" mode of power usage which characterizes patriarchal society (Eisler 28), and to note that discussions of personal explorations of power within women's lives must be understood in the contexts of the larger shifts in power as analyzed in these novels of sacred history.

At the opening of the novel, Morgaine explains both her ability to tell her tale and the necessity of the telling. She asserts:

> I have always held the gift of the Sight, and of looking within the minds of men and women; and in all this time I have been close to all of them. And so, at times, all that they thought was known to me in one way or another. And so I will tell this tale [x].

Through the figure of Morgaine, Bradley seems to claim a connection to consciousness which allows her to speak of the legend of Arthur. Significantly, she does not claim an absolute truth; only that she will tell the side of the story we have not heard. Morgaine comments:

> For this is the thing the priests do not know, with their One God and One Truth; that there is no such thing as a true tale. Truth has many faces and the truth is like to the old road to Avalon; it depends on your own will, and your own thoughts, whither the road will take you, and whether, at the end, you arrive in the Holy Isle of Eternity or among the priests with their bells and their death and their Satan and Hell and damnation [x].

In her revision of a male Christian monomyth, Bradley attacks not only previous redactors, but also their claims to absolute truth. Implicit in the above idea is the notion that the tales we tell or believe do shape the realities we create, the concept underlying magical storytelling examined earlier in regards to Chernin's work. Bradley's readers have experienced the separation and denial characteristic of a culture based on the tales of the priests of death and damnation. Through *The Mists of Avalon*, Bradley offers us a different type of tale, one which gives us a glimpse of life where the Goddess and women are central and powerful, sexuality is sacred, and nature is valuable for its own sake.[18]

The Mists of Avalon, then, does more than retell Arthurian legend from the point of view of a female character. By combining the perspective of female experience with a feminist analysis of the implications of the change from Goddess worship to God worship, Bradley transforms an androcentric narrative into a text within the new tradition of contemporary sacred storytelling. Through such rewriting, she offers her readers the opportunity not only to share in female history, but also to understand how that history of power affects their personal identities, lives, and futures.

Although her text shares many similarities with *The Flame Bearers*, there are two important differences. First, the stages of exploration of power issues are far clearer in Morgaine's story than in Rae's. Second, the ending of *The Flame Bearers*, which finds Rae transported both in time and space, imparts a sense of living tradition largely transmitted through intuition. The ending of *The Mists of Avalon* is also hopeful, but relies on the reader to make the connections to present-day appearances of Goddess religion. However, both novels posit themselves as transmissions of information which are vital for the creation of the female present through re-creation of the female past.

The Mists of Avalon is an example of the retelling of a Christian legend, while *The Flame Bearers* retells Jewish legend. I have also chosen to discuss Bradley's *The Firebrand*, so that the third major western European narrative component, that of the Greek classical tradition, may be examined in regards to its feminist reevaluation. While all three projects share an interest in retelling from a female character's point of view, an exploration of female experience and identity, and the reinscription of Goddess history in the west, in *The Firebrand* Bradley goes further in exploring the consequences of these ideas for men and women's lives.

Bradley's second rewrite of a central cultural legend, *The Firebrand*, is a treat for any female student who ever sat in a classics or "great books" course which included the *Iliad*, and asked, "Why are women being treated as prizes to be handed back and forth among males?" and "Why are these gods and goddesses so capricious?" only to be told by a professor, "Oh, that's just how it was." Having successfully denied Christianity as "just the way it was" in *The Mists of Avalon*, Bradley challenges the Pagan manifestation of patriarchy which was Hellenist Greece. She does so by having the ignored prophetess of Aeschylus' work, Kassandra, tell the tale. This change from masculine to feminine narration does more than give voice to a previously unheard, female side of the story; it also allows for a probing of the social and theological dimensions of the Trojan war.

The novel opens by depicting the skepticism which greets stories of female power. Bradley accomplishes this task by relating the visit of a harper to the house of Kassandra, years after the Trojan war has transpired. After he receives his customary welcome, he begins to play and chooses for his subject a song of the Trojan war: in his words, a song of great men and gods. Infuriated, Kassandra forbids him to tell "those stupid lies" (12). When he politely informs her that is the way it is sung everywhere, she responds that "it may be sung that way, from here to the very end of the world ... but it didn't happen that way at all" (12). She continues:

> At first in this land there were no Kings, but only Queens, the daughters of the Goddesses, and they took consorts where they would. And then the worshipers of the Sky Gods, the horsefolk, the users of iron, came down into our country; and when the Queens took them as consorts, they called themselves Kings and demanded the right to rule. And so the Gods and the Goddesses were in strife; and a time came when they brought their quarrels to Troy [13–14].

He seems skeptical, and Kassandra realizes "This has been my destiny always: to speak truth and never to be believed" (14). Kassandra's destiny has been the destiny of most women: to speak our truth and never have it believed. Kassandra's stories of queens and goddesses are greeted with skepticism by the harper, and contemporary findings of matrifocal goddess-oriented cultures are greeted with a similar skepticism by some who have too thoroughly learned the lessons of patriarchal academia, which has always been hostile to women. They tell us, "But that is not the way I have heard it sung." Therefore, one nuance of the element of fire in Chernin's and Bradley's choice of titles can be related to the power of women's truth-telling as powerful, inflammatory, and capable of destroying falsehood.

Just as feminist scholars hope for an audience among open-minded women and men, so too does Bradley hope to finally give Kassandra an audience believing her critique of patriarchal religion and power. An audience, in fact, who may be willing to see the Trojan story as not one of heroes, but rather of men who seem "little more than animate weapons" (435), who dispose of women "as prize[s]" (449). The Trojan war which Bradley gives the reader is one where the supposed hero, Achilles, is seen in his true colors when he rapes the corpse of the Amazon Penthesilea (526). Likewise, we see Ajax, another ostensible hero, rape Kassandra while his partner rapes and kills a child (560). Ultimately, Greece is depicted as a world where men do evil "at the bidding of Gods made in their own image" (602). Through Kassandra's tale-telling, we witness not only the other side to the story of the fall of Troy, but also glimpse the change from matrifocality to patriarchy, which connects with Kassandra's struggle to define the source of her vision and power. By extrapolation, the reader can consider the effects upon contemporary society of the evils committed in the name of a man-made God, and further contemplate how that knowledge can serve in the redefinition of power relations by and between women and men, as I discuss later in the story of Zakynthos and Kassandra.

Like *The Flame Bearers* and *The Mists of Avalon*, *The Firebrand* also explores the transition from the Goddess to gods and goddesses. In the beginning, only the Goddess was worshiped, although, as Penthesilea tells Kassandra, "each village and tribe had its own name for Her. There were many" (115–16). Though there were various guises of the Goddess, she was understood to be one. And, as Kassandra finds during her dedication to the Goddess, the Goddess is also the self. Kassandra asks to see the face of the Goddess, and receives the reply, "Do you not yet know that you are I, and I am you?" (137). Like Morgaine, Kassandra must acknowledge the Goddess within. The idea of immanence, however, does not set up the ego as deity; instead, immanence implies that not only is the self holy, but so also is the earth and nature, as we have seen in the previous two novels. Thus, homage is also paid to the Goddess as the force which works in and through nature, hallowing all natural processes (272).

The Firebrand refers to the assertion that when the patriarchal "Sky God" worshiping peoples came in from the north, they attempted either to set their own gods above the Goddess, or alongside goddesses, when the first was not possible. An example of the former is the story of Apollo and the Python. The Python was sacred to Gaia, the Earth Mother, and Delphi, the site of her oracle, was seen as the center of the earth. Apollo, according to legend, slew the Python, and erected a temple to himself on the site, where the priestesses, or pythonesses, would prophesy in his name (Eisler 87). This explains the presence of serpents in his temple at Troy, which first drew Kassandra to the service of Apollo.

In pondering this story of matricide, Kassandra thinks, "Apollo Sun Lord had called her; He had given her His serpents; one day He would lead her to knowledge of the Serpent Mother's mysteries as well" (69). This indeed happens, though indirectly and in a way Kassandra does not foresee. An example of the latter method of subversion, of gods being placed alongside goddesses, occurs when Kassandra vicariously shares Paris's vision, and sees Hera, Athena, and Aphrodite. She notes their differences from the goddesses she is familiar with, and wonders "those Goddesses were all defined as wife or daughter to Sky Father.... Perhaps in a land where the Sky Gods rule, can only those Goddesses be seen who are perceived as servants to the God?" (119), thus echoing analyses by spiritual feminists such as Christ (*Laughter of Aphrodite* 171–78).

Morgaine's perceptions of the roles of Mary and Brigid also parallel this thought. Even though Kassandra eventually serves Aphrodite in her love for Aeneas, she does so on her own terms, and does not accept the patriarchal theological trappings associated with certain names of the Goddess. Through this action, Kassandra represents the viewpoint of feminist spiritualists such as Spretnak and Stone who dig beneath the layers of patriarchal theological sediment to reconstruct goddesses as they may have been viewed in earlier times, to literally and figuratively remember them.

As one might expect, the shift from viewing deity as a self-sufficient female to that of a dependent female who answers to a male god or gods had an effect on social order as well, and Bradley examines this issue closely in *The Firebrand*. Some might argue that the cultural shift precedes the reformulation of mythology, or more likely, that they occur simultaneously. Penthesilea accurately informs Kassandra that "the Father-principle [is] ... a worship of male power and ability to father sons" (67). This makes the connection between God worship and patriarchy, a connection which becomes very clear in a study of the rise of kings and city-states.[19] Although Hecuba's rearing with the Amazons tells her that only a mother has rights over her children, Priam asserts his rights as king and father over the lives and deaths of his children, and Hecuba realizes her consent and marriage have brought this situation about (29). If a woman does not consent to patriarchal control, however, she can expect the worst, physically and spiritually. Thus, when Hector catches Kassandra at arms practice, he warns her: "I have seen women warriors ravished and not one man protest. If a woman refuses such protection as is lawful for wives and sisters, there is no other protection for her" (168).

Similarly, women are to be protected from fully using their minds as well. When Khryse the scribe and priest finds that Kassandra is a quick learner, he refuses to teach her more writing, employing the standard arguments that "it will damage their minds [and] dry up their wombs," and otherwise upset the "natural order" (223). Parroting oft-used arguments against full female participation in life, Bradley clearly asserts that when the Goddess is subordinated, human females are similarly subordinated. They are pressured into a childlike dependence on men, rather than encouraged to develop their talents, strengths, and leadership abilities.

Like Rae and Morgaine, Kassandra continuously questions and rejects such arrangements. She tends to be more vocal in doing so than the other two protagonists. Perhaps this trait corresponds to her legendary status as a prophetess. Astutely, she understands that in such a society, "to be a woman … [was] to lose all that made her herself" (41). She is also suspicious of marriage and childrearing as woman-recommended remedies for a woman's ills, especially when such ills consist of dissatisfaction with the status quo of male rule (268). Such instances reinforce her "belief that women everywhere conspired with their oppressors" (578). Few women have the rebel spirit which Kassandra possesses, or her willingness to question. Even fewer are willing to pay the price she does, never to be believed.

Kassandra's pattern of journeying is very close to Morgaine and Rae's. Her willingness to question leads her on a spiritual journey from certainty to doubt, and finally to resolution. Like Rae and Morgaine, Kassandra experiences part of her journey as an actual priestess. As she changes from Amazon, to priestess, and then to Zakynthos's partner, the reader witnesses Kassandra's struggle not only to be believed, but also to clarify her own beliefs. Thus, the female reader might not only empathize with this struggle, but also gain some affirmation through Kassandra's self-belief in the face of disbelief from others.

Kassandra's training in a rigorous female tradition is closer to Morgaine's, with Rae's training as a priestess far gentler in comparison. When Hecuba sends Kassandra to her kinswomen, the Amazons, for fostering, she finds herself among like-minded, independent women for the first time. She accustoms herself to physical hardship, and even kills a man who attacks her (112). With the Amazons, Kassandra learns of the Goddess as she is worshiped by the women. Later, in Colchis, Kassandra undergoes initiation rites into the service of the Goddess, a ritual descent into the underworld, where she passes all three "gates," thus marking herself as a born priestess (134–38). These latter events especially parallel the experience of many spiritual feminists.

The alienation the former protagonists experience in the "outside" world is also duplicated by Kassandra. Her experiences with the Amazons make Kassandra even less prepared for a life in Priam's court, where she is expected to serve as a gracious and genteel example of her father's possessions and power. By implication, a woman's immersion in Goddess spirituality makes her even less likely to fit in as a dutiful daughter of the patriarchy. After Kassandra takes vows to Apollo, she begins to wonder if she is reneging on her vows to the Goddess (177). This dilemma haunts her for some time, only to increase rather than lessen. When Khryse steals the mask of Apollo in order to deceive Kassandra into lying with him, she is so enraged that she swears "By the Mother of All, I wouldn't lie with you if you were truly possessed by Apollo!" (228). Apollo takes exception to this oath; yet when he calls Kassandra his chosen one, the Goddess replies, "Yours, Sun Lord? She was given to Me before ever she came to birth in this mortal world, or felt Your touch!"

As punishment for Kassandra's words and choice, Apollo curses her, vowing that none will believe her prophecies (232). Dismayed, she begins to wonder if "a God, when a man and a woman contended, could not take a woman's part, whatever the rights of the matter? She was the property of the God, just as if she had married a mortal man" (263). Years of her sincere love are spurned by Apollo for her one trespass, and significantly the "sin" is one of the assertion of her sexual autonomy. Kassandra's increasing disillusionment resembles the concerns of spiritual feminists who observe that even when a woman has served in a male religious tradition for years, any disobedience or questioning singles her out for harsh punishment.[20]

Such treatment only serves to increase a woman's questioning and doubt about the nature of patriarchal religion. As the war wears on, and shows further evidence of being a quarrel among gods as well as humans, Kassandra's doubts about deities grow. What kind of gods quarrel like this?, she repeatedly asks. When Penthesilea's corpse is raped by Achilles, however, Kassandra finally realizes for having served in Apollo's house (526). If the Gods would not act, she would. While Morgaine's action in the face of doubt eventually strengthens her belief, the opposite is true for Kassandra. Donning the mask of Apollo, she takes her bow and an envenomed arrow, and fatally wounds Achilles (528). Although this action is personally rewarding for Kassandra, it does not quell her doubts and questions. She asks Apollo:

> "Can You not save Your people? If you cannot, why are You called a God? And if You can and will not, what kind of God are You?" ... She was suddenly aware that she had asked the last question anyone ever asked of a God, and the one that would never be answered [550].[21]

In her crisis of faith, Kassandra apprehends that the power called Apollo has been shaped by men's perceptions and can no longer deserve her worship. Although in *The Mists of Avalon* male deity does exist in the form of the Horned God, he is subordinate to the Goddess in his role as consort, and Bradley does not focus on him. *The Firebrand*, however, examines the role of male deities after the usurpation of the Goddess, which results in a portrayal of male deity as resembling patriarchal human males: paternalistic, controlling, and judgmental.

In her concluding note of partnership between men and women, Bradley emphasizes that the reclamation of women's sacred history is of benefit to both sexes. Like contemporary spiritual feminists, Kassandra rejects the patriarchal forms of gods and goddesses, and returns to an earlier concept of the Goddess, but one which is modified by the idea of partnership; neither kings nor queens shall be omnipotent.

After she accepts the gift of her life, and that of her child, Kassandra no longer fights a war within herself, and gives herself to the Goddess as the source of life. The primary inspiration for Goddess spirituality is an observation of the processes of life itself, not reliance on a single text or doctrine. At the moment of her acceptance, Kassandra is approached by a woman who is later revealed as a man, Zakynthos, who had sworn to search "for a woman in whom the Amazon's spirit still lived" (600). Having found that in Kassandra, he wishes to found a city "where women are not slaves, and where men need not spend their lifetimes in war and fighting" (601). Not surprisingly, Kassandra agrees to go with this heterosexual feminist dream man, and "somewhere, a Goddess smiled. She did not think it was Aphrodite" (603). It may not be an ideal world, Kassandra realizes, but at least it would be "as much better as men and women could make it" (602).

This speculation on the effect of Goddess religion on the personal relationships between men and women goes beyond the endings of either *The Flame Bearers* or *The Mists of Avalon*, and presents what Orenstein terms a "utopian motif" (*Reflowering* 163). While few men in western culture at large resemble Zakynthos, many who follow a tradition of Goddess spirituality do, and wish to help contemporary spiritual feminists build a world that is life- and woman-affirming.

Kassandra rejects the idea of all-powerful deities, and ultimately accepts the power of the Goddess as seen in the natural world, and is willing to place the onus for change and control on ordinary women and men. By doing so, she exhibits belief in herself, regardless of what others might think. She dares to create a new life based on equality, even if the rest of the world is to go on telling stories of powerful gods and great heroes. By giving this ending to Kassandra's story, rather than simply assuming she was disposed of along with Agamemnon, as the *Iliad* supposes, Bradley dares to suggest the possibility of new futures for women when they know their true histories and venture to tell their own stories. Her retelling of sacred history indicates a call for action, not nostalgia.

Alice Walker: And a Womanist Shall Lead Them

In her "Open Letter to Mary Daly," Audre Lorde criticizes Daly for using African women's texts and lives in a racist manner, portraying women of color as "victims and preyers-upon each other" (*Sister Outsider* 67). Lorde challenges Daly's

> assumption that the herstory and myth of white women is the legitimate and sole herstory and myth of all women to call upon for power and background, and that nonwhite women and our herstories are noteworthy only as decorations, or examples of female victimization [69].

"An Open Letter" examines the presence of racism within the feminist spirituality movement, and reveals how words intended to heal can also harm. I have never come across a published response by Daly to Lorde. Though I do not know why this is so, it possibly fits the pattern where white women take offense at black women's anger, and refuse to engage in further dialogue. In *Sister Outsider* Lorde mentions several instances of this pattern. In part, this defensiveness is a natural human reaction, as few people wish to be told they are wrong. Nor do white people wish to have their racial shortcomings pointed out to them. Resistance can also come from black women. Minister and professor Katie Cannon argues:

> Every reflective and well-intentioned African American scholar who is seriously concerned with "the liberation of a whole people" must work to eradicate the criterion of legitimacy that implicitly presumes an absolute incompatibility between womanist critical scholarship and White feminist liberationist sources [131].

For true dialogue to take place, conversations between women of different races/ethnicities cannot dead-end. It is counterproductive to belief in interconnection, and spiritual feminists in particular should be wary of this trap. Writing this, I reflect on the various voices who told me whether I should or should not, could or could not include black women's fiction in my study (yes, feminists can be "gatekeepers" too). For the most part, black feminists told me I should, and some white feminists told me not to. This encouragement on the part of black scholars suggests to me that even though many feminists are now aware that one may be taken to critical task for not "getting" the same reading as someone who shares the same identity nexus as the author, that there is still value in the effort. As Cannon observes, "we must answer the inescapable questions of appropriation and reciprocity." Failure to do so, to fall into "either-or" thinking, is "to play the game of androcentric, heteropatriarchal academese without understanding it" (135). Dialogue between texts, voices, and identities emerges, and though we will not find a universal sameness, we can find coalition. Given this context, I will briefly address my inclusion of African American women's texts in this chapter and throughout the work.

Through my concurrent reading of African American women's magical realism texts and fantasy and science fiction by European American women writers, I noticed many thematic similarities between the fiction, but also became aware of African American women's emphasis on racism as a primary form of power-over, and their reliance on an African spiritual tradition which paralleled European American feminist articulations of immanent value, but derived from a non–European heritage. My inclusion here of Walker's *The Temple of My Familiar* is indicative of the parallels between women writers of African and European descent.

This endeavor is not unproblematic; critics such as bell hooks have shown how white criticism on African American texts is itself privileged because of racism (*Talking Back* 44). I am proposing my reading of these texts as a spiritual feminist literary critic, not as a personal authority on African American spirituality. The reader is encouraged to refer to books such as Marilyn Richardson's *Black Women and Religion: An Annotated Bibliography* for further sources. Writing as a European American spiritual feminist, I am endeavoring to combat racism within the feminist movement as a whole, and the feminist spirituality movement especially. The African American authors I discuss in this chapter are very clear about racism as a form of power-over and a denial of immanent value. The protagonists in these texts are consciously combating racism, as are their authors; until European American women have taken up that task as well, comments about community and the web of women will ring hollow. Thus, feminist spirituality must combat all forms of power-over, and these texts challenge all their readers, especially those of European heritage, to do so.

The living tradition of community healing from which these authors write is instructive for all who wish to further true sisterhood by understanding the "ways in which racism and sexism are immutably connected rather than pitting one struggle against the other or blatantly dismissing racism" (hooks, *Feminist Theory from Margin to Center* 53). Hooks contends that one of the main differences she sees in the black and white worlds is "a profound unshaken belief in the spiritual power of black people to transform our world and live with integrity and oneness despite oppressive social realities" (*Sisters of the Yam* 8). This belief is a point of connection with the emphasis placed by many spiritual feminists on social transformation.

In *The Temple of My Familiar*, Alice Walker explores more deeply the spirituality first tentatively articulated in *The Color Purple*. When the critic's perspective is informed by both an understanding of contemporary feminist spiritual theory and practice, and Walker's own concept of "womanism," she finds that the events, times, people, and places of the novel form an interconnected pattern which emphasizes the presence and vitality of the life of the spirit, a life in which women and men find renewal and power. Walker defines a womanist as "a black feminist or feminist of color" who appreciates women's love, culture, and social characteristics, yet "sometimes loves individual men, sexually and/or nonsexually, [and is] committed to survival and wholeness of entire people, male *and* female" (*In Search of Our Mother's Garden's* xi). Noting the intersections of her perspective with the descriptions of feminist spirituality we have seen articulated by European American feminists results in what can be described as "womanist spirituality," a term which has since become circulated by African American writers on spirituality.

Cannon connects womanist spiritual struggle to its presence in African American women's literature. She notes that it "frees womanist scholars from the matrix of dominant Western ethics so that we can get some sense of the sublimated ethical concerns and the 'handing on' of moral insights that communicate emancipatory praxis" (76). Walker's presentation of womanist spirituality in *The Temple of My Familiar* involves an understanding of the Goddess in history, woman as Goddess, and "womanspirit" concerns such as healing, psychic awareness, and reincarnation, linked to an African American feminist critique of the predominantly white feminist articulations of the above subjects.

Like Caroline Arewa, author of a book on the chakras, she would argue that "history has masked the spiritual achievements of the African race" (xx), and in a similar vein feels that all spiritual lineages should be traced back to Africa. The critique of racism as a form of power-over broadens the perspectives on domination we have found thus far in the other examples of fantastic fiction. With this critical foundation, the surprising transformations undergone by the novel's many characters, black and white, old and young, male and female, are more readily understood as healings which spring from a new perception of personal power. These characters move from states of alienation, separation, domination, and oppression to egalitarian relationships characterized by partnership, cooperation, and recognition of the immanence of the spirit. As Annette Van Dyke notes, the progress of each character is linked to that of the others (73).

At the center of the web of characters, which includes two couples (Fanny and Suwelo, and Carlotta and Arveyda), is the remarkable Lissie, whose own transformation and recognition of her Goddess nature allow her to be a catalyst for the other characters' development. Unlike the previous protagonists, Lissie is not a priestess in the most literal sense. Rather, she is woman whose multiple selves are the different faces of the Goddess. As a womanist Goddess, she shares her wisdom with men as well as women.

Lissie informs Suwelo that her name means "the one who remembers everything" (52). Thus, she represents the voice of both female knowledge and African knowledge which has been lost to the world, yet is now ready to be revealed by means not always accepted by white supremacist patriarchy. For Lissie these means include past life explorations, invisible ink writings, and tape recordings. In this way she illustrates Cannon's assertion that "the starting point for womanist epistemology is the oral culture bequeathed to us by our grandmothers, mothers, aunts, and sisters" (133).

To those who do not believe that Lissie's stories are true, especially when she discusses her past lives, she states "I pity you" (65). Through her past life experiences, Lissie provides the reader with different versions of history and legend, including two versions of the "fall," the significance of Medusa, the relationship of Isis to the Madonna, and the witchhunts. Rather than picking one legend as do the previous authors, Walker uses these multiple stories to challenge patriarchal history and a "whitewashed" Goddess.

While at first she tells Suwelo that she has always been a black woman, she later recants and confesses to having lived lives as lions and as white men, including one of the first white men, the life of whom she relates to Suwelo as a version of the fall (359–62). At first, this young man knows only that he is of age to mate and then join the men, who live separately from the women. He makes love to his dearest female companion, and when he falls asleep, she rubs him with an ointment his mother has used to "make [his] skin strong and protect it from the sun" (359). When she tells him he looks skinless, he is shocked and goes to the nearby pool, where he washes until he sees his paleness. Highly upset, he runs away, striking his friend's familiar dead in the process (360–61). He is left to live in solitude, wearing skins to cover himself, and having only the companionship of dogs (362).

In this version of the fall, separation is caused by color, and linked to violence. Walker implies here that the violence of white men is caused by this primordial separation from the community of black women. Like Walker, Lissie knows herself to be considered "other" by the currently dominant culture. Yet the story of her life as the "mutant" white man turns white men into the "other" at the same time it demonstrates inclusiveness by acknowledging the shared African roots of whites and blacks. The oppressed, Walker argues, can easily turn into the oppressors themselves unless they recognize interconnection. Rather than using the journey motif as Bradley and Chernin do, Walker uses Lissie's white and male past-life experiences to argue against the use of power-over (domination) by demonstrating that it fosters corruption and separation.

Because her incarnations include other genders, symbolically Lissie is not only Everywoman, but Everyperson, and thus the techniques which guide her life are held out as useful tools for both men and women, an idea which corresponds to Walker's womanism, and spells out new spiritual possibilities. As Walker asserts in *Living by the Word*, " all people must be our people ... and *we* must be 'every person' in any event if we are to assume the largest possible freedom for ourselves" (166).

Through one of Zede's (Carlotta's mother) stories, Walker further refutes the Christian notion of the fall and the concept of an omnipotent, punitive deity. Zede relates a story that implies that humanity's problems did not start with disobedience to a dictatorial father god, but rather with the loss of reverence for life as symbolized by women or the mother Goddess. A teaching handed down from woman to woman for generations says that in her village, women were originally the priests, but "it was the men who made them so" (48). The women's ability to give birth causes the men to imagine "a mujer muy grande, larger than the sky, producing, somehow, the earth. A goddess. And so, if the producer of the earth was a large woman, a goddess, then women must be her priests, and must possess great and supernatural powers" (49).

Eventually, after generations, the men rebel against this order, and set themselves up as the priesthood. Zede points out: "What the mind doesn't understand, it worships or fears. I am speaking here of man's mind" (49). In this story, male fear and misunderstanding are responsible for the alienation of the sexes. The difference between the male concept of Goddess and Lissie's concept is that Lissie understands Goddess power as a mode of embodiment and connection. The male mind can only see it as an external controlling force, one ultimately to be rebelled against and controlled, especially in the form of actual women. Walker depicts the model of domination as originating with men. Her sympathetic portrayal of Arveyda and Suwelo suggests, however, that men can successfully combat this tendency, and in fact have an obligation to do so; that Lissie speaks most directly to Suwelo is further indication that Goddess re-membering can restore men to a sense of right relationship.

For Walker, domination also takes the form of racism, and is often found linked with sexism, which distinguishes her novel from the others discussed earlier. Unlike the white novelists' Goddess stories, Walker concentrates on the destruction of the Goddess as a black Goddess, a story revealed through Nzingha's, Fanny's half sister, recounting of her education in Paris. A lecture on a depiction of Perseus slaying Medusa prompts a discussion of Medusa's hair (dreadlocks, perhaps) as representing the snake as an African fertility symbol. Nzingha continues:

> if you are from Africa you recognize Medusa's wings as the wings of Egypt, and you recognize the head of Medusa as the head of Africa; and what you realize you are seeing is the Western world's memorialization of that period in prehistory when the white male world of Greece decapitated and destroyed the black female Goddess/Mother tradition and culture of Africa [269].

Continuing in the idea that what man fears, he must destroy, Walker evokes the power of African Goddess tradition as something which Hellenist Greece had to destroy in order to make a claim for cultural supremacy. Her discussion also calls to mind the current debates about the indebtedness of Greek culture, so highly valorized in the western educational tradition, to Egyptian culture in particular and African culture more generally.[22] The resistance with which many scholars treat the idea that the fountainhead of white civilization could be indebted to black history reveals the power Walker finds in the image of the beheaded Medusa.

Nzingha also tells Fanny that "I knew Notre-Dame was built on the site of a shrine to Isis, who was later called the Black Madonna" (268). She also notes how Isis stands behind the image of the Black Madonna, and how Christianity took over sites of Goddess shrines as sites for worship (268). Eloise McKinney-Johnson is one of the scholars who argues that "Isis' profound influence upon major concepts of the Virgin Mary and her Christ child continues today in the many portrayals of the Black Madonna" (67).[23] Further, Walker connects Isis with Athena, arguing that Athena's birth from Zeus' forehead represented "the destruction of the African Goddess Isis and the metamorphosis of Isis into the Greek Goddess Athena" (270). In disgust with her teachers at the Sorbonne, Nzingha leaves and returns to her home in Africa, refusing to be taught that "a civilization founded on the destruction of the black woman as Goddess in her own world was superior to what I had at home" (270). Walker insists on the racial dimensions of the destruction of Goddess cultures at the same time she critiques the racist tendency of white spiritual feminists and academics to ignore race in their discussions of Goddess traditions, or to act as though Goddess worship began in Greece.

In a similar fashion, Walker also employs Lissie to introduce the issue of race in the era of the European witchhunts. Whereas Baudino (discussed in Chapter 3) depicts the witchhunts as fostering division between men and women, and between those with "gifts" from those without, Walker portrays the witchhunts as the final split between black and white women. This part of the story is written to Suwelo in "invisible ink," ink which disappears as it is read, a metaphor for the erasure of blackness in white society. Lissie points to the Moors as thinking that "the Christian religion that flourished in Spain would let the Goddess of Africa 'pass' into the modern world as 'the Black Madonna'" (195). However, as the church taught that "both the color black and the female sex were of the devil" (196), and that women healers were witches, these women of color were targeted for extermination. The result?

> The connection between black woman and white was broken utterly; the blood sisterhood that African women shared with European women was gone as if it had never been. In France, there is nothing. Notre Dame. Our Lady. Not our Black Lady ... [and] Mother Africa, cursed by all her children, black, white, and in between, is dying today, and after her, death will come to every other part of the globe [198].

The idea of the death and dismemberment of the Goddess becomes more than a legend; it becomes a metaphor for the destruction of true sisterhood and the world due to a denial of life and a misuse of power. In *Oya: In Praise of the Goddess*, Judith Gleason mentions seeing an ancient cup with two female faces, one white and one black, whose braids join them. She remarks, "only their faces ... are different. Inside that antique cup continues to brim liberation" (14). Writing on the relevance of the West African Goddess Oya for all women, Gleason echoes Walker's assertion that once, women were not separated by race, and that bridge can be rebuilt. Walker deftly weaves myth and history into a prophetic tapestry that speaks to the relevance of the Goddess, and the redefinition of power she implies, for healing the rifts between all peoples, and between people and the earth.

As Walker has written elsewhere, "Earth itself has become the nigger of the world.... While the Earth is enslaved, none of us is free" (*Living by the Word* 147). In the advocacy of interconnection, someone must speak for the animals and others who cannot speak for themselves, "And that is why," Lissie tells Suwelo, "goddesses and witches exist" (199). In the fallen state which exists when the richness of the Earth Mother in all her guises and manifestation is torn asunder and forgotten, women with special abilities, goddesses and witches (like Lissie), in their sibylline way, tell the story that the rest of the world has forgotten or made invisible. Through *The Temple of My Familiar,* Walker positions herself as one of these prophetic storytellers.

In contrast to European patriarchy's role as dominator, Lissie articulates a view of Goddess as self/selves and cosmic interconnection, an idea we have seen demonstrated as the source of right action in the other novels. She contrasts Hal's earnest yet partial love for her with Rafe's total acceptance of all her selves, black, white, male, female, and animal:

> Hal loved me like a sister/ mystic/ warrior/ woman/ mother. Which was nice. But that was only part of who I was. Rafe, on the other hand, knowing me to contain everybody and everything, loved me wholeheartedly, as a goddess. Which I was [371].

A woman who sees herself as Goddess, sees herself in relationship to others, and this fosters an ethics of cooperation rather than domination. This is the lost knowledge of which Lissie reminds the other characters and the reader. While women of European heritage can relate to this idea, Walker's reclamation of Goddess identity for African women must be recognized as a use of the redemptive power of magical storytelling.

Lissie resists gender and racial oppression through storytelling rather than violence. Violent resistance is neither totally absent nor deplored; Mary Ann Haverstock's liberation of Carlotta and Zede is an instance of political action by a white woman, as well as African resistance to white rule — both portrayed positively. However, as Everyperson, as Goddess, Lissie is an idealized figure, and represents a more joyous vision where resistance is achieved through joy with oneself and one's relationships. Unlike the protagonists who engage in literal battles, Lissie's primary mode of resistance to white patriarchy is creating a pleasurable life for herself. Living as a African American woman in a Eurocentric society, Lissie knows both racial and gender oppression. At the same time, she is successful at carving out a satisfying life for herself, while wary of the trap of thinking herself superior to others. Ultimately, Walker proposes that one cannot wait for the struggle to be over before experiencing pleasure; the struggle may never be over, but pleasure can be found in the present moment. Her own acknowledgment at the end of the novel supports this idea: "I thank the Universe for my participation in Existence. It is a pleasure to have always been present."

Walker affirms that telling new stories — or the true, lost, older versions — does have an impact on the lives of others. When we allow them to shape our consciousness, we change, and when we change, those around us also change. In the novel, Lissie's stories impact Suwelo enough that he can understand Fanny's discovery of self, encapsulated in a message she receives from the goddess Nut: "Whatever I embrace, becomes." Upon reflection, Suwelo decides that "what she meant was that we must, all of us, turn toward whatever it is that we do want, in our lives, in our loves, on the planet, and whatever we don't want, just have sense enough to leave alone" (279). True power lies in interconnection, in the ability to encompass, embrace, create, and manifest. While this concept is radical for some, it can be taught by those who live and imagine it. As Carlotta remarks to Suwelo, "It isn't impossible to teach the alternative reality, especially when it's your own" (379). Walker's stories teach the reader to embrace womanist reality and history.

As has been seen in Walker's, Bradley's and Chernin's work, the project of rewriting history, of telling the stories of women, is a necessary part of the task of liberating the female imagination through the use of fantastic/speculative fiction. Shinn comments that "[f]antastic literature by women redefines our past so that we may perceive other possible futures than the one which seems to be carrying us to our destruction" (*Worlds Within Women* 12). Through the genre of fantastic fiction, authors like Bradley, Walker, and Chernin can escape the confines of rigid academic proof, and go straight to the project of re-creating history and legend.

In telling these stories, authors make a relationship between the impersonal level of myth and the personal self. The Goddess, whether as symbol or source, implies creation, and in this case the creation which is needed is the project of giving birth to ourselves. To paraphrase a male creation story, this may begin with the word. Through magical, sacred story-telling, women authors not only correct the biases of male monomyths, setting themselves up as "soothsayers" or truth-tellers, like Kassandra, but also illustrate the struggles each woman in a patriarchal society must endure before she can regain a sense of connection with others and power within herself. This process is the magic of fantastic fiction as a source of gender and racial empowerment.

Orenstein believes that eventually these stories will be "seen as parts of a larger mythic construct ... [and] function as elements of a vast feminist matristic mythos of life's origins and women's history" (*Reflowering* 148). Appropriately, the feminist literary project of rewriting or retelling history and legend comes first in my treatment of spirituality in contemporary women's fiction, for an understanding of the female past enables women to create different, meaningful futures. As Shinn suggests, the future shaped by patriarchy is not pleasant, and one only has to recall the Four Horsemen of the Apocalypse to picture where "el Shaddai" is leading us. In contrast, the values of feminist spirituality as found in the creative histories of a Goddess-focused past call for an egalitarian society characterized by peace, racial harmony, respect for nature, and celebration of sexuality.

3
Finding and Defining Personal Power

Central to feminism, no matter how one defines it, are two questions: What is power? How should it be used? Spiritual feminists are very concerned with these questions as well, and their concern is reflected in the literature they create. While the previous chapter focused on mytho/historical shifts of power between religions, races, and genders, this chapter focuses more directly on female characters as individual women in search of their own power as spiritual, responsible beings.

Like their real life feminist counterparts, the protagonists of these novels are seeking an alternative to patriarchy's definition of power as the ability to dominate, conquer, or exploit. Often they have been victimized by persons, usually male, white, or both, who live according to the patriarchal definition. In the process of re-covering and creating meaningful lives, these women must redefine the concept of power in order to share love and act meaningfully. Christ and Spretnak term the period of loss which precedes the search for a meaningful life "experiencing nothingness." They note that "[e]xperiencing nothingness, women reject conventional solutions and question the meaning of their lives, thus opening themselves to the revelation of deeper sources of power and value" ("Images" 330). Such a woman or protagonist may find that

> Because she can no longer accept conventional answers to her questions, she opens herself to the radically new — possibly to the revelation of powers or forces of being larger than herself that can ground her in a new understanding of herself and her position in the world [329].

Fantastic or speculative fiction serves as an ideal medium through which the artist and reader may explore new understandings of power, because it offers wide latitude for postulating visions of the "radically new."

Many spiritual feminists are already exploring new definitions and visions of power. Starhawk, a popular feminist thealogian, writes in *Dreaming the Dark*:

> This book is about the calling forth of power, a power based on a principle very different from power-over, from domination. For power-over is, ultimately, the power of the gun and the bomb, the power of annihilation that backs up all the institutions of domination [3].

In contrast to this type of power, which she views as central to patriarchy, Starhawk discusses "power-from-within," our ability to "be able" which "arises from our sense of connection, our bonding with other human beings, and with the environment" (*Truth or Dare* 10). Individuals who realize their power-from-within may link with others in "power-with," whose source "is the willingness of others to listen to our ideas" (10). When this happens, personal spirituality becomes political in its ability to challenge standard patriarchal definitions and attributions of power, asking "questions [which] are broader than the terms 'religious' or 'political' imply; they are questions of complex connections" (*Dreaming the Dark* 4). This new feminist idea of power relies on connection rather than division: connection to the earth, to one's self, and to others.

Connection is also emphasized in Sally Gearhart's use of the term "energy re-sourcement" because "it suggests we must go to a new place for our energy. To re-source is to find another source, an entirely different and prior one ... that allows us to stand in the path of continuous and cosmic energy" ("Womanpower: Energy Re-Sourcement" 195). In terms of women in search of power, this means

> that there is a source or kind of power qualitatively different from the one we have been taught to accept and to operate with; further, the understanding, the protection, the development of that source and the allowing of it to reach its full dimensions could mean the redemption of the entire globe from the devastation of the last ten thousand years [196].

Gearhart and Starhawk differ in that Gearhart feels that this is a uniquely female experience, an attitude reflected in her novel *The Wanderground* (Rosinsky 78–79). Starhawk, who would agree that women's positioning outside traditional patriarchal positions of power-over enables them to more readily conceive of other types of power. She also holds open the possibility of this experience to men. Riane Eisler echoes Starhawk's sentiment concerning the inclusion of men in her view of "the representation of power as linking," which she finds in such Goddess symbols as the chalice or the circle, both important images in the Goddess-focused, "gylanic" partnership societies she discusses in *The Chalice and the Blade* (193).

An important subtext of feminist spirituality which cannot be overlooked is the idea that the female self can be a powerful agent of change, and that the female self is already imbued with the ability to define and shape reality. Cynthia Eller remarks that "[r]ituals, songs, poems, literature, even academic analyses of feminist spirituality speak with one voice on the desirability — and usually the reality, albeit neglected — of women's power" (212). She further notes that "it is not enough for a woman to think of herself as a strong and powerful person who happens to be female; she needs to think of herself as a powerful woman" (212). Here, a powerful woman is one who is powerful both within and beyond her body. Feminist speculative fiction portrays female characters who discover this inherent power in themselves. Many of the novels discussed in this chapter either mention or feature goddesses who are catalysts in the female protagonists' search to redefine power, and who serve as symbols of the powerful female. Novels which focus more specifically on the protagonists' need to develop clear understandings of the Goddess as a power, symbol, construct, or manifestation, are left to Chapter 4, "The Quest for the Goddess."

In this Chapter, I will explore Mercedes Lackey's *Oathbound* and *Oathbreakers*; Gael Baudino's *Strands of Starlight*; Octavia Butler's *Wild Seed* (fantasy novels); and Patricia Kennealy's *Keltiad* series, especially *The Silver Branch* (science fiction novels). Though these novels span several varieties of speculative fiction, they are all what Gloria Orenstein, writing about a wide range of feminist literature, calls "tales of power." They are stories which "may be considered as medicine stories, for they promote a healing of the wounds we might identify as 'de-souling' or as a loss of the spirit" (*Reflowering* 30). Orenstein further argues that the search for female power is a discovery process rather than a creative process. In other words, female power has always existed, but has been clouded by the force of patriarchal constructs. Thus, she writes that "[t]oday's feminist matristic literature has the awesome task of dismantling those patriarchal cultural constructs which have masked the historical verities of female empowerment over aeons of time" (130). In the novels under consideration in this chapter, the female protagonist must recognize patriarchal constructs of power and come to an understanding of her connection with others, with nature, and with spirit (not that the three are found divided in such novels) so that she may claim her identity, her power, and paradoxically, her independence. These have always been there, but have gone unrecognized and un- or under-utilized.

The figures of the sorcerer/sorceress and the warrior have traditionally been imbued with a great deal of power, and in masculinist examples of the literature, the sorcerer and the warrior embody the patriarchal "values" of domination and manipulation. As several of the novels in this chapter demonstrate, in feminist uses of the sword and sorcery subgenre (Wolfe 128), power is still expressed through these figures, but this power is qualified and restrained by an ethics which prohibits destructive force for purposes other than self- and community-defense.

In commenting on this modification, Charlotte Spivack points out that "the female protagonists also demonstrate physical courage and resourcefulness, but they are not committed to male goals" (8). Thus, one can argue that feminist authors such as Butler, Lackey, Baudino, and Kennealy are claiming this tradition even as they rewrite it, in a similar fashion to the rewriting of myth and history examined earlier. Also, one observes that while authors differ on the extent to which such defense should go, they emphasize that female identity and feminist values are worth defending and fighting.

Mercedes Lackey: The Power of Women United

Mercedes Lackey (along with Butler, Baudino, Abbey, and Kennealy) is one of the newer generation of writers following in the footsteps of Bradley, Vinge, Norton, and other feminist writers of speculative fiction. Like them, Lackey is engaged in the process of revising the science fiction and fantasy tradition. Charlotte Spivack describes one of the characteristics of feminist fantasy as "a feminine revisioning of the fantasy quest and its heroes, the fantasy world and its occupants, and above all, the meaning of magic at the heart of fantasy," even when a writer is not consciously rebelling against more traditional models. Spivack would call a work feminist whenever it contains "a feminine perspective on plot, character, theme, structure, and imagery" (8).[1] Although Lackey prefers the term "humanist" to "feminist" (personal interview), her novels consistently explore a range of concerns which most would indeed describe as feminist in nature, and are highly concerned with magic and its meaning for women. Her female protagonists are strong warriors and mercenaries, magicians, rulers, and councilors, though they are by no means infallible or all-powerful. In spite of this perspective, which has clearly found an appreciative audience, Lackey has not received the critical attention she deserves, especially for one who has published over forty novels, including the popular *The Heralds of Valdemar Trilogy*, *The Last Herald-Mage Trilogy* (one of the few fantasy pieces with a gay male protagonist), and the *Vows and Honor Duology*.

The two novels of the last set, *The Oathbound* (1988) and *Oathbreakers* (1989), are especially relevant to this chapter because they deal with issues of female power as manifested in oath making and the honoring of one's oaths, or vows and honor. What sets this fantasy series apart is that the primary oaths are between the two female protagonists, Tarma and Kethry, rather than between males.[2] Thus, the novels explore how power is defined and manifested in terms of female identity and allegiance. In addition, each woman has a specialty which gives her ethical responsibilities in regards to power: swordsmanship for Tarma, and sorcery for Kethry. Through these familiar sword and sorcery figures, Lackey explores the dynamics of power and responsibility on the personal, partnership, and societal levels. Though they do not share a sexual relationship, Tarma and Kethry are "she'enedra," or sisters by a Goddess-blessed blood oath. This background enables Lackey to investigate power issues from the female protagonists' point of view, using what Spivack has called a feminist heroic perspective, which has as its goal both "self-fulfillment and protection of the community" (8). Each protagonist must understand that while the victim of power-over can easily see its errors, the harder task entails eliminating the residual effects of patriarchal domination as they exist within an individual. Each woman must learn to see her own power within, and then recognize a similar power in others. Once again, the feminist connection between the personal and the political arises.

Through Tarma's struggle to rebuild her clan, Lackey comments on how societies are constructed and how they establish control. For Tarma, a Shin'a'in, community primarily exists in the form of the clan. When her clan is slaughtered, leaving Tarma as the sole survivor, she becomes a Kal'enedral, swordsworn to the Warrior aspect of her Goddess. Kal'enedral are characterized not only by their accuracy as fighters, but also by their cool, impartial, desexualized demeanor. At the beginning of *The Oathbound,* Tarma and Kethry, still relatively new to each other, are determined to work together to re-found Tarma's clan, since Kethry is able to bear children, whereas a Kal'enedral cannot. The clan will be reconstructed, but not along traditional male/female lines; both clan head and clan mother are female. Their clan will include not only the biological children Kethry will have, but also adoptees from other clans, reinforcing the idea that this female-headed clan further challenges the emphasis on blood lines as a determiner of connection, an emphasis often found in male-dominated cultures, including the Middle Eastern nomadic tribes on which the fictional Shin'a'in appear to be loosely modeled. Thus, Lackey stresses nurturing, not patrilineal bloodlines, as the true basis of families. Such an argument supports single mothers and lesbian couples in their contemporary struggles for acceptance as families.

Before Tarma and Kethry's plan can be implemented, however, they must first prove the validity of female vows. Lackey depicts the challenge to the validity of the duo's vows as an example of the patriarchal tendency to see female bonds as lesser than the bonds between a man and a woman, or between a man and anything else. When the two reach the Shin'a'in elders, an old man who refuses to acknowledge the validity of the duo's vow accuses Kethry of faking the sign of the bond through sorcery. In response, Tarma calls him out for doubting the word of a Kal'enedral, who by virtue of their bonds, are upholders of justice among the Shin'a'in. In doing so, she is prepared to fight for recognition of the female pair as legitimate, as well as the recognition of her personal female vow to the Warrior; a stamp of validation is placed on this bond by the natural world when a hawk, totem of Tarma's clan, alights on their upraised and linked arms (104). After this legitimation, the way is cleared for the pair to lay the groundwork for founding the clan. The scene affirms that while patriarchal society may view female connections with skepticism, women's bonds are nevertheless affirmed by a higher, natural order whose law is more valid than human opinion.

This novel is one of the first I discuss which examines rape and other forms of violence as catalysts for the formation of an awakened feminist consciousness. While a thorough discussion of literary presentations of rape is beyond the scope of my text, it must be noted that, as in many other genres, fantasy literature has its share of rape scenes or characters who have been raped, not always female.[3] Whereas masculinist texts treat rape either as a prelude to a male act of "heroism," or as a subject viewed with titillation, feminist fantastic fiction presents rape in a way which acknowledges its pervasiveness in the lives of women in patriarchal societies, while also emphasizing the need and ability of women to redress such violence.

Annis Pratt describes the presence of rape in fiction as the "rape trauma archetype" and views it as emblematic of patriarchal attempts to enclose and limit female autonomy (24–26). While the protagonists she discusses appear to be effectively limited by rape, the opposite occurs in authors such as Lackey and Baudino, who create protagonists who are transformed by their rapes into women who escape patriarchal limitation.

Rather than remaining powerless victims, female protagonists in fantastic fiction are usually motivated to learn some type of ability, either martial or magical, which eventually allows them to exact some measure of justice previously denied them, for themselves and often for others as well. Certainly, for most rape survivors, this is a fantasy indeed, since women rarely find justice through the court system, and if they seek justice outside the courts, tend to be prosecuted with more rigor than most rapists ever experience. Given that estimates for the incidence of sexual assault among all women range as high as twenty-five percent,[4] a significant number of female readers of the literature might have been assaulted themselves. They can experience the textual pleasure, at least, of viewing female figures bringing their violators to some form of justice. And, in the dialogic form which I see operating among the author, text, and reader in feminist speculative fiction, the textual presentation may help heal by inspiring the reader to re-vision herself as powerful rather than as a victim, capable of meaningful action in regards to working to change the society that produces such treatment of women.

In "Spiritual Techniques for Re-Powering Survivors of Sexual Assault," Carolyn Shaffer recounts the results of spiritual revisioning in helping one woman recover from sexual abuse: "She is a warrior exposing with a lawsuit the abuse she received in the name of medicine; she is an artist incorporating visual art with sacred, healing dance; she is Goddess and woman, transforming the world as she transforms herself" (468).

Further, Lackey acknowledges rape as a profoundly life-affecting experience for women. Both Tarma and Kethry experience rape as an event which motivates them to make lifelong vows. Sold at age twelve by her brother to a wealthy, sadistic man, Kethry escapes from him and goes to the White Winds school of sorcery for training of her suddenly erupting psychic abilities. When she meets Tarma, Kethry is a journeyman mage, and she carries a sword named Need, whose inscription reads, "'Woman's Need calls me, as Woman's Need made me. Her Need I will answer as my maker bade me'" (32).[5] Named for the extra, almost supernatural help women need to survive in patriarchal societies, Need works only for women, and only provides her bearer with the skills she lacks. For Kethry, Need enables her to be an expert swordswoman as well as a mage, but cannot supply her with magical aid. Like Tarma's bond to her Goddess, Kethry is soul-bonded to Need, and must answer the call to defend women whom Need perceives as in danger. As a result, the union of Tarma and Kethry is very much a true partnership between women and their causes; Kethry agrees to help her sister renew her clan, while Tarma must also accompany Kethry on the journeys Need leads her on. Through this partnership founded on sacred vows and soul bonds, the two women learn about human cooperation, limitation, and caring. Symbolically, their partnership implies that bonds between individual women are the precursors to a true sisterhood which fosters interconnection and cooperation.

In this novel, the heroic challenges each woman must face involve unlearning behaviors fostered by patriarchal society. The women's responses to these challenges also indicate that rather than being some innate, genetic construct, power-over behaviors can be changed into ones of beneficent interconnection. For Tarma, one of the main challenges is to find some reason for living besides revenge for her clan. When she finds that reason in her bond with Kethry, she must further learn not to act like a patriarch by limiting Kethry's freedom. In order for their soul-bond to carry over further on the personality level, Tarma must step out of her self-imposed isolation and learn about her partner's past, hopes, and fears.

Tarma's efforts reveal another theme: When women share each other's stories, they are able to confront the wounds of the past and work toward healing them. Shared stories, a staple of feminist consciousness which arose in conjunction with the consciousness-raising groups from which the feminist movement gained its strength, act as agents of healing and transformation (Christ, *Diving Deep and Surfacing* 127). Logically, this power extends to female-authored texts, such as the novels under discussion, which can use the language of fantasy to articulate the experiences of women's psyches. For female reader as for character, this process offers new ways of seeing one's place and powers in the world.

In *The Oathbound,* for example, Kethry has to face her greatest fears which are bound up in her past. Circumstances force Kethry and Tarma to go to Mornedealth, whose name suggests Kethry's attitude toward returning to where her brother and "husband" still live. Upon hearing Kethry's story, Tarma offers both emotional and physical support (34). Additionally, Kethry realizes that one hurdle she must face before moving up to adept status is to resolve any past conflicts which would drain her or tie up much needed energy (36). Thus, we see the pair exhibiting help and encouragement to each other — Tarma helps Kethry with her past, while Kethry helps Tarma with her clan. After they enter Mornedealth, Wethes does kidnap Kethry. As he gloats over her bound body, she kicks at him, and from his reaction realizes that he is actually terrified at any signs of resistance, which is no doubt why his sadistic sexual appetites centered around very young girls. This realization marks a turning point for Kethry in terms of both self-realization and personal power.

While sympathetic to the profound effects of violence on women, here Lackey indicates that women are responsible for broadening their physical powers of resistance in order to combat more effectively the continual threat of physical assault found in patriarchal culture. In contrast to the limitations imposed by the rape trauma archetype discussed in Pratt's study, Lackey acknowledges women as empowered to shape their lives and not remain victims.

The bond between the two characters, which is one of both sisterhood and a type of marriage, could be considered "lesbian" in the broadest sense of the term as "woman focused" (Zimmerman 206). As lesbian couples have discovered, however, it can prove difficult for partners not to fall into gendered patterns of behavior promoted by society. Women cannot be equal partners if one assumes the role of the male/husband of the patriarchal family; they must avoid paternalistic behavior which views the "other" as lesser or weaker. One major challenge to this principle of equality between the two characters is Tarma's protectiveness toward Kethry, which manifests itself as the two pursue their main adventure in *The Oathbound*, the banishing of a demon named Thalkarsh. In dealing with the demon, Kethry's desire to escape this paternalistic behavior, and Tarma's thoughtless adoption of a paternal rather than sisterly stance, result in placing them in life-threatening danger.

Lackey literally and figuratively explores the temptation women face to use the traditional expressions of female power allowed to women in patriarchal societies: power through serving a male, sexually or otherwise. Need involves the duo because Thalkarsh's worship depends largely on the painful yet self-willed sacrifice of women lured by the demon's ability to assume an intensely sensual identity which inspires a corresponding sexual response on the part of his victims. Thalkarsh tries to tempt Kethry into accepting a position with him. He tells her:

> Is it the bonds with that scrap of steel that trouble you? Fear not — it would be the work of a single thought to break them. And think of the knowledge that would be yours in the place at my side! Think of the power [183].

His mesmerism is almost successful, until the cut from her grip on Need's blade brings Kethry back to a realization of the oaths she has made to women as a class as Need's bearer (woman's need asserts itself and cannot be denied), to natural law as a White Winds sorceress, and to family as Tarma's partner. Through realizing the importance and power of her connections with others, she is able to defy him (184). In anger, he turns to Tarma, whose Goddess-given shielding greatly protects her from his attentions. Instead of trying to sway her with the offer of knowledge and power

[over], Thalkarsh presents her with a vision of herself with a beauty to match his own. In the brief second she allows herself to follow this vision, he almost succeeds in weakening her Kal'enedral bond (185). Angry at herself and him, Tarma helps Kethry break his demon-focus so that he loses his earthly control. Both Tarma and Kethry can resist because they are bound to a cause. For spiritual feminists, the vow is a commitment to explore their spiritual selves and inner power, and not to "backslide" by giving their power away to men.

In order to more clearly demonstrate that female heroic protagonists are strong and powerful, but not omnipotent, Lackey considers several varieties of weakness: perceived female weakness, character weakness, and human weakness. After Kethry performs a magical sex-change illusion operation on a rapist-bandit-murderer named Lastel, he joins Thalkarsh, whose first move is to make Lastel a woman in actuality, as this makes Need useless against him/her. Lastel is enraged to find himself trapped in the type of body he has labeled weak. It leaves him vulnerable for he no longer sees himself as capable of power, much as the women he abused. A different weakness stalks the duo, however: rashness and pride springing from a desire to prove themselves adequate to any task without outside help. Kethry persuades Tarma that the two of them can battle Thalkarsh, and feeling defensive, Tarma agrees (252–53). In their eagerness not to appear weak, they actually weaken themselves. The demon surprises Tarma, and transforms her into the vision he had given her earlier, wiping out her mind and passing her around for gang rape (269). Kethry, now in Lastel's body, rages at herself: "'If I hadn't been so damned sure of myself—if I hadn't been so determined to prove you were smothering me—it's all my fault, it's all my fault! What have I done? What has my pride done to you?'" (276). Eager to escape being seen as vulnerable due to her gender, Kethry has caused her partner to experience that vulnerability in the worst way.

Clearly, when a woman claims her power, she must realize that those operating from power-over will try to deny or "enclose" that power, to use Pratt's terminology. When that happens, she must be willing to acknowledge the limitations of individual power and allow for help from others. In this novel, such help comes in both male and animal forms, indicating that sympathetic others do not always have to be female, and that escape from enclosure is possible. Lackey avoids a reductionist/essentialist approach which posits femaleness as the sole criterion for goodness. Tarma's willingness to sacrifice her partner in order to save Kethry's soul saves the sorceress. However, Tarma, due to Thalkarsh's workings, is left with her Goddess-bond violated, and an intense sense of loss which could drive her mad. Kethry calls on Tarma's Goddess, who replies:

> I am nothing but another face of your own Lady Windborn—
> how could I not know you? Both of you have been wrong—but
> you have wrought your own punishment. Now forgive your-
> selves as you forgive each other—and truly be the two-made-
> one— [296].

Thus, the Goddess affirms that human weakness is inescapable, but carries its own punishment. Rather than espousing an ethics of behavior which calls any deviation from perfection a sin, Tarma's deity posits human weakness as worth watching out for, but also as a part of life which must be accepted. From acceptance flows forgiveness, a necessary ingredient for a lasting partnership.

Another necessary ingredient is a concept of love which is based on sisterhood, an idea which emerges from the spiritual feminist belief that every woman is a face of the Goddess. As Z. Budapest comments, "Her name is every woman's name" (*Holy Book*, Part II 198). The episode above also signals Tarma's change from family "patriarch" for she now has a new definition of both her clan and love. Praying to her Goddess, Tarma understands "[w]hat is your Clan but your sister?" and the true meaning of "love must live free" (301–2). Unwittingly, Tarma has been trying to control her partner, an idea abhorrent to the very ideal she is trying to perpetuate. Their tangle with Thalkarsh teaches both the serious consequences of such control, and the deep love of the pair which enables them to be willing to sacrifice for one another, willing to give each other freedom.

What the reader finds in the bonding of Tarma and Kethry is the struggle to give up forms of power-over ranging from outright force to more subtle gender role-playing, which can be tempting, and instead to live according to power with, the power of equals united. First, each woman must see this power within herself; next, she must acknowledge it in others. Central to this task is the ability to tell one's story and hear another's, and then act on the self-discovery found therein, calling for help when needed. To do otherwise is to live in a world where "vows and honor" are impossible.

In *Oathbreakers,* Lackey uses fantasy to extend a feminist discussion of vows, honor, power, and justice beyond the personal and interpersonal realm, showing how these same issues are at the basis of either a just or unjust society. Here, personal growth is seen as the foundation of any lasting societal change regarding the use of power. Thus Lackey makes a typical feminist connection between the personal and the political. As they track down the oathbreaker who brings these issues into play, Tarma and Kethry must once again grow personally in order to aid in the dispensation of justice for those who abuse their power. For spiritual feminists, growth in personal consciousness underpins the political transformation of societal consciousness. As Hallie Iglehart comments, "[t]he feminist movement, without a healthy spirituality, can never be effective because it addresses only one part of our oppression" (408).

Rather than explore such issues by the popular feminist method of creating a utopian backdrop against which dissonant elements or persons appear,[6] Lackey continues to use the "generic medieval" setting with sword and sorcery action. One advantage to this usage is that while the societies depicted are low technology,[7] they more closely resemble our own because violence, struggle, and the misuse of power are already present and must be contended with. Unfortunately, the dynamics of racial oppression are often missing from these depictions, though authors such as Octavia Bulter and Rosemary Edghill indicate a growing concern with the issue of racism.[8] Even so, instead of viewing this approach pessimistically, one can see the optimism presented when changes can occur among these people/societies. This realism is one of the primary values in feminist fantasy fiction of the sword and sorcery variety, as contrasted with utopian literature.

While Lackey uses these conventions, one can see that certain feminist revisions occur, especially in her connection of the defense of a woman with the defense of social order. In *Oathbreakers,* Tarma and Kethry join with a mercenary troop, composed of both women and men, known as Idra's Sunhawks. Kethry's magical school does not forbid her the use of magic in battle; it just prevents her from gaining her magical energies through coercive means.[9]

Nonetheless, certain aspects of the Sunhawks suggest a feminist revision of traditional mercenary principles: Though they fight for a living, the Sunhawks abide by a code of ethics, and even have a home base which allows for the raising of families and provides for retirement, thus valuing fighters. Idra herself is not the usual mercenary leader, who in both fantasy and history was often a male unlikely to inherit lands or a title; she rescinded her place in line to the throne of Rethwellan, "preferring freedom over luxury" (21). Freedom to create one's own destiny is viewed as preferable to a cushioned but rigidly formatted lifestyle.

When a conflict arises over which of her brothers should succeed to the throne, Stephen or Raschar, Idra goes to help settle it, and disappears; Tarma and Kethry search for her. They soon find out that their defense of a woman becomes the defense of a whole society, as they discover that their search for Idra also becomes a search to discover the moral nature of each of the men-who-would-be-king involved. While their task leaves the principle of hierarchy itself unchallenged, which does fit the medieval setting, it proposes that moral character, rather than might, should determine leadership if the society is to prosper.

Lackey suggests that recognition of the power in one's self leads to an awareness of power through interconnection with the natural world. One of the few standard tenets of feminist spirituality is that one is already interconnected with all other life forms or forces; one must simply become cognizant of the relationship in order to draw upon the universe as an unlimited source of power which the woman can shape to suit her purposes (Starhawk, *The Spiral Dance* 10). This principle underlies contemporary references in feminist spirituality to magic and manifestation, and can be seen in Lackey's representation of Kethry's development as a sorceress.[10] Kethry's first challenge is to perform the ritual which will make her an adept, which is important in that she will no longer have to draw the energy from herself, but can instead draw on a connection to the universe. When Kethry calls forth "the White Wind itself— the Wind of the Five Elements," it grows "into a geyser of power and light and music that surrounded her and permeated her until all she could see and hear and feel was the light and the force" (190, 192).

The synesthesia in this image reinforces the concept of interconnection. With Kethry's new status, "forces that she had been incapable of reaching were hers to command from this moment on. Not carelessly, no— and not casually — but never again, unless she chose to, would she need to exhaust her own strength to cast a spell" (193). Thus, she has reached a pinnacle of magical power marked by interconnection, which indicates that her usage of these greater powers will be just if she remembers their source. Further, if one substitutes "action for change" for "spell," this passage closely reflects Gearhart's description of energy re-sourcement noted above.

Sexual violence as a form of power-over also appears in this novel, related to another violation of interconnection, injustice. Kethry and Tarma find that Raschar, who currently holds the throne, was responsible for and participated in the kidnapping and gang rape of his sister, who finally committed suicide under the torture. Unquestionably, a man who violates both blood ties and common decency in such a heinous way cannot be allowed to hold a position of power. Stefan, whom most had thought of as a rake, is proven while he is in hiding to be the rightful king, as a magical sword found by Tarma and Kethry demonstrates. Obviously, appearances are not reliable, and the sword's judgment of Stefan's character is confirmed by the fact that he has given up his carousing and chosen to marry. While both choices for ruler are male, Lackey subtly ties in the question of rulership with how each man treats individual women, and works in a denouncement of imperialist behavior by condemning colonizing attitudes toward women.

The responsibility of using power wisely becomes the key once one has it, and Lackey depicts the question of justice in an imperfect world as often amounting to the choosing of a lesser evil. Along with Jadrek, a scholar, Tarma and Kethry pronounce the oathbreaker judgment on Raschar; this "Outcasting" is a spell, involving a mage, priest, and honest man who charge the oathbreaker with violating the sacred vows of kinship and kingship (236). This combination represents the unification of the metaphysical, moral, and mundane worlds, whose integrity has been violated. While leading a coup against Raschar, Kethry explains some spells she has constructed to Jadrek, who comments, "That — is not a nice spell"; she responds, "these aren't nice people" (250). Further, she notes, "I only know that the alternative ... is less moral. ... I never thought that becoming an Adept would bring all these moral predicaments with it." As Jadrek observes, "power brings with it the need to make moral judgments" (251). Here, Lackey emphasizes that recognizing the misuse of power does not automatically mean that one will then make flawless moral judgments and executions of power. Nor is she using "the end justifies the means" approach. The point she makes is that one must always strive for justice, and be willing to take a moral inventory regarding one's actions.

Can one's actions include violence as a dispensation of feminist justice? The previous dialogue concerning deadly spells suggests so, as does the fulfillment of the Outcasting spell. When Kethry completes the outcasting spell, she invites the spirit of Idra herself to deliver judgment upon Raschar, which Idra does with "something colder than hate, and more implacable than anger" (270). After Idra completes this task, the Sunhawks return to Stefan and the people of Rethwellan a bundle "with just about enough left of Raschar to be recognizable" (271). While this is shocking, the reader is left with little doubt that justice has been served, albeit in a coldly unbending manner. In contrast to human weakness as discussed earlier, which can be forgiven, in Lackey's moral cosmology the violation of sacred trust and blood ties deserves the harshest punishment possible, for as Raschar's case reveals, the breaking of such bonds threatens the infrastructure of society itself. Therefore, the severity of his punishment is a literal "facing up" to his actions and their consequences. Lackey's position is not held by all spiritual feminists, and stands on a spectrum of varying attitudes toward the employment of violence versus nonviolence when seeking justice. Again, Lackey's stance reflects a combination of complex psychological dynamics with a realistic approach, as opposed to a more utopian vision.

Yet not all of *Oathbreakers* revolves around punishment; the balance to that aspect of the novel is its emphasis on love as a healing force which is active in the present. The earlier declaration of Tarma's Warrior Goddess that she is another aspect of the Lady Windborn, Kethry's deity, foreshadows the idea of seemingly opposite forces as different manifestations of unchanging principles of reality. Kethry's love for Jadrek implies that women need an intellectual equal to be truly satisfied. Yet the love between Tarma and Kethry is no less redemptive for being nonsexual in nature; Tarma's love for Kethry brings her back from death itself after she loses a magical battle. Tarma, in her refusal to lose her partner, calls upon the aspect of her Kal'enedral bond as priestess to the Warrior, "power she had never taken, never used" (205). The warrior speaks: "That you call My Name can mean only that you seek a life, jel'enedra ... the giving of a life — not the taking." When She asks Tarma if, in return, she is willing to live without renewing Tale'sedrin, Tarma responds, "[a]sk anything of me; take my body, make me a cripple, take my life, even make Tale'sedrin a Dead Clan, it doesn't matter. Because without Kethry to share it, none of that has any meaning for me" (206). The Warrior approves, and heals Kethry, telling Tarma:

> It is well that you have opened your heart to the world again, My Sword. My Kal'enedral were meant to be without desire, not without feeling. Remember this always: to have something, sometimes you must be willing to lose it. Love must live free, jel'enedra. Love must ever live free [207].

In these words, which echo Tarma's realization at the end of *The Oathbound,* we see that Tarma's actions to heal Kethry bring about her own healing as well. Where before she had nothing to live for except the renewal of her clan, a hope for the future, Tarma finds that her present friendship and love for Kethry are far more valuable. This discovery marks her transition from vengeance-born killer to one who can kill, but act as a life-giving priestess as well. That both aspects are powers of the Warrior underscores the ethics of balance present throughout Lackey's works. Kethry's physical and Tarma's emotional renewal balance the judgment Raschar receives; both are necessary, and point toward a hopeful future.

These sword and sorcery heroines do not transcend the earthly world in their journeys; rather, they attain personal growth, and find renewal in partnership. In Lackey's work, the bonds between women who can find their inner strength become so strong that they effect change in the larger body politic. In terms of feminist spirituality, inner transformation is "magical" in that it makes possible visions of connection which can transform the world as well. Just as Lackey's novels posit a hopeful vision despite grim realism, spiritual feminists believe that the reclamation of women's inner power leads not only to personal happiness in the present but also to a future world which recognizes the value of all living things. Sjöö and Mor comment on this redemptive power of feminist spirituality: "[I]f we do not want to die, then we must evolve.... We return to the cosmos only by becoming lovers of life, rather than life's victims, voyeurs, and policemen" (430).

Patricia Kennealy: When a Woman Rules

Some may know of Patricia Kennealy from the movie *The Doors*, which depicted her relationship to Jim Morrison and, in a rather unflattering light, her involvement with Wicca, the pre–Christian religion of Old Europe. However, upon reading *The Tales of Aeron* series within *Keltiad* ouvre, one realizes that Kennealy's involvement with the European pagan tradition has led to an intensely researched and involved study of the Celtic tribes, their legends, and their religious traditions; both the prefaces of these novels and the texts themselves attest to this fact.[11] In Kennealy's *Tales of Aeron* series, we see a movement from Lackey's emphasis on the power of women's bonding, to an examination of power-within and how its expression can affect the larger body politic. Aeron, the royal protagonist, has a great deal of "outer" power, but must learn on an inner level the proper use of her personal and political powers.

Though the first volume, *The Copper Crown,* was copyrighted in 1964, it was not published until 1986, followed by *The Throne of Scone* (1987) and *The Silver Branch* (1989). However, in the chronology of *The Tales of Aeron* themselves, *The Silver Branch* comes first. The novels are a blend of science fiction and fantasy, in that the magical and psychic realms exist comfortably alongside the advanced technology of starships. Kennealy does not return to a remote Celtic past; instead, her fiction places the Celts in the future, where they have settled since fleeing Earth and the persecution of the pagans during the time of Patrick, a subject covered in her recent novel, *The Deer's Cry*. In this new location, the "Keltic" lifestyle has continued relatively unchanged over the millennia; the action takes place during the 3500s, "Terran" years. Thus, Kennealy's Kelts exhibit the love of learning, magic, religion, strength, and honor which many have found to be true of Celtic society. By placing her Kelts in a futuristic, technological society, Kennealy appears to affirm both her personal involvement in contemporary Wicca and the relevance of neo–Pagan religion in a technological society.[12]

Sword and sorcery again appear as types of power which women must learn the just use of, and which are united in Aeron. Skilled in many facets of learning and expertise, she is something of a superwoman. However, Aeron does have one major failing — her "traha," or overbearing pride and arrogance. Giving her heroine this flaw allows Kennealy to explore the responsibilities and limitations of power, whether it be that of a ruler or a mage; in a sense, the idea of oneself as all-powerful or invulnerable as part of this hubris allows for an exploration of the dynamics of limitless power-over. Since Aeron is both mage and ruler, the way in which she handles or fails to handle power affects not only her own soul, but empires and planetary federations, thus rendering her tale an epic portrayal of the implications of the way one uses power. Relying primarily for brevity's sake on *The Silver Branch* (*SB*), which shows Aeron's development and her crisis with power, and *The Throne of Scone* (*TS*), which covers her eventual resolution and renewal, I will discuss how her story constitutes a critique of power as manipulation, while supporting the idea of power as an internal and cooperative force which carries its own laws of cause and effect.

Like Lackey's "generic medieval" setting, Keltic society is hierarchical, which some might find at odds with a feminist vision. However, close reading suggests that Kennealy is taking recognizable elements of historical Gaelic peoples, and refining them from a feminist perspective. In the idealized vision of Keltia which Kennealy presents, all of those who hold rulership positions are considered bound in honor and service to those under them, the king or queen most of all. Also, Keltia is notable in that none of its people go without food, shelter, or work, unless they wish it. In addition, most of the magical and military training programs, even the most elite, are open to any rank or gender, as long as that person carries talent. Keltia is very egalitarian, and women are found in all areas of expertise, enterprise, and governance.[13]

By giving Aeron the personality trait of seeking the limits of her abilities and then expanding them, a tendency which proves to be both her bane and her saving grace, Kennealy allows her readers to conceive of having a female identity whose only limits are those placed by the self, but whose actions have repercussions for her society. As a future ruler, Aeron receives rigorous training in all her areas of talent in order to serve her bond to her people properly. At times, she rebels against this strict upbringing, and this conflict between the needs of the private self and the public self is hardly new to literature; Shakespeare's Prince Hal in *Henry IV Part I* is a classic example that comes to mind. Still, females with powerful public selves are found less regularly in fiction. Fantasy offers feminist authors the means to explore strong female characters without experiencing the confinement of strict historical accuracy.

Like Lackey's, Kennealy's treatment of power emphasizes that balance and knowledge are necessary tools for its correct exercise. In this regard, knowledge consists not only of the means to do something, but also a knowledge of the full consequences of one's actions. This belief echoes the spiritual feminist reliance on personal responsibility as a regulator of behavior, rather than external judgments of sinfulness. As Susan Sered mentions, the deterrent for spiritual feminists "is not hellfire or Judgment at the end of days, but the fact that the consequences are also inherent in the structure of this world" (157). When Aeron goes to study under the order of female Druids, she is determined to prove her own worth, and that she is not there merely because she is royalty. A quick and apt student, she learns not only the smaller spells, but also

> the greater spells, the spells to bless or to blast, to send or to bind. Spells too there were that none should teach, and that none should ever seek to learn. But since to forbid knowledge was contrary to wisdom, there was no bar even to these, for a determined student to get the mastery ... and some did [SB 132–33].

Aeron informs the Magistra "[I] knew all at once that I had such power to my hand as could build or blast a world, merely by the willing of it." To this her teacher responds, "And how did that knowing cause you to feel?" The answer: "Terrified. Exhilarated. And, my sorrow to say, very pleased with myself'" (148). Her teacher compares Aeron's powers with those of St. Morgan, Arthur's legendary sorceress sister,[14] but comments: "Aeron is headstrong ... though she is swift and sure off the mark, she often bends her bow before her target is fairly seen, and uses a boar-bow to shoot where a bow strung for rabbits would suffice" (179). These words prove to be prophetic. Aeron's "traha" causes her to mistake ability for knowledge; she can cast powerful spells, but her lack of forethought means that she is unable to accurately foresee their consequences. This problem resembles the use of scientific powers by patriarchy; inventions and techniques ranging from pesticides to biological warfare have been developed and used simply because they can be, without sufficient thought regarding ethics and consequences.

Kennealy makes clear that balanced judgment, feeling leavened by reflection, is necessary to wield magical or martial powers. As with magic, Aeron also excels at swordsmanship. Her teacher remarks "Certainly she will be the best swordsman to sit upon the Throne of Scone for many reigns." Yet he further comments, "When it comes to a choice, she will follow feelings over judgment every time. Not that feelings have no place ... but the idea, and the ideal, is to balance all. With her it seems ever to be 'neck or naught'" (199). While Aeron's great talent and practice in both swordwork and sorcery earn the admiration of her teachers, both qualify their praise by noting her lack of restraint and forethought.

In any spiritual or moral practice, balance is tested during crisis situations, events which require one to implement the practical value of one's wisdom. As predicted by her teachers, Aeron fails this test when her parents and fiancé are murdered in an attack. Viewing their bodies, she becomes filled by "an anger that totally consumed bereavement and grief and pain, that fed on them to fuel its flames" (316). Considering herself "prepared to accept all consequences and ... not count the cost," Aeron flies undetected to the enemy outpost Bellator, warning its inhabitants only so they are aware of the sorcerous doom she has decided to pronounce as judgment, casting aside all the prohibitions against such use of magic:

> Then Aeron ceased to speak, and raised her hands before her face, wrists set back to back in form of the sacred sun-cross — its use here anything but holy — and turned all her power down the forbidden path ... shutting out the cry of her own deep soul in protest, and the voices of all those other souls that clamored suddenly all about her, the spirit-presences of those she loved, all gainsaying her action [325].

She burns Bellator down to bedrock, killing not only soldiers, but also artisans, children, and others, for a total of two million. Both the magical power involved and the death toll are epic; here a woman's anger and her ability to retaliate are indeed formidable. But rather than applauding such a display of might, Kennealy's explanation that this is an act which shocks both Aeron's soul and her beloved dead lets the reader know that the answering of power-over with another act of power-over is unacceptable, especially since the innocent are harmed. Like Lackey, Kennealy indicates that brutality does not equal justice, even in female hands.

When a woman is out of balance, she is likely to experience the phase of the heroic journey known as the descent, often rendered as a descent into the underworld. While the male journey as discussed by Campbell shares this stage, for women the descent frequently consists of grief and depression, either because a woman's belief systems have failed her, or because she has not lived up to her own values. In *The Heroine's Journey,* Maureen Murdock describes women's descent into the underworld as "filled with confusion and grief, alienation and disillusion, rage and despair" (88). Suffering from personal guilt and severe karmic and magical backlash,

Aeron experiences Annwn, the Keltic underworld, where she is "poured out like metal for the casting, hammered like a blade upon some titan's anvil"(*SB* 339). This image captures how a soul-wrenching experience can reshape a woman and make her stronger, like forged steel.

In Aeron's story I find a theme examined earlier in regard to Tarma and Kethry, that hope for women undergoing the descent lies in the acceptance of responsibility for one's actions, as well as forgiveness for acting imperfectly. In Aeron's case we are told that "in that far extremity Aeron came face to face with herself and with her pain and with her deed; and embraced them all three, and in that moment she began to live again" (339). Her return to consciousness is hastened by her magical teacher, who tells her: "[y]ou are already on a path of brightness, Ard-rían; I have Seen it. It began in darkness, and it will pass through still greater darkness, but it will end in a greater light than Keltia has seen for long" (353). In women's spirituality, there is always a chance to test what one has learned. Redemption lies not in some remote heaven, but rather in the chance to effect changes, personal and otherwise, in the here and now. As Starhawk remarks in *The Spiral Dance,* immanent spirituality "does not foster guilt, the stern, admonishing self-hating inner voice that cripples action. Instead, it demands responsibility" (26).

Aeron's opportunities to test her healing and the lessons she has learned about the wrongful use of power occur in the last two novels of the trilogy, and Kennealy uses female jealousy as the catalyst for these events. Kennealy employs the character of Arianeira to indict the ways in which women can be each other's worst enemies. Gwydion's sister, Arianeira, is threatened by both Aeron and Gwydion, and especially the alliance of the two. Unable to hold a position of rank, Arianeira fumes at others' talents and status, rather than develop her own. Power-within implies that each person has gifts and talents to use, and that being the "only" or the "best" is not necessary in order to be effective. As Starhawk says, "We do not have to earn value. Immanent value cannot be rated or compared. No one, nothing, can have more of it than another" (*Truth or Dare* 15).

Failure to realize this truth can make one a puppet for power-over opportunists, symbolized in this case by the Fomori and Cabiri empires. Arianeira's jealousy of and dissatisfaction with Aeron cause her to bring down the Curtain Wall, a magical shield in space which has protected Keltia for centuries, thus leading to a full-scale invasion of Keltia, particularly Tara, the throneworld; once again, personal imbalance threatens societal stability. Women who do not realize their immanent value cannot live sisterhood, and thus betray it and themselves into the hands of patriarchy.

Faced with war on a nearly galactic scale, Aeron is urged by those around her to use magic to save her home, but she refuses, sensing that the first to use magic in the battle (one of her opponents is also a sorcerer) will doom him/herself to be the loser (353). Here we see a new thoughtfulness on Aeron's part which reflects the idea that knowledge includes realizing the consequences of the use of one's power.

Kennealy shows us through Aeron's search for the lost Treasures of Arthur in *The Throne of Scone* that a woman should continue to develop her resources and options, for these make the power of choice even more powerful. Aeron, together with a friend and councilor, embarks on a search for the lost Treasures of Arthur, magical weapons forged by the Sidhe themselves, the Shining Folk.[15] This element of her story lends it epic weight, so that in Kennealy's saga Aeron is ranked with the legendary Arthur. When Aeron discovers Arthur's body, this emotional moment releases all the unexpressed grief over her familial loss, Bellator, and the ensuing war, which she has held inside herself: "[b]ut all of it came back upon her now, no longer to be denied; and now she did not put it by but let it break over her, throwing wide the gates of her soul to let it in." At this point, she realizes that not only had "[a] kingdom's long search had been ended here, but also a woman's long burden, and both by Arthur's hand" (*TS* 219). While on the surface this scene might seem rather male-oriented, Kennealy is redacting the legend of Arthur as the Fisher King, whose whole land suffers when he is ill. Likewise, when Aeron as a female ruler is unhealed, then her world suffers. Thus, Aeron's moment of release also signals a readiness for and an acceptance of her leadership role, which in turn means she can now possess the "Treasures." Spiritually, the scene also points to the necessity of grief and release, and, more generally, to the necessity of healing in conjunction with the recognition of personal power.

Kennealy stresses that Aeron's spiritual wholeness is the product of a new sense of restraint and an understanding of the difference between power wielded justly and unjustly, and life versus destruction. She realizes that the certain victory brought about by the unrestrained use of the Treasures would not be "any victory worth having" (331). This realization brings her to the conclusion that she must battle her enemy, the Cabiri sorcerer Jaun Akhera, one on one, each with no other magic but his or her own. Their battle is not merely one of ruler against ruler, nor even one of longstanding enmity between peoples, but one between power-over and power-with (339). They fight fiercely, until desperate and in great pain, Aeron invokes the Mother Goddess herself in the shape of "the spirit of the planet" to create a rift in the earth which swallows Jaun Akhera and most of his armies (351).

Literally and symbolically, Aeron's claim to just rulership is approved of and backed by the Goddess herself, which gives Aeron's victory the sense of a righteous and lawful balancing. Although she can call on the Goddess, Aeron cannot command her; thus, the Goddess's actions validate Aeron's position. Much like Kethry's invocation of the White Wind, the Goddess's role further suggests that inner balance and self-reliance make it easier for one to receive aid from a higher power in times of need, for one is working with natural and spiritual currents, rather than against them.

Perhaps one of the hardest challenges for women is to recognize their strength, and to feel comfortable with others recognizing it as well. This is true even for Aeron, a veritable superwoman. Her victory and alliances with Earth do more than restore her to her throne as queen; they put her in the position of empress if Keltia takes its new place in the galactic order. She shies away from this: "'Empress': It is too much change, and even the sound of it mislikes me" (351). Yet Gwydion, her mate, persuades her that her future role, no matter what her title, will in fact be that of empress (353).

In the simplest terms, Kennealy show us that when women act, they change themselves, and have to learn to put new words to new roles and behaviors; they initiate a process with no discernible end. This process is reflected in speculative fiction, which seeks to find the words for women's changing reality. Aeron bows to the one true human fate: the process of continual change. She can do so because in her life's journey, she has grown from the point where she could only see power and action in the power-over terms of destruction, to the point where she understands the balance needful for the exercise of personal and political power. This allows her to accept herself as empress, for now she knows that it is not the title which makes one wrong or overbearing in the use of power, but rather the self-knowledge, or lack thereof, of the wielder.

Gael Baudino: From Victim to Judge

A reading of Gael Baudino's first novel, *Strands of Starlight*, also demonstrates how knowledge of the aims and tenets of feminist spirituality is necessary to interpret and contextualize the moral dimensions of such a text. For example, the fact that Baudino is a practicing minister of Dianic Wicca has important implications for the interpretation of the figure of the Goddess in the novel, and for an understanding of her emphasis on female healing. Like other spiritual feminists, Baudino portrays the Goddess as many or even all things. Most importantly, she depicts the

Goddess as the matrifocal representation of the power of integration and interconnection, rather than the power of domination and exploitation, which for Baudino is embodied by the patriarchal church and the Christian God. Baudino's Wiccan beliefs demand that her representation of the Goddess, healers, witches, and the witchhunts be read as more than symbolic. Their representation also resonates with the lived religious practice of contemporary feminist Wiccans who value the transformation of the female self into a self-actualized, powerful being. Like Kennealy's treatment of Aeron, through the story of Miriam, Baudino explores the redefinition of spiritual and material power. Miriam's movement from powerless, exploited victim to committed yet caring warrior, from human to Elf, reflects the desire of spiritual feminists to shape a reality based on the idea of power as an inner strength born from one's recognition of union with the ground of being, the Goddess.

Baudino creates a feminist revision of history in regards to the Inquisition, especially that portion known as the witchhunts, which is specifically Wiccan and feminist. Feminists such as Mary Daly, Ehrenreich and English, Sjöö and Mor, Starhawk, and Anne Barstow have all offered interpretations of this event as the logical extension of Christian misogyny. The Wiccan community as a whole has also claimed this event as a rallying cry for religious freedom. "Never Again the Burning" is a popular slogan, and Charlie Murphy's "The Burning Times" serves as the unofficial Pagan national anthem. Baudino's treatment of the witchhunts is in keeping with both these perspectives. Using the witchhunts as a backdrop allows Baudino to contrast the patriarchal values of the Catholic Church with the matrifocal values of the Elves. Elves have long been a staple of legends, tales, and fantasy literature based in the European tradition. In Baudino's portrayal, elves embody the principles of feminist spirituality, and further connect her subject matter with European witchcraft.[16] After discussing the contrasting patriarchal and matrifocal values displayed in the text, I will show how Miriam's life before and after her transformation displays concerns of spiritual feminists.

Through the union of Aloysius Cranby with Roger of Aurverelle, Baudino critiques the worst that patriarchal church-state has to offer. Cranby is a bishop who feels that the best stepping stone to the papal throne is a crusade against the Free Towns, which are known to have connections with the few remaining Elves. Another priest in the novel cynically reflects, "Did Cranby honestly believe that the Throne of Peter was to be bought with blood? Probably. After all, it had been before" (312). Cranby's detached torture and questioning of Miriam in an effort to gain information against the Elves is just another step in his drive for domination. Roger of Aurverelle admires Cranby because "these eunuchs, these spiritual castrates who went about in women's clothes — they were something different. Cranby came the closest he had ever seen to being a real man" (324). A large man who also loves to hunt and rape peasant girls on his lands, Roger attacks Miriam and spurs her quest for revenge.

In contrast to the patriarchal church-state, represented by Cranby and Roger, stand the Elves, represented by Varden and Terrill. They are male, which at first seems odd in that they are the main communicators of the tenets of this matrifocal society. The effects of Baudino's strategy are twofold: First, it refutes the notion that feminist spirituality is relevant only for women; and second, it prevents a simplistic breaking down of power dynamics in the novel to "men versus women." By including men who act in a nonsexist manner, Lackey and Kennealy also employ this distinction between opposing value systems and differing genders. The characteristics of Elven society which parallel those of spiritual feminists are Goddess worship, nonviolence, and awareness of the interconnection present in the universe, which Elves term "the Dance."

As Goddess worshipers, Elves choose to call the Goddess "the Lady," an ancient titular prefix also used by many neo–Pagan groups today (Starhawk, *The Spiral Dance* 17–18). The similarities extend to the Elven definition of the Goddess: when Miriam asks Terrill who the Lady is, he replies "Simply: everything" (262). However, the Goddess allows herself to be perceived as a woman. Terrill notes that "She wears this form for our convenience.... In this, we are privileged, and we love Her dearly. As She loves us ... She made us ... She is us" (263). Here, Baudino's definition of the Goddess via Terrill attempts to counter the most frequent misunderstanding about contemporary Goddess thealogy, which is the notion that women are simply performing a sex change on a deity (Goldenberg 109). Instead, the Goddess is immanent divinity, whose presence is known in the heart of the mundane, in the processes of the natural world and everyday life (Starhawk, *The Spiral Dance* 91–93). Cranby, in his petition to lead a crusade against the Elves, charges:

> It is well-known that the Elves worship a woman, consummating their rites in obscene blasphemies. Furthermore, they claim that this woman-god of theirs is tangible, and that she can be perceived by the believer directly, before death, and that this perception can be constant and joyful [36].

Since this conception of the Goddess enables the Elves to "revere women, and treat them with respect, ascribing various noble virtues to the daughters of Eve," this heresy is doubly threatening to the patriarchal hierarchy of the church. For Elves as for spiritual feminists, a Goddess-oriented, woman-affirming belief system directly opposes patriarchal religion and its view of women as subordinate and sinful.

The second resemblance of Elves to spiritual feminists is their typical nonviolence. Like most spiritual feminists, Elves have no sense of themselves as morally superior to or separate from another being; this is the expression of immanent value noted earlier by Starhawk. Elves hesitate to take life, and are essentially nonviolent except for defensive purposes.[17] For example, they refuse to cut living trees for firewood; instead, they gather dead wood from the forest floor. The Elves will kill when they feel the consequences of not killing would be worse, which reminds Lackey's readers of Kethry's dilemmas upon becoming an adept.

Varden and Terrill observe that since they are immortals, they have quite a bit of time to reflect on the consequences of their actions, and as Elves they have a more acute awareness of the life possibilities they end when killing someone. Once again, the need to measure the impact of one's actions is more important than the ability to act in and of itself. Thus, Elven attitudes toward violence correspond to a degree to Starhawk's statement of nonviolence as following from a belief in immanent value, but they part from its utopian manifestation by allowing for a broader range of self-defense.

The Elven awareness of potentialities, combined with their sense of connection with others and the natural world, forms what the Elves refer to as the Dance, a name which appears to self-consciously echo Starhawk's *The Spiral Dance*. The vision of interconnection forms the third parallel of the Elves to contemporary spiritual feminists. Here is one of Miriam's first visions of the dance of life:

> She was seeing everything in all its wholeness, in all its intricate connection. The world was bright and fresh — even the dying leaves and the dead grass — as though created that very instant. But she saw beyond the instant, too, into past and futures. She saw the possibilities inherent in the smallest particle of earth, saw the endless cycles of season and of life and death, the days stretching off behind and before her, weaving through one another and through her in the Great Dance [164–65].

For the Elves, such perception is not the stuff of an occasional mystic vision, but rather is their everyday perceptual mode. Among spiritual feminists, the awareness of one's interconnection and interdependence with life is both a tenet and a goal, as persons search for an integrative alternative to the alienation fostered by patriarchal religion (Mary Daly, Starhawk, et al.).

Miriam's transformation from victim to Elf is the before and after story of the effects of spiritual feminist values on a woman's sense of herself as a powerful being. Before her exposure to "Elven" values, Miriam's life is characterized by persecution, lack of control, and victimization. In a sense, these experiences are necessary for women to break from patriarchal values and open themselves to the alternative values proposed by spiritual feminists. When the reader first sees Miriam, she is feeling anything but powerful. Born with a miraculous healing gift that causes others, including her parents, to cast her out of their society as a witch, she manages to escape the dungeons of Hypprux after being tortured. In fiction as in history, in 1350 women who heal and do not wear cleric's robes, such as midwives and others, are targets for the Inquisition (Ehrenreich and English 7–19). Miriam is a healer in a world opposed to such powers in women, and that world has at its command a wide range of control measures, against which a small, frail, dark-haired and dark-eyed girl has little hope of standing. Symbolically, she represents the woman who does not yet understand the nature of her special powers which place her in opposition to the hierarchical order. Miriam's initial lack of development contrasts with Lackey's and Kennealy's more consciously powerful heroines.

Patriarchy suppresses women's voices and choices, and as Christ has noted, the silencing of women's stories narrows women's concepts of reality (*Diving Deep and Surfacing* xxiii). Even more damaging to Miriam than the loss of control she experiences during torture is her lack of any control over her healing gift. Even during her escape, ill and exhausted, Miriam heals the mayor of Saint-Blaise, and when he thanks her, remarks, "I didn't have any choice. I never have any choice" (5).

This issue stands at the very heart of the novel and Miriam's struggle. At the beginning she has no control over the characteristic by which others define her, her healing. Her situation is a metaphor for the patriarchal view of the Other. Traditionally, women have lacked control over how others define them. For white women, the definition is primarily one of gender, while black women are defined by both race and gender. Women, whether of African and European descent, must struggle to define themselves on their own terms. Like other women on the spiritual journey, Miriam progresses as she learns of the choices open to her and their implications for her life. She also chooses how she will define herself, which suggests a view of the spiritual journey as a journey of interpretation.

The question of victimization and vengeance becomes part of her situation as well, for as with other fantasy heroines such as Tarma and Kethry, rape presents women with the choice of viewing themselves as victims or as survivors. Miriam finds Roger of Aurverelle near death, and unable to control her gift, she heals him; he then rapes her. With the only determination of will which can carry her past suicide, she hardens her despair into a vow of vengeance upon Roger. She reflects: "She would not cry anymore. The Church had persecuted her, her power had violated her, and now on top of those outrages was piled yet another" (54). Onto Roger, the author of her final violation, she projects all her anger at a male-dominated system which exploits and dominates others. Miriam feels that her only choices are either his death or her own, and she is already enough of a fighter to choose his death. Her anger is also a recognition of rape as the physical manifestation of societal misogyny, thus echoing analysts such as Susan Brownmiller on the use of rape as a tool which enforces patriarchal domination (*Against Our Will: Men, Women, and Rape*).

Miriam's transformation by Elven magic can be interpreted here as the application of Goddess energy to a woman's life. First, she finds someone who will hear her story and help her realize her physical strength. Varden, the Elven healer, has the capability to give her the fighter's body she will need if she is to become a swordswoman, but he attempts to dissuade her, for it goes against Elven ethics to perform magic to aid someone for the purpose of killing another. When healing her, however, Varden was forced to relive her rape as she perceived it, and this does make him sympathetic to her plea. By implication, men who have been sensitized by their Goddess worship are more readily able to empathize with women's lives, as seen earlier with Zakynthos and Kassandra, thus positing yet another positive effect of Goddess reverence. Varden senses that Miriam's existence is pivotal, and that his refusal of aid would only end in her death, so on the Pagan Beltane, or Elven "day of completion," Miriam is transformed into a tall, strong, and beautiful woman. During this process, she finds herself faced with a woman who holds out her hand, and Miriam, unafraid, takes it. We later find that this is Mirya, an Elf who was raped and murdered by humans, and Miriam now bears her likeness.

As seen with the other heroines, power-within is a spiritual power, not just a physical power. Therefore, Miriam's physical transformation sparks her change from human to Elf, a psychological transformation based on the integration of spiritual feminist principles. Baudino suggests that the incorporation of Goddess energy into a woman's life is not only a process of healing but also one of alteration. First, though Miriam is bent on vengeance, the Elves try to teach her nonviolence.

Terrill, the swordteacher, tries to instill in Miriam a sense of the life and death powers she now carries, hoping to caution her from overreacting. His fears are warranted; as soon as she is proficient enough to be given a real sword rather than a practice one, she kills. In turn, this act unleashes a chain of events which almost causes the death of her closest friend, Charity, and which forces Varden, very reluctantly, to kill Aloysius Cranby. From this fiasco, Miriam learns to look further ahead into the possible futures in order to weigh her actions, thus echoing Aeron's lesson in Kennealy's *The Silver Branch*. Central to this episode is the twofold attitude toward violence I noted earlier: Baudino posits Miriam's struggle for defense as a positive one, but also makes clear the ease with which any act of violence begets more violence.

The Mirya/Miriam connection is a clear example of the tenet of interconnection, and is important in three ways. First, their union is a mutual choice: Mirya selects Miriam, but it is Miriam who reaches out to her. Thus she is consciously selecting a particular idealized form, Mirya, to incorporate into her identity, marking her transition to "Elfdom" as more conscious than unconscious. Second, while Mirya's Elven nature broadens Miriam's perspective and has a moderating influence on her, Miriam equally obtains the justice which Mirya was denied. Finally, both were healers, and their union symbolizes the necessity of women to claim all aspects of themselves in order to achieve healing. Just as Lackey's Tarma had to claim her priestess self as well as her warrior self in order to achieve a combined healing balance, Miriam the healer and Mirya, a healer but also a developed warrior, heal each other.

Further, Miriam's growing acceptance of herself as an elf symbolizes the spiritual feminist rejection of human life in a patriarchal society and conscious choice of matrifocal values. When Miriam returns to Hypprux to rescue the midwife Mika from the same dungeons which had once held her, an act which symbolizes the ripple effect of these tenets, Miriam is able to contextualize and interpret her own anger:

> she knew that her anger still existed, but she had begun to understand that it did not stem solely from her violation. Rather, it grew out of her society as a whole.... She herself had once consented, but no more. She had withdrawn her permission, had, in fact, withdrawn herself from the human race. She was connected to the mortal world still, as she was with everything, but she would not allow it to direct her [293].

In recognition of her new strength and sense of inner power and choice, she chooses this moment to rename herself by adopting the name Mirya, which in Elvish means "the sudden blooming of a flower" (199). She has accepted life as an Elf, or "Fairy: . . . 3; member of a Heathen nation who is feared, hated, and oppressed by Christians but Survives in the Realm of the Wild" (Daly, *Wickedary* 123). Significantly, conjoined with her decision to direct her own world is Miriam's action to help save another woman who is being victimized. Therefore, help is portrayed as integral to interconnection.

Like Walker, Lackey and Kennealy, Baudino implies that the highest goal of feminist self-development is not tying up all of one's energy fighting patriarchy, but going further by living a life where the woman controls both the definition of pleasure and of the female self. As Miriam becomes more elven, she is increasingly perceptive of the Dance and its patterns, and is also able to perceive the Goddess or Lady as well. Her faith in the Christian god shattered, she dedicates herself to the service of the Lady instead (222). And, as her awareness expands, Miriam begins to imagine a future for herself beyond her revenge, much as Tarma was forced to do.

As Kethry discovers in *Oathbreakers*, spiritual feminist ethics does not always provide a woman with easy choices. Miriam's opportunity for justice is more complicated than she first envisioned. First, much of her satisfaction at holding Roger at sword's point is diminished by the fact that he does not recognize her as the small girl he raped; her body is entirely different now. Second, after Miriam has slit his throat and he lies dying at her feet, she becomes aware by looking at the patterns that his death will leave a void which will lead to the certain destruction of the Free Towns and all those she loves. So, she does what she had sworn never to do: she heals him. While Miriam is at it, she does what perhaps every rape victim and many women in general have longed to do: she changes a man's mind, literally. As she does so, she also sees some of why Roger became the type of man who vents his hatred through rape, and finds that some of his pain is similar to her own. Miriam heals this, and transforms him into a man who will no longer rape — or lead a plot against the Free Towns. Miriam realizes that "[a]s terribly as she had been raped by Roger, it was as nothing compared to the magnitude of the violation she had perpetrated on him" (361). But it was what she *chose* to do, and the wiser Miriam now knows that no choice is perfect, and that she will accept the responsibility for what she has done. Instead of adopting an "ends justify the means" approach, Baudino, like Lackey, acknowledges that power also carries with it uncertainty and ambiguity.

In addition, Miriam sees the connection between the personal and the political, between her own revenge and the need to save the Free Towns and all that they stand for, and bases her choice on this. Baudino represents the reconciliation of the warrior self and the healer self, a unification which incorporates Baudino's own dual identity as literary "warrior" with musical healer.[18] Finally, Miriam's healing of Roger implies that while women's healing is primary, ultimately men must find healing as well, for they control the tools of destruction. Some spiritual feminists share this view (Starhawk, *The Spiral Dance* 230–34).

Baudino's work continues the emphasis we have seen on feminist ethics of power as a decision-making process which involves both interconnectedness and responsibility. As these sword and sorcery heroines learn of their inner and joined powers, they must also extirpate internalized patriarchal values. Through fantastic fiction, Baudino, along with Kennealy and Lackey, acknowledges female oppression at the same time she affirms women's ability to liberate themselves and others.

Octavia Butler: Healing and Resistance

As a prolific African American writer of speculative fiction, Octavia Butler's presence introduces a note of difference in the symphony of speculative fiction that is currently dominated by both mainstream European American male and European American feminist writers. In one of her *Patternist* novels,[19] *Wild Seed,* the reader finds a multivalent treatment of oppression and the possibilities of resistance. The novel serves as a critique of male dominance in African American society, and also suggests that female healing can produce important changes in male behavior. Butler explores issues of oppression and healing not only through the backdrop of the slave trade, which provides one narrative of oppression, but also through the focal story of Anyanwu, a healer, and Doro, psychic enslaver and breeder, a relationship which serves as a vehicle for the issues of male dominance, eugenics, and speciesism. By looking first at the issue of slavery, then Anyanwu's relationship with Doro, I will show how she, as "wild seed" resister and healer, illustrates the ability to transform power–over behaviors.

Enslavement of Africans is central to the novel in several ways. First, it provides a historical subtext, as Butler reminds her audience of the horrors and destruction of the slave trade, as perpetrated by a supposedly "civilized" people. Second, it invites comparison with Doro's own brand of slavery. Third, it allows Butler to demonstrate the struggle to keep Africentric traditions, such as healing methods, alive in America. Finally, the narrative of slavery intersects with that of male–female dominance and comments upon it.

From the novel's opening, set in the western part of the African continent, to its depiction of antebellum Louisiana, the slave trade and its effects are ever present. Sandra Govan notes that this connection to the "Black American slavery experience ... is a fundamental departure for science fiction as a genre" ("Homage to Tradition" 79). Further, Butler, like the writers of past slave narratives, clearly desires to "educate and politicize in no uncertain terms" (Govan 81). Butler politicizes in terms of African American female identity. To underscore the brutality of the slave trade, even the callous Doro must be affected by it. At the beginning of the novel, when Doro investigates one of his seed villages, where he has settled a group of his psychically gifted children, he finds that "slavers had been to it before him. With their guns and their greed, they had undone in a few hours the work of a thousand years" (*Wild Seed* 3). Reminders of this sort of thoughtless waste continue throughout the novel.

Both Anyanwu and Doro have been slaves at some point in their lengthy lives (9, 116), but their experiences as African slaves do not adequately prepare them for such seventeenth century realities as the typical European slave ship and the conditions of the middle passage. In addition to the physical torment of slavery, the psychological damage must be noted as well. In America, Anyanwu remarks to Doro, "haven't you seen the men slaves in this country? They are never permitted to learn what it means to be a man. They are not permitted to care for their children" (215). Thus, in addition to dislocation and the use of force, the role of humans as breeding animals is another vicious aspect of slavery with negative consequences for African American women, men, and children.

How does Doro's version of slavery compare to that of the white man? Anyanwu sees that his enslavement of others is not made different by his existence as an African. Instead, Doro shares the desire to dominate others, including women, which the white men also display. One of the first things one might note is that although Doro sometimes chooses to wear the body of a white man, he was originally a Kushite, or Nubian (7). In this way Butler indicts patriarchal power regardless of race. Neither the fact of Doro's African past nor his own treatment as a slave prevents him from forcing others to do his bidding. While his desire is not for monetary profit, he is nonetheless the beneficiary of his exploitation of others' lives. Thus, Butler condemns both the white engineers of the slave trade and those black men who are willing to adopt their tactics, thus threatening other Africans and their descendants. Like European slavers, Doro is perfectly willing to use whatever degree or threat of force is necessary to put people in the locations he desires. Usually the threat consists of the likelihood that Doro will take over the body of any recalcitrant person, thus removing their soul and effectively killing them. This is also a rather persuasive means to another end, which is Doro's breeding program. At his command, sister will lie with brother (121). Clearly, Doro is more alike than different from other slavers. His justification for his actions is very paternalistic; he sees himself as a good master, promising a degree of protection in return for obedience. His people are highly loyal to him. However, Anyanwu is not fooled; when he tries to tell her how his form of slavery does not waste people, she responds, "Shall I be glad that your slaves will not be wasted?... Or shall I fear the uses you will find for them?" (68). Because her longevity has given her both independence and the wisdom of years, Anyanwu never believes that Doro is good or kind; after all, he coerces her as well by threatening her children. Thus, we can see that as an oppressor, Doro is different from the other slavers only in degree, not kind. In fact, Doro is very equal opportunistic; he will control any of his seed people regardless of race, class, or gender.

The reader may also view this male control of breeding as representative of the historical desire of males to usurp control of the female creative force. Anyanwu's disapproval of Doro's program represents a justifiable female suspicion of male control of reproductive capabilities, a concern especially relevant for Third World women, who are more frequently exploited in drug testing and sterilization abuse (Davis 215). Eugenics is a recurring topic in Butler's works. I view her interest as arising not only from a desire to speculate on possible uses of such programs in the future, but also from an awareness of the forced breeding done on the slave plantations in the American south. This dual motivation may account for the similarly divided attitude toward eugenics which is displayed in the novel; eugenics is alternately blameworthy and praiseworthy.

This attitude also reflects differing types of reproduction and relation to the body. Jenny Wolmark comments that "Doro's existence depends on the 'taking' of bodies, so, for him, possession and power are inseparable; Anyanwu is able to regenerate and recreate her own body, thus avoiding the relations of oppression that are crucial to Doro's existence" (45). Anyanwu's reproduction emphasizes nurturing and protection of her "witch children."

Butler indicates that men, represented here by Doro, lack a wise woman's concerns about interrelation and the effects of one's actions on the community. Thus, the reader is encouraged to view selective breeding, in this case for the specialization and enhancement of psychic talents, as a violation of natural law. Butler accomplishes this through the reader's sharing of Anyanwu's reactions to Doro's activities. One reason for her dislike toward Doro's breeding program is that Doro does not recognize any kinship limits or taboos; incest is not a problem to him, whereas for Anyanwu it is an "abomination." "He had spoken of this before. Of incest, of mating her own children together with doglike disregard for kinship" (121).

Of further distaste to her is the knowledge that he will threaten or use force to get his way, if necessary. Also, the living products of Doro's eugenics program provide the most damning argument against the practice, as evidenced by the tragic results of their own lives. Examples include the tortured Thomas, who drinks himself into oblivion because he cannot tune out the thoughts of others; Isaac's mother, who commits suicide for the same reason; and the Sloanes, so tormented by their own perceptions of pain that they unthinkingly abuse their children (138). Such disastrous results speak loudly for the cost in human terms when science is applied blindly and mechanically, as Doro does, and serves as an indictment of genetic manipulation in the absence of an ethical foundation, a contemporary controversy.

However, there is a positive side. Anyanwu can approve of Doro's actions to the degree that he operates from an affirmation of those persons/qualities commonly outcast from Eurocentric patriarchal societies, as seen earlier in *The Flame Bearers* and *Strands of Starlight*. Doro is also described as a "breeder of witches" (29), and this term is not used pejoratively. Doro's children are those with psychic abilities, the "different ones" who are "ground down" by those to whom "the hearing of voices, the seeing of visions, the moving of inanimate objects when no hand touched them, all the strange feelings, sensitivities, and abilities were evil or dangerous, or at the very least, imaginary" (149). Doro remarks to Anyanwu that "every witch-scare one person's foolishness creates can hurt many. We are all witches in the eyes of ordinary people, and I am the only witch they cannot eventually kill" (97). These psychic abilities, which provide Doro with "tastier" kills, by implication also sweeten or enrich life.

Butler suggests that burning or stamping out the visionaries and seers among us is as bad as increasing these traits to an unbearable level. Anyanwu's sympathy for, and related status to, these societal outcasts combines with her desire to have a child whom death will not take away from her, and this causes her to lend her nurturing and love to the products of Doro's experiments. This is one example of her use of healing to nurture and to improve the quality of life for those around her. Because of her willingness to do so, Anyanwu can eventually persuade Doro to modify his callous approach to the only project which gives his unending life meaning.

The magnitude of Anyanwu's task in the novel — to not only survive Doro's domination, but to change him — has been made clear by the preceding description of Doro as a type of ur-patriarch. To understand how Anyanwu can do so, the reader must first comprehend the Goddess, healer, and "wild seed" aspects of her character.

Although the character Anyanwu is not revered as a Goddess who exists outside the human realm, certain aspects such as her name, shape-shifting abilities, longevity, and position as ancestress do grant her stature which is more than human. And certainly they are like Goddesses of African tradition, which have a close relationship with their human worshipers and are strongly linked with ancestor reverence. Her character reflects an African focus on community, interconnection, and ancestor reverence. Anyanwu is the name of an African solar deity, and Doro's nicknaming of her as "sun woman" places an emphasis on her life-giving powers. Govan cites Butler as asserting that Anyanwu "is partly based on the Onitsha legend of Atagbusi, a shape-shifter much honored by her people because she used her abilities to help them" ("Connections" 87n). In addition to this legend, Anyanwu's shape-shifting abilities also suggest a connection to various goddesses with such ascriptions as "Lady of the Wild Beasts." Finally, her longevity, and resulting numerous generations of offspring, cast her as a divine ancestress, a title which her chosen American name, Emma, acknowledges (278). Shinn sees Anyanwu as "clearly the female principle of life itself … [a] Great Mother" figure ("The Wise Witches" 212). All of these features contribute to a perception of Anyanwu as Goddess-like, and qualify her image as mother, an image which makes critic Dorothy Allison "scream with frustration" because of what Butler's female characters will do to protect family and children, which Allison perceives as reinforcing stereotypes (471).

As important as her Goddess qualities is her role as a healer. Unlike Doro, who uses his unique abilities only for self-serving purposes, Anyanwu uses her abilities primarily to aid others through healing, and only secondarily for self-defense. She can and does kill when necessary, but prefers to eagerly and methodically explore anatomy, herbalism, and other forms of healing. Through this depiction of Anyanwu, one finds Butler, like Ehrenreich and English, alluding to the work of the wise woman as the foundation of medicine. However, Butler claims this tradition for African women rather than European women.

As the title suggests, the fact that Anyanwu is considered wild seed is significant, and alludes to African American women's unique position in European patriarchy. To Doro, wild seed is offspring that has appeared without his knowledge; as breeding stock it can strengthen his other strains, which are highly inbred. In his opinion, however, "wild seed always had to be destroyed eventually" (90). Isaac, his son, tells Anyanwu that "wild seed resists sometimes…. But he [Doro] always wins. Always" (102). Clearly, this situation is analogous to women who defy the patriarchal order. In this case, Isaac is mistaken; Anyanwu's sense of independence is never truly broken. Lacking the conditioning which would encourage the adoration his other people give Doro, Anyanwu ultimately proves resistant and defiant; she is prepared to defy Doro even if it costs her life. This is an act of resistance which only a "wild seed" could accomplish.

Having escaped from Doro's control for over a century, only for him to find her in Louisiana with her own family of "witch children," over whom he asserts his control, Anyanwu sickens of the struggle and begins to will herself to die. Doro finally realizes that what Isaac had told him was correct: Anyanwu offers him his only chance for a lifetime (that is to say, immortal) partner. After begging her not to leave him, Doro begins a process of change. Although he cannot entirely stop killing others, he will no longer callously kill those who serve him, and he will no longer command Anyanwu, her children, or her household (277–78). Anyanwu, the wild seed, does the impossible: She resists, and wins.

How should the reader interpret this ending, whose "uneasy compromise between Anyanwu and Doro is a crucial pointer to those possibilities for on-going change and development with which all of Butler's fiction is concerned" (Wolmark 45)? One possibility is to look at the healing of male-female relationships as the logical extension of an ethics of interconnection.

First, the reader notes that Anyanwu and Doro, as immortals, are invested with traditional archetypal qualities as female and male. Govan likens the pair to Adam and Eve ("Connections" 84). Hoda Zaki argues that Butler's view of human nature is essentialist, or biologically deterministic (242). Certainly, the two characters have many traits which are stereotypically masculine and feminine. Doro, as male, displays the qualities of aggressive, penetrating force; his realm is also that of the spirit. Likewise, Anyanwu, as female, is connected with the body, nurturing, submission, and to a degree, redemption. Nonetheless, Butler subverts these straightforward ascriptions. Doro is preoccupied with the material creation of his people; Anyanwu can attack and devour. At times, both wear the body of the "opposite" sex. This subversion of gender associated qualities weakens Zaki's argument that Butler's ascriptions are essentialist.

There is, however, enough difference between Anyanwu and Doro that this critic has no trouble reading Doro as the embodiment of the worst patriarchal males have to offer. Even Doro's final cooperation is self-serving. Only a threat to his sense of security can deter him from his stance as dominator. Given this portrayal, Butler implies that men will never give up their control unless women are willing to deprive them of their presence and cooperation, thus threatening men's sense of security. A corollary of this idea is the notion that unless women are willing to risk doing so, male domination will spiral out of control until males no longer have any "human" traits such as compassion and love, as Isaac has suggested will happen to Doro without Anyanwu's influence.

This reading goes beyond a story of gender and racial struggle to one of interspecies domination. Anyanwu understands that life coexists in a complex web in which humans are not justified in acting on whim. The first hint of such a possibility occurs when Anyanwu discovers that the dolphins are intelligent creatures which should not be casually slaughtered (91). The second indicator is Doro's treatment of humans as though they were sheep or cattle. As in other Butler novels, humans can be outraged when an entity is strong enough to exert power over humans. Thus, Butler's fiction provides an explicit critique of speciesism that is relevant to contemporary society as it faces various forms of ecological crisis, including the extinction of species at an unprecedented rate.

Can women stop men from oppressing them, and can humans cease their other forms of oppression? No doubt some women are resistant to the idea that global healing, in all its levels, should originate from them. What a task! Yet Butler strongly indicates that men will not reform themselves unless women withdraw their complicity with their own oppression and demand change, being willing to die for it if necessary, as African Americans in the civil rights movement demonstrated their willingness to risk death in order to fight racial oppression. At this point the narratives of racial and gender domination intersect and comment upon each other. Not all persons find themselves capable of risking alienation and death in order to defend their rights. Many women, like those who adore Doro, give in to patriarchal males only to find themselves discarded casualties, puppets, or tokens. Others, the rare feminist wild seed healers, may prove to be a strong, resistant strain, from which a new breed of sensitives could spring forth, to create utopia out of dystopia. Such action means reclaiming control of female creative power, and keeping it out of the hands of men who would abuse the creation of life. Butler suggests that a feminist healing of male-female relationships can have a ripple effect on other relationships in the web of interconnection. It might not be likely, but it is a possibility, and this sense of hope makes Butler's novel a comic or unifying one that reveals the pivotal importance of redefining power.

Speculative fiction allows these authors to explore the ultimate possiblities of female power, an issue which continues to beat at the heart of feminist activism and debate today. By acknowledging that victimization is part of many women's experience, yet need not define, much less limit, that experience, the authors I have discussed show that a woman's strength not only shapes her personal reality, but is a force to be reckoned with by all of society's structures, regardless of degree of partriarchal/racial oppression.

Though Butler, Lackey, Baudino, and Kennealy differ in their positions on the continuum of proper actions for feminist self-defense (understood in its largest sense), they all use various elements of sword or sorcery to stand as reminders of the female ability — indeed, responsibility — to transform the world through the combined efforts of our considerable physical and mental power.

4

The Quest for the Goddess

Although the female protagonists in the previous chapter are heroic, strong female characters who act and achieve in the course of their journeys, the heroines in this chapter have a more specific sense of mission, one which is strongly dependent on a personal relationship with either a particular aspect of the Goddess or the Great Goddess principle as a whole. In Marion Zimmer Bradley's *City of Sorcery,* Lynn Abbey's *Daughter of the Bright Moon* and *The Black Flame,* and Joan Vinge's *The Snow Queen,* the journey clearly takes the form of the quest, and the relationship of the personal to the divine as a source of empowerment becomes the central issue. Like women in the contemporary feminist spirituality movement, these protagonists find that the Goddess is a figure which simultaneously supports them and challenges them to new levels of self-reliance. For each, coming to a personal understanding of the Goddess in her life involves a heroic quest which ultimately affirms interconnection with all life, even though the quest is essentially an individual one. The female heroic quest also confirms their identities as powerful women exhibiting aspects of immanent deity. At the same time that these protagonists exemplify a spectrum of female heroism, their quests also typify the Amazon tale/ bildungsroman. Their quests differ in regards to the solitary nature of the quest, and the degree to which a personal quest affects the world. The selected texts are all by European American authors, though not because of a conscious decision to select on that basis. There are elements of the quest for the Goddess in various African American texts: Fanny's growing awareness of the Goddess in *The Temple of My Familiar* is an example. However, in the narrow sense I am defining this pattern, I have not come across a text which focuses on one protagonist's quest to understand one

Goddess. As will be seen in the following chapter, African American women are typically more concerned with familial and community healing, and perhaps have steered away from a more isolated individualism typical of the western tradition, a tradition more readily visible in European American women's texts. A brief discussion of the use of the quest, the concept of female heroism, the role of the Goddess/Goddesses, and the influence of genre follows, preparatory to examining the quests in the novels themselves.

In discussing the female heroic quest, critic Maureen Murdock recounts how she felt upon hearing Joseph Campbell's pronouncement that women do not need to make the heroic journey because they are already "there":

> This answer stunned me; I found it deeply dissatisfying. The women know and work with do not want to be there, the place that people are trying to get to. They do not want to embody Penelope, waiting patiently, endlessly weaving and unweaving. They do not want to be handmaidens of the dominant male culture, giving service to the gods. They do not want to follow the advice of fundamentalist preachers and return to the home. They need a new model that understands who and what a woman is [2].

Critic Dana Heller echoes this sentiment in her assertion that "[i]n Campbell's view, women are accessories for the male's heroic adventure" (2). Further, Murdock observes that women's quests involve "learning how to value themselves as women and to heal the deep wound of the feminine." The journey begins with a

> rejection of the feminine defined as ... dependent, overcontrolling, and full of rage. It continue[s] with total submersion into the familiar outer heroic journey, complete with masculine allies, to achieve the boon of independence, prestige, money, power, and success. This [is] followed by a bewildering period of dryness and despair which [leads] to an inevitable descent to the underworld to meet the "dark feminine" [3–4].

Her comment highlights the fact that the traditional male model of the quest is not always applicable to women's lives. As we shall see, women's quests end in unification and (re)connection rather than achieving a special prowess which sets one apart. Murdock's Jungian approach causes her to view the Goddess in terms of anima, and this journey or quest as a primarily psychological event. However, her emphasis on contemporary women's lives, as well as her positive view of the quest, makes her model of the journey more useful than Pratt's (136–43) for my analysis. For the authors under consideration here, the literary presentation of this inner psychological event also includes an outer religious/spiritual event, thus adding to the levels of complexity found in representations of the female journey.

Thus, knowledge of the "Goddess" refers to the psychospiritual states which mark the stages experienced during the healing of the split from the experience of one's power as (a) female. For these protagonists, the split is from a femininity as typically, and usually negatively, defined by their respective cultures. After this split, each woman goes on to succeed in a nontraditionally female or feminine role.

As Murdock tells us, this stage necessitates a stage of breakdown and questioning. Like modern feminists, each woman must decide how to define and view herself, using her lived experience to break down the rigid, restrictive codes passed down by society regarding the meanings of femininity and femaleness. What Murdock describes as the meeting with the "dark feminine" can also be seen/depicted as the search for and meeting with the Goddess. In connection with this idea, the motif of a descent to the underworld, both physical and psychological, is frequently encountered in these stories, as Pratt has also observed (142). In the novels I examine, Murdock's depiction of the journey's end as the emergence of a balanced and fulfilling female identity corresponds with each protagonist's achievement of growth and balance, conjoined with an understanding gained through personal experience of what the Goddess means to her.

Two of the categories of feminist science fiction and fantasy identified by Kathleen Cioffi are the Amazon tale and the bildungsroman. These are useful, if not entirely separable, starting points for a discussion of the types of questing heroines found in speculative fiction (85). The Amazon character achieves a legendary stature either through physical or psychic prowess, sometimes both. Often, however, the possession of such striking powers alienates her from others. In turn this isolation may spur a quest for a deeper inner understanding of her life and its meaning.

Cioffi describes these tales as demonstrating "an important tension not found in novels with male warriors as heroes: the tension between the heroine's role as a woman and her role as a super-hero … their worlds say that a person cannot be both a warrior and a woman" (86–87). Both Bradley's Magdalen Lorne and Abbey's Rifkind experience this conflict in their quests, and through their stories we are reminded that "[t]hough at first glance the Amazon story may appear to be feminist wish-fulfillment fantasy, it can be in reality a serious exploration of the nature of a strong woman's role in a society that expects weakness from women" (87). The Amazon is also an expression of the idea that in order for a woman to combat patriarchy, she must exhibit physical as well as psychic strength. I find Cioffi's evaluation of the feminist uses of the Amazon figure more accurate and useful than Lefanu's dismissive criticism (35).

Rifkind's story, along with that of Vinge's Moon, may also be viewed as a bildungsroman, a story where the protagonist "goes through a search for self that takes her through various traumatic experiences but finally results in her becoming a whole and committed person" (Cioffi 90). In contrast to the traditional male quest

> to retrieve some sort of sacred talisman that would reunite the community with the gods, the goal of the feminist science fiction heroine is more explicitly to find herself, and only in the process of rediscovering her true identity does she also save her society.... Thus the feminist science fiction bildungsroman combines the traditional journey of mythology with the modern journey to consciousness that women are making today [91].

For women struggling against the restrictions of a patriarchal society, the maturation into a deeper level of consciousness and self-actualization is heroic, and women writers frequently use the bildungsroman to depict the female heroic quest. When feminist authors combine this form with fantastic fiction, they are free to depict a "coming of age" which shows women achieving selfhood in ways which are only rarely, if ever, encountered in our culture. Although Pratt grants this potential to science fiction, she proposes that the protagonists transcend their gender limitations (35). I would argue that rather than transcending their gender, the protagonists in the novels I discuss *affirm* their gender through the symbol of the Goddess. Race is not highlighted in these examples, but is implicit in the construct. The imaginative potential in such larger-than-life depictions is of feminist value for female readers, for it inscribes a wide variety of abilities and power as specifically female.

Significantly, the combination of the bildungsroman and the Goddess occurs primarily in women's fantastic fiction. Why is this? First, given the reluctance of American patriarchal society to accept the findings of feminist theorists concerning Goddess worship, one can see that the umbrella of speculative fiction would prove more embracing for this topic than that of "realism," for instance. In *Feminist Fabulation*, Marleen Barr asserts that "feminist fabulation" is an important postmodern literary strategy which writes against patriarchal reality (xxi). Second, it reflects European American western women's historical severance from the Goddess, which began in the Dark Ages and reached its nadir in the witchhunts of the European continent. Having lost that linkage to the memories of their foremothers, it is more difficult for European American women writers to depict the Goddess in contemporary life than to create another world, another realm, or another history in which this psychic union is possible. As Dana Heller remarks:

> genre may function for the woman writer as technological or cognitive estrangement functions for the protagonist (and the reader) of future quests: the female's heroic quest, incompatible with current social reality, finds its expression in a form structurally detached from current time, place, and any dominant perception of the "real" [37].

While fantasy fits this purpose nicely, what of science fiction, where the technological becomes juxtaposed with what we have grown up considering magical or supernatural? In my treatment of *The Snow Queen* I argue that such juxtapositioning serves to challenge binary oppositions such as nature/culture, or technological/ spiritual.

In a woman's quest, the Goddess tends to be incorporated in one of two ways; this is true both for contemporary women and for the protagonists of these speculative novels. First, the protagonist may be challenged to add a certain aspect of the Goddess into her life. For example, if she is used to caretaking and mothering others, she might have to learn to cut away those who drain her resources; her story becomes one of taking on the aspect of the Crone as destroyer. Or, the format of her journey may be that of one depicted in Goddess mythology, such as Psyche's tasks, Demeter's loss of Persephone or Inanna's descent. These three motifs, in fact, are so frequently discussed in nonfiction treatments of feminist spirituality, such as *The Heroine's Journey* and *Truth or Dare,* that one would be surprised *not* to find them in fictional tales as well, especially those by European American authors. Estella Lauter remarks that "[i]f we think of myth as a structure for dealing with shared crises of self-definition in the face of the unknown, we need only locate mythic stories created by women in order to know which of our experiences have been most critical or enduring" (8). The persistence of the spiritual quest in women's stories attests to its critical importance in women's lived experience. It is presented here as related to the creation of new mythologies based on the contemporary reintroduction of Goddess spirituality.

Marion Zimmer Bradley: Of Amazons and Goddesses

The first quest novel is an Amazon story, Marion Zimmer Bradley's *City of Sorcery,* one of her Darkover novels. The setting is the planet

Darkover, a hierarchical society ruled by families bearing great psychic powers called laran. Many of the novels detail Darkovan interaction after being rediscovered by the now highly technological Terrans from whom they originally sprang. One subset of Bradley's numerous Darkover novels is that concerning the Free Amazons, or Renunciates. Ironically, the former name is used by most Darkovans to emphasize the "renegade" character of the women, while they use the term Renunciates, which is more evocative of that which women sacrifice in order to carve a free space within a patriarchal society. Other women on Darkover live constricted lives, either chained symbolically by the marriage bracelets or *catenas,* in the Domains; by literal chains, in the Dry Towns; or by those of duty, in one of the Towers where psychic work is done. Women who are willing to forsake the comfort and security of socially sanctioned male protection form the guild-houses of the Renunciates and develop their own crafts, such as midwifery or tracking, freely choose their lovers from either sex, and experience independence as well as the bonds of an organized sisterhood. Anne Kaler traces Bradley's Renunciates to the Beguines of medieval Europe. *The Shattered Chain* (1976) sets forth the story of the Renunciates, while *Thendara House* (1983) continues the saga of Terran and Renunciate interchange, particularly in the relationship of Magda and Jaelle.

The physical journey of the group to find the City of Sorcery parallels the spiritual quest of its members, especially Magda and Camilla (another Renunciate), to find a higher degree of spiritual fulfillment, understanding, and purpose. Success on this quest first depends on their ability to differentiate between the Dark Sisterhood and the Sisterhood of the Wise, which ultimately proves to be the choice between using and misusing the force of endings and destruction. The women's ability to choose rightly hinges on their perception of the Goddess as Crone, and on the power of naming. Given this, it strikes one as ironic that Bradley would employ darkness as a negative term suggestive of a racial slur, when in fact the Crone is positively linked to images of darkness.

What starts out as a rescue attempt becomes a group quest for strength, unity, insight, and knowledge of the Goddess. While I choose to focus primarily on Magda's journey as part of this group, elements of other characters' quests are often integral to her own, and invite mention. One noteworthy aspect of Magda's journey is that she takes it in the company of other women, some of whom support her. In *City of Sorcery* (1984), Magdalen Lorne (Magda), along with Jaelle and Camilla, accompanies two women from Terran headquarters, Cholayna and Vanessa, in pursuit of Alexis Anders, a Terran, and Rafaella, a Renunciate. The latter two women have gone off in search of what is known as the Dark Sisterhood, which had previously contacted Alexis on one of her missions, thus setting the story in motion. In its misuse of power, this Dark Sisterhood is intended to contrast with the Sisterhood of the Wise, but as the group starts out in pursuit, very little other than vision, rumor, or conjecture is known about either group.

As a heroine, Magda is literally and figuratively an Amazon, and as often happens in contemporary society, a woman's own strength becomes the fulcrum to undermine her in a society where women are not supposed to be too powerful. As Cioffi notes, this is not a problem experienced by male heroes. Magda's self-doubt causes her to wonder what her next steps on her journey should be. Such instances of doubt emphasize that for questing women, the journey, or process, is as important as the goal or destination. A woman of immense achievements, the word most frequently attached to Magda is "legendary" (18). She infiltrated the Renunciates, yet kept her oath and remained in them, with Jaelle as her freemate (a type of ritual marriage), and went on to form the Bridge Society where Terran women could interact with the Renunciates. She also began work with the "Forbidden Tower," one dedicated to helping anyone with laran develop it, even one of Terran descent.

Like Cioffi's Amazons, Magda finds that her immense achievements sometimes distance her from other Terran women who are afraid to approach the "Lorne legend." Her situation is created by the privileging of competition over cooperation. Women in patriarchal societies frequently see other women as the enemy in competition for the scarce rewards given to females. This is especially true for white women, who usually do not consciously ally along racial lines; the dynamics of racism de facto puts them together. Some Terran women fear that Magda's accomplishments will make their own less recognizable, and thus they approach her with hostility. When Magda enters the mind of Alexis Anders to find a clue to her amnestic condition, Lexie wakes, saying, "Hellfire, Lorne, are you involved in Medic too? Isn't there any pie on this whole planet you don't have your fingers into?" (46). During the journey ahead of her, Magda begins to doubt herself, wondering if in fact she is too overbearing and controlling, and she begins to blame herself for Lexie's search for the Dark Sisterhood, "feeling that this whole trip was somehow a reflection of her failures — with Lexie, Vanessa, Cholayna, and perhaps especially, Rafaella" (161). Her doubt is representative of the self-questioning which spurs the female heroic quest.

Spiritual feminists generally agree that a woman's interest in the Goddess usually occurs when her current worldview is no longer meaningful, and she is ready for a paradigm shift. As Murdock notes, "[W]hen a woman decides not to play by patriarchal rules anymore, she has no guidelines telling her how to act or to feel. When she no longer wants to perpetuate archaic forms, life becomes exciting — and terrifying" (8). At this pivotal point women are most open to the Goddess. Similarly, Magda's indirection and doubt cause her to be open to new direction and belief. Like many heroes, she receives guidance on her journey in the form of visions. Magda has a vision of robed figures, accompanied by the sound of calling crows; she perceives them as the Dark Sisterhood, "guardians of some sort" (48). While the others remain skeptical, Jaelle suggests that if they can find the priestesses of Avarra, a Darkovan Goddess whose province is death and decay, they may be led to the Sisterhood of the Wise, and ultimately the City of Sorcery (97). Rumor holds that whoever reaches the city will have any questions she has answered; thus, while the trip begins as a rescue mission, members of the party begin to formulate the particular desires or requests they have of the Goddess. Magda, concerned over issues of control, and haunted by the feeling that guild-house life no longer contains her, wants to know what direction her life should take (70). The desire to enact a physical rescue gives birth to the desire for self-knowledge, or existential rescue. In order to be successful in their journey, the women must come to understand all of the Goddess' faces.

While Vanessa, Cholayna, and Jaelle begin the journey primarily out of the desire to aid their friends and engage in an adventure, Camilla, like Magda, has a deeper reason for going along. Camilla's desire for an explanation of the suffering of the innocent fuels her journey, and is representative of contemporary thealogians' need to articulate the perspective(s) of Goddess spirituality regarding humankind's perennial questions, such as those concerning the existence of "evil." Thus, the Goddess is not merely a projection of the female self. The Goddess is the cosmos in its entirety, and thus all the questions concerning relationship with deity must also be asked of the Goddess, as Camilla does. Kidnapped and brutally raped and abused as a young girl, Camilla chose the illegal and dangerous *emmasca* operation, a neutering procedure, to remove all physical traces of her womanhood lest she be touched again by a man. An illegitimate child of one of the most powerful men of the Comyn, or ruling caste, she is disowned by him after her kidnapping. In return, she refuses to accept any connection to her relatives, and Camilla also disavows the laran which the Comyn bear. Understandably bitter after such experiences, her words to Magda regarding the existence of the Goddess and any possible influence she might have, pose one of the most basic metaphysical questions a person can ask:

> "Don't you suppose that I — prayed? I cried out for help with all my strength. Not only for human help, I cried out to all the

> Gods and to any supernatural forces that might have been hanging around to help me. If they could have heard you, where were they when I cried out to heaven, or even hell, for help? If they heard you, why did they not hear me? And if they heard me, and did not answer — what sort of Gods or helpers were they?" [52].

In order for Camilla to understand the answer, she must first come to love the face of the Crone, who sometimes gives women gifts they would rather not have had.

In *City of Sorcery* the primary Goddess figure which is explored by Bradley is that of the Crone, typically regarded as the waning/dark aspect of the triple moon Goddess. The Farrars remind us that the Crone is:

> Wisdom, the Jewelled Hag. She has seen it all; she has compassion for it all, but a compassion undistorted by illusion or sentimentality. Her wisdom is much wider than intellectual knowledge, though it includes intellect and does not despise it. Maid and Mother live within her as stored experience, and she within them as potential [*Witches' Goddess* 36].

To this, Starhawk would add that "She is the Old Woman, the Crone who has passed menopause, the power of ending, of death. All things must end to fulfill their beginnings.... Life feeds on death — death leads on to life, and in that knowledge lies wisdom" (*The Spiral Dance* 93). A woman's psychic journey is not complete without the incorporation of the Crone's wisdom into one's life, for she validates age, wisdom, and purposeful destruction as aspects of female power.

There are several Crones in the novel; one of the first is encountered by Magda during astral projection. She is afraid of her because the old woman scorns her abilities and seems generally menacing (142–44). The old woman is still threatening when Magda next encounters her (164). Yet when the Crone mocks her and Jaelle's psychic shielding, asking them "So, so, so, you think you can keep me out, silly girls?" Magda replies, "Mother, not you" (250). Intuitively, Magda recognizes her as the Crone, who though she brings death to all things, is not cruel for the sake of cruelty. Rather, she is the challenge and the challenger, the shadow side that each woman must face when she pursues knowledge about herself.

Bradley makes this connection by introducing one of the priestesses of Avarra as a Crone figure, a logical extension since Avarra, whose symbol is the crow, is the Darkovan equivalent of the Goddess as Crone. When the group is greeted by this old blind woman, Magda is startled: "Nevertheless for a shocking instant Magda thought it was the old woman she had seen in the overworld" (290). Just as the old moon is "dark," with an accompanying emphasis on insight, the old woman whose vision is dim is a being of great insight.

When the old blind woman next appears, Bradley suggests that her audience dismiss its "Terran notion of a witch" and learn to accept the wise woman as "Mother":

> By the flickering firelight she seemed anyone's idea of a witch. But, Magda thought, not the ordinary Terran notion of a witch; something older, more archaic and benevolent, a primitive cave-mother of the human race, the ancient sorceress, priestess, clan-ruler in the days when "mother" meant at once grandmother, ancestress, queen, goddess. The wrinkles in her face, the gleam of the deep-sunken eyes beneath the witchlike disorder of her white hair, seemed wise, and her smile comforting [300].

Magda again recognizes this when she refers to her as "old mother — she used the title in the most respectful mode" (301). Bradley may be invoking Hecate, the moon witch, who was originally a full Crone deity in her own right, and whose attribute of governance of the crossroads is evident in the questioning of the group by the old woman. Since Magda is at a crossroads regarding the direction her life should take, this connection and sense of recognition on Magda's part is a logical one. It also points to the need for her to embrace her own Cronehood, for she has already explored the Amazon (maiden) and mother aspects of her identity. The aspects embodied in the Crone are those which patriarchy is most reluctant to value in women.

Another aspect of the Crone is revealed in another older priestess who is "tall ... her face swarthy, with wide-spaced eyes under slender gray eyebrows" (294). She is recognizable as a Crone figure by her emphasis on death. She often reminds various members of the search party that death is natural, not a punishment. One should note here the clear difference Bradley is making between Goddess religion and Judeo-Christian patriarchal thinking, where rulership and judgment are the norm in life and religion, and death is the wage of sin. The priestess explains to Rafaella after Alexis has been killed, and Rafaella is busy questioning who deserved to die: "Oh, I see. Thee thinks death a punishment for wrong-doin' an' life the reward for good, like a cake to a good child or a whip to a naughty one. Thee is a child, little one, an' thee canna' hear wisdom" (417). The sign of maturation into Cronehood is one's soul-felt acceptance of this wisdom into one's own life. Before the group can embrace the wisdom of these Crones from the Sisterhood of the Wise, they must first understand why Acquilara, leader of the Dark Sisterhood, is only a warped notion of a wise woman.

Implicit in the depiction of Acquilara is a critique of any attempts to paste Goddess thealogy onto what is actually a desire on the part of some women to engage in traditional patriarchal power-over. Acquilara claims to represent a Goddess; for her, "She is the Dark One, cruel and beyond the comprehension of mortal women, and her worship is secret. ... Her only truth is Necessity" (232). However, Magda's group is suspicious of her claims, and soon begins to realize that she is not a priestess of Avarra. In fact, the difference is clearly symbolized by their representative birds: Acquilara's token is the hawk, who preys on the living, while Avarra's symbol is the crow, the scavenger which feeds off the outworn and lifeless (239).

The "real power" (371) which Acquilara offers to teach them involves psychic and magical skills used to gain domination over others for the sake of personal aggrandizement, and thus Acquilara embodies the power of destruction in a perverted, unbalanced way. Her goal is nothing less than eventual control of Darkover (372), which is indicative of her alignment with imperialist behavior, as opposed to true sisterhood. Before the women can enter the city where the Sisterhood of the Wise dwell, they must be wise enough to distinguish between the destructive power of Avarra, which can be impersonal, but not cruel or vicious, and the sense of negation for profit's sake which Acquilara represents. After all, true knowledge of the lesson of the Crone means that one understands the transitory nature of the ego in the face of time, and Acquilara's desire not only to refuse to relinquish the ego but to aggrandize it reveals her lack of understanding of the ego's true position.

Naming creates reality, highlighting the role of communication and symbol systems in our perception of consensus reality. When one asks, "Who is wise?," one must perforce operate under an assumed definition of wisdom, which a subject under question either exhibits or not. The links between power, self-definition, and ultimately wisdom are highlighted by the role of naming in the novel.

Personal naming is the first area in which the reader can note this connection. Magda is also Magdalen and Margali, names which point out the contrast and conflicts between the Terran (rational and technological) and Darkovan (intuitive, psychic, and place-oriented) sides to her personality, and her eventual synthesis of their strengths. When Marisela calls Camilla by her true name, Elorie Hastur, Camilla reacts violently, though she had just mocked the idea that names carry power. Marisela replies, "And still you say names have no power, Camilla?" (345). Later, when Marisela tries to explain why the group should not name Acquilara, she remarks that "naming them could attract their attention; thoughts, as we know, have power" (351). Thus, what one chooses to be called is an indicator of the power to create the boundaries of one's identity, and by extension, experience.

In addition, sisterhood itself must be named and defined in order for the members of the group to make their choices of which mode of power to follow. To do so, the women must first learn to live sisterhood. Thus, Bradley asserts the value of experiential epistemology, where lived experience yields the most valuable knowledge. Their initial search is motivated by a sense of bonded duty, which is one aspect of sisterhood, but it is only a beginning. To ensure their physical survival, the members must develop the qualities of tolerance and cooperation; they must develop the bonds of "power-with" which mark true sisterhood. This stands in marked contrast to the sense of competition and domination which characterizes Acquilara's approach, and reminds us of the lessons of power discussed in the preceding chapter.

The reader comes to understand that the Sisterhood of the Wise accepts Acquilara's role as tempter to those who seek them, in order that those who are motivated by competition will not reach their city. By the end of the novel, both Rafaella and Alexis reject Acquilara after she orders them to kill Cholayna, which they refuse to do; as a result, Alexis dies during the struggle. But Camilla's sacrifice goes beyond even this instance of female loyalty. In order to rescue Magda and the others, Camilla makes use of her long-denied and suppressed laran, thus acknowledging the part of her past which is Comyn and allowing the Dark Sisterhood to be defeated. Symbolically, the act of sacrifice for the good of one's sisters overcomes a superficial unity based on greed and dominance.

As the legend has indicated, Magda and Camilla are among those who may go to the City of Sorcery to study with the Sisterhood of the Wise. Camilla's wisdom results from the growth which allows her to see that had her life as a Hastur been uninterrupted, she would have come to desire power in the way that Acquilara did. Because of the severity of her experience at the hands of men practicing power-over, Camilla eventually rejects that mode, and accepts the past which has brought her to her present. Likewise, when asked "What is thy truest will?," Magda decides to spend time with the Sisterhood; instead of mothering and leading others, she will focus on her own needs. For both, Goddess-knowledge leads to self-knowledge, and vice versa. The novel is open-ended in that the reader sees Magda and Camilla begin to move into their psychic and spiritual potentials, but the blueprint for their development is not given, since that is a new journey which is different for each woman.

For Magda and Camilla, understanding the Goddess Avarra as Crone means that they must come to terms with the role of loss and destruction in their lives as women and in the greater cycle of life. They have gained the qualities of the Crone for themselves. The type of heroism necessary for their successful completion of this quest for knowledge is one based on cooperation. Yet the quest is never truly over; rather, the quester moves to another curve on the spiral. The quest of the group for the City of Sorcery is allegorical in that it parallels differing ideas about the value of feminist spirituality within contemporary feminism. Some feminists are skeptical of its existence, and even when faced with it, refuse the opportunity to continue the spiritual journey. Others who are willing to admit that the psyche's powers have not been fully charted find their search rewarded with new information on the powers they hold within themselves, as well as those exhibited by the universe at large. Ideally, like the women in *City of Sorcery*, both skeptics and believers can work together within feminism with an ethics of cooperation, and resist the temptation of the patriarchal ethos of power-over.

Lynn Abbey: The Warrior Who Heals

Another Amazon figure who must discover the meaning of the Goddess is found in Lynn Abbey's *Daughter of the Bright Moon* (1979) and *The Black Flame* (1980), where we are introduced to Rifkind, a protagonist described as "priestess, warrior, healer, witch." [1] Abbey's efforts to create a memorable Amazonian figure in this duology are noteworthy for several reasons. As with Kennealy's Aeron, we find sorcery and swordsmanship combined in one character. Unlike Aeron, however, Rifkind lacks support from her community, and must struggle against her isolation. In contrast to Magda and Camilla, Rifkind does not journey with a sisterhood of equals, although she does attempt to create a sense of female lineage between herself and the much younger females she does encounter. Although both Rifkind and Aeron must confront issues of power and control, Rifkind's spiritual journey differs in that she questions both her Goddess and herself. Like Miriam, Rifkind must grow to accept that her service to the Goddess is equally that of a warrior and a healer, and reconcile these seemingly contradictory roles. As a heroine, Rifkind's dual roles as healer and warrior must be examined against the backdrop of barbarianism which characterizes the early Rifkind.

From this vantage point, Rifkind's quests can be examined and are found to contain elements of both the Amazon tale and the bildungsroman. The first quest, detailed in *Daughter of the Bright Moon,* involves her struggle to choose between the use of overpowering force which her clan taught her to admire, and the need to work with the forces of life which her healer's training has taught her. Like Magda, Rifkind must learn to claim the powers of life and the powers of death. In *The Black Flame,* Rifkind moves from a devoted yet unquestioned relationship with her goddess, the Bright Moon, to one which acknowledges her own power and the limits of the deity she serves. Her questioning and shifting resemble that of women in the contemporary feminist spirituality movement. Their relationships to the Goddess are neither uniform nor static. Women draw what they need, feeling free to redefine both the need and the source, even as some acknowledge the Goddess as larger than self.

Like many of the other protagonists, in *Daughter of the Bright Moon* Rifkind struggles to define herself against the prescribed standards of femininity set by patriarchal societies, both her own and those of the lands she travels through. Like Tarma, Rifkind and her clan are loosely modeled on Middle Eastern nomadic desert tribes. They are characterized by a male-dominated warrior elite, with women having few opportunities for status other than daughter, wife, or concubine. Rifkind is an Asheeran, a name which echoes that of the Middle Eastern goddess Ashera, also known as Astarte and Ashtoreth (Stone, *Ancient Mirrors of Womanhood* 113). The connection here is somewhat ironic given the inferior status of women in the Asheera, a name which describes the land occupied by the tribe as well as the tribe itself. However, Rifkind's bond to a female lunar deity, the Bright One, may explain Abbey's terminology. Unlike Tarma, whose bond to her clan is the driving force behind her desire to be a warrior, Rifkind, as her name implies, finds no solace with her clan, nor does she have a figurative sister or sisterhood to turn to. She is only allowed to take up the sword after being physically abused by her brother, who is heir to the chieftainship (115). When he challenges her again after she achieves mastery of her weapons, a feat unheard of for a woman in her society, she is forced to defeat him in front of the entire tribe, an act which earns her "the enmity of all her people for humiliating the logical successor to her father" (119). For Rifkind as for other women, transgressing the patriarchal order results in outcast status, a motif Annis Pratt terms "woman as outsider" (*Archetypal Patterns* 67). Unlike most of Pratt's protagonists, Rifkind is eventually able to create a place for herself in this tribal society.

As noted before, acute circumstances usually precede the beginning of a woman's heroic quest. When her brother's enmity turns into lethal threats, Rifkind undergoes an apprenticeship with Muroa, a clan healer and priestess, which marks the beginning of her development as a healer and priestess. However, like Kassandra, the prophetic voice she develops is dismissed. The opening of the novel finds Rifkind looking upon the massacred remains of her clan, which had failed to heed her warning, and suffered extremely for it. Like Tarma, Rifkind is left to find a purpose to her life, a use for the gifts she has developed, with only her own resources and Goddess-bond to guide her.

As one reads the duology, one is able to trace the evolution of Rifkind from a skillful warrior and somewhat bloodthirsty loner to a woman who remains strong but learns to show kindness, compassion, and forgiveness. Rather than providing the reader with a stereotypical feminine character, Abbey's depiction suggests instead a movement toward balance in the psychological makeup of her character; Rifkind must learn to temper her tendency to judge and execute with mercy, lest she become a bully little better than her brother. The actions which teach her this lesson reflect the need for the sometimes conflicting aspects of her personality, the healer and the warrior, to become balanced and thereby mutually reinforcing. Similarly, in striving to explore their own power, women sometimes go through a stage of imitating male aggression before they learn to temper true assertiveness with the qualities they threw away because patriarchal culture deemed those qualities weak and disempowering. In this sense they are like Camilla, wishing to destroy the aspects of themselves considered feminine, and therefore weak by the dominant culture.

Nonetheless, Abbey portrays the early Rifkind, blunt, barbaric, and humorless, in a manner which wins our sympathy. As Lady Inelda attempts to teach Rifkind to act "ladylike" at the Dro Darian court which Rifkind must infiltrate, the reader understands the baring of teeth which passes for a smile on the face of the warrior forced to learn to dance and trail her sleeves (154). Undoubtedly, such attempts to "pass" resonate with all women who have bent to gender-associated societal expectations in order to achieve goals considered by themselves to be of higher importance. Perhaps they too have experienced the sense of isolation and lack of connection which Rifkind faces as she pursues her quests, and understand the strained conformity which serves to continually remind her of the fact of her Otherness.

In *Alien to Femininity,* Marleen Barr argues that Rifkind's dual identity as swordswoman and witch embodies "both the 'masculine' power to inflict pain with a sword and the 'feminine' power to eradicate that pain" (89). Rifkind's desire to heal as well as fight ultimately empowers her ability to adapt, grow, and balance her personality. As the duology progresses, Rifkind begins to understand how the nature of her Goddess, the Bright One, is linked with Vitivar, a "male" moon deity whose death dealing aspects are generally viewed as negative. As she comprehends their polarity, Rifkind also learns how to create life, achieving balance on the wheel of what Estes terms the "life/death/life" cycle of the instinctual woman (130–31). Note that both Rifkind's growth and Estes' cyclical view of a psychologically whole woman claim purposeful destruction and death as inherent in women's normal makeup, and thus do not posit these qualities as inherently male, as Barr does. In terms of the triple Goddess image, Rifkind is independent and can defend herself, like the strong Maiden, and she also has the ability to deal death, as does the Crone. The aspect Rifkind must develop during her quest is that of the Mother.

Rifkind's own lack of a mother, her search for substitute mothers, and her attempts to act as a mother can be seen as a commentary on the psychospiritual need for women to create a powerful lineage of female strength and nurturing if that is not provided for them in their surroundings. The type of nurturing needed is one which promotes a strong sense of selfhood, not stereotypical femininity. Rifkind's biological mother died giving birth to her, and only later in life is Rifkind strong enough to seek out two foster mothers, Muroa and the Bright One. Muroa teaches her skills and rituals, but the Bright One as "goddess/mother" (Barr, *Alien* 90) marks her at initiation, simultaneously providing acceptance and access to new realms of spiritual power. Barr notes that rather than looking to a man for this sort of fulfillment, "Rifkind looks to the Bright One to provide her with a sense of nurturing, intuition, and compassion. Rifkind's relationship with the moon helps to make her a whole human being" (90).

Cynthia Eller observes that "[s]ome spiritual feminists say that having a divine mother is a way of compensating for the frailties of human mothers, giving women a more perfect mother, one who will never separate from them or prove herself inadequate to her daughter's needs" (143). Instead of viewing this act as a desire to continue to make human mothers unrealistically powerful, one can view this use of the Goddess as an important way in which women receive healing from themselves.

Like other powerful women, Rifkind finds it difficult to pass on her hard-won wholeness because the women she would pass it on to have been negatively shaped by patriarchal ideas of power-over and traditional female powerlessness. Rifkind seeks to perpetuate her female healing tradition by tutoring the girl Linette, as Muroa had done with her. While Barr discusses this idea, she also fails to note that Rifkind fails miserably during this first attempt; at the urging of Adijan, Rifkind's former swordmaster who is also a cult priest, Linette attempts to use her budding magical powers to dominate nature, and thus eventually has them stripped from her (*Daughter of the Bright Moon* 276–78). Further, in *The Black Flame*, Linette almost dies while a courtesan to Lord Humphrey, one of Rifkind's antagonists; while Rifkind saves her, there is no indication that Linette will carry on a female-focused tradition.

On the other hand, in that same novel Rifkind's relationship with Jenny, Ejord's half sister, is more positive. While Rifkind does not guide her spiritually, she does influence the girl through her example of strength, courage, and independence. The former serving girl is able to act as a leader by the end of the novel. Another striking omission on Barr's part is any reference to the actual pregnancy which Rifkind experiences in *The Black Flame*. Perhaps this is because the novel ends with her still pregnant; no gender is ever ascribed to the child except by the father, who assumes it will be male. Since this is not confirmed by Rifkind herself, this might just be an example of male projection. I read the ending of the novel in a similar fashion to that in *City of Sorcery*, literally pregnant with possibilities, a beginning within an ending. The reader does not witness Rifkind's journey through the stage of physical mothering. Rather, Abbey suggests a spiral image of female development combined with a symbol of a new female legacy.

In *Daughter of the Bright Moon*, Rifkind's quest is to do battle with An-Soren, a renegade mage. Ultimately, this struggle reflects the choice Rifkind must make between power-over and power–with/in. Like many of the protagonists I have discussed, she must use all her resources in order to fight a male antagonist's entrenched and fortified powers.

That power remains a neutral force until wielded either in a cooperative or coercive manner is symbolized by the matching rubies worn by Rifkind and An-Soren. Rifkind's ruby was given to her by her mother, and thus represents an indirect heritage. The reader later discovers that the ruby is no mere jewel, but rather a powerful enhancer of psychic abilities. Robin Roberts observes that jewelry is often used in speculative fiction as a symbol of magical technology (93). Rifkind slowly awakens to her jewel's power after An-Soren psychically attacks her. An-Soren has chosen to use his ruby in order to enforce his domination over the land of Dro-Daria, where he has already fomented civil war. If he can obtain the use of Rifkind's ruby, either through forcing or tempting her, his power will be unlimited. Like contemporary women, Rifkind can choose to comply with forces of domination or to resist them.

Abbey clearly places the violation of Goddess/nature onto men, in contrast to Bradley's creation of the Dark Sisterhood, a group with similar purpose and goals. This difference suggests that Abbey is focusing blame on patriarchy, while Bradley also wishes to show how women have internalized patriarchal standards and methods. In both instances, the conflict is between what Mary Daly describes as "biophilic" (biophilia: "the

Original Lust for Life that is at the core of all Elemental E-motion; Pure Lust, which is the Nemesis of patriarchy, the Necrophilic State") and "necrophilic" approaches to power (*Wickedary* 67, 83). Although Lord Humphrey believes that Rifkind fights An-Soren because of his request, he is incorrect. She feels an ethical obligation to fight the sorcerer because her powers are aligned with a Goddess of nature and order, and as a healer Rifkind must stop the threatened usurpation of nature (151–52). That An-Soren's powers are a violation of natural law is indicated by his previous association as leader of the Dark Brethren, a group which abandoned its association with the Bright One, and was subsequently punished (135).

When patriarchal forces appeal to women's ambition, they usually attempt to keep women working within the confines of the status quo, which ensures that female effort will eventually support male control and "success" as defined by the culture, and not contribute to women's quest for growth and autonomy. A prelude to An-Soren's offer for Rifkind to share in the power of domination occurs when one of the mountain cults of Glascardy, led by Adijan, invites Rifkind to join them and forsake her Goddess. Paralleling Thalkarsh's offer to Kethry, Adijan tells Rifkind that he can "cleanse" her of her vow to the Bright One, and "dedicate [her] to a god with some real power" (172). Just what kind of power he offers to Rifkind is indicated by Linette's mockery of Rifkind's insistence that "[i]t is forbidden to destroy or pervert an existing life-force to create another. We can transform lower existences to higher ones, or restore things to their proper form — that is the only way."[2] Linette responds: "You don't understand anything about power, Rifkind; you don't have any imagination" (225). In a society shaped by power-over, power which flows from a knowledge of and unity with life force is denigrated as lesser than, not "real," power. The wisdom of Rifkind in rejecting this offer is underscored by the words of Hanju, a being whose name means "life force": "Stay with the Bright Moon, too. She is distant and slow to change, but she lacks ambition — you'll need that" (245).

Like Magda and the other Renunciates who must refuse Acquilara's offer of power-over, to be successful in her spiritual quest, Rifkind must refuse An-Soren's offer. An-Soren appeals to ambition when he has a chance to confront Rifkind, yet ultimately she refuses and is able to defeat him, though in the process she destroys the ruby of which she is so fond (374). He tells her that by joining forces with him, Rifkind "will serve no greedy goddess — only [herself]" (329). Though she does not succumb to the temptation, even considering it for a moment makes "the agony of the Bright One's anger and her own betrayal ... a part of her" (329). This sense of loss fuels Rifkind's determination to defeat An-Soren, for she realizes that there could never be sufficient compensation for the willful separation of oneself from the flow of life force and cosmic healing which the Bright One represents. Likewise, spiritual feminists understand that whatever external price they pay for not playing by the rules of the Father God and his loyal sons is negligible in comparison to the sense of vitality and connection they experience through Goddess spirituality.

While exterior battles abound in both novels, in *The Black Flame* Rifkind's struggles increasingly reflect her internal change and growth. Events cause her to reappraise the gods in general and her Goddess in particular, to explore other aspects of the Mother Goddess, to rely on her sense of strength and her own judgment, and to heal the source of her pain. These aspects of Rifkind's external struggles create a corresponding spiritual growth by forcing her to look inside herself for the answers she seeks, an idea we have seen conveyed in the Wiccan "Charge of the Goddess": "And you who seek to know Me, know that your seeking and yearning will avail you not, unless you know the Mystery: for if that which you seek, you find not within yourself, you will never find it without" (quoted in Starhawk, *The Spiral Dance* 91).

The representation of gods and goddesses in fantastic fiction varies widely, from an understanding of deity as a poetic construct formulated by the human mind in order to make sense of super-rational realities, to a much more anthropomorphic portrayal, complete with such human tendencies as squabbling and bickering. *The Mists of Avalon* includes the former, while the latter is the case in *The Black Flame*. Rifkind begins to understand that her outer quest, the search to find the Well of Knowledge and the Black Flame, is an action which marks her as a player on a game board governed by a generation of gods, among them the Bright One, who are not the first of that land, though they wish to remain the final pantheon. Because misuse of the Well "impinged on the natural powers by which the gods maintained themselves," Rifkind must not allow it to fall into evil hands, this time those of the sorceress Krowlowja and the demonic powers she allies herself with (146).

Whereas the Bright One remained fairly remote as a goddess in *Daughter of the Bright Moon,* in *The Black Flame* she appears at several points, actually conversing with Rifkind. In one instance, both her limitations and her love for Rifkind are revealed. Rifkind has trespassed and the other gods demand her death; the Bright One tells her "[t]here are many lifetimes, Rifkind. You will return to me. I will keep your spirit safe. … I love you most of those who have served me" (112). However, Rifkind reveals that she has information which the Bright One lacks, and is able to save herself by passing it on to the pantheon (113). Clearly, these gods are not omniscient and all powerful; Rifkind must re-evaluate her position:

> Rifkind refrained from telling Jenny that she no longer had anything but the wildest guesses about the alliances of the gods and the natural forces at their commands. Her own notion of a benevolent deity overseeing Her healers had suffered repeated and possibly irremedial harm in this as yet uncompleted night [120].

Even though Rifkind now views the pantheon as acting more like humans than she had ever realized before, she still grants that these deities have a sphere of influence which necessitates a great responsibility on their part in order to prevent the sort of misuse which threatens the balance of nature: "It is easy to appreciate the temptations of such powers as the gods possess.... The menace of power is more than mere corruption" (243).

As in *Daughter of the Bright Moon*, one way Rifkind views her relationship to the Bright One is as a path of service. When Domhnall, the man who becomes her lover, suggests that she view herself as a leader, she replies "I serve the Goddess and those who need me — people do not serve me"(227). This service should not be seen as homage, but rather as the responsibility of interconnection, which in these novels is ecofeminist in its association of female-focused values with the preservation of nature and its balance. In addition, Rifkind is not a powerless servant; there is a reciprocity of power in the relationship: "There is a certain mutuality of faith betwixt the Bright One and myself" (157). This sense of acceptance enables Rifkind to have the determination necessary to fight Krowlowja and her forces:

> I do what I do. It is as simple as that. The Goddess has always known what I am. My future and past were known to her at my initiation. She would not have given me the crescent of Her honor without accepting me as I am. It is not for me to question why She would want, or need, a healer whose first instincts are to snarl and fight [176].

Like Rifkind, women who view themselves as participators in relationship to the Goddess feel accepted as women, a feeling many comment was lacking in their other spiritual experiences or practices. Eller astutely notes:

> The primary symbolic function the goddess has for spiritual feminists is as female self-image. The goddess, the many goddesses, are external projections of a new, desirable internal conception of self. They are figures that reflect back to women what they already — if imperfectly — are: powerful women [213].

Healers who "snarl and fight," as well as other types of women whom patriarchal judgment has branded as odd, different, or even perverse, find this acceptance, whether discovered through imagery, practice, or mystical experience, one of the great attractive forces of the contemporary feminist spirituality movement.

Just as spiritual feminists rarely divide an experience of the Goddess as either purely internal or purely external, the representation of the Goddess in feminist speculative fiction conveys this same fluidity of perception. Rifkind's Bright One seems to be external, yet in many ways is internal and represents Rifkind's highest capacities. As a result, Rifkind grows in proportion with her ability to translate the Goddess' acceptance of her into self-acceptance, thereby producing a new trust in her own judgment. One example of this self-trust is Rifkind's decision to pursue her relationship with Domhnall. Whereas the Goddess had wisely withheld permission for Rifkind to marry Ejord, in her relationship with Domhnall, Rifkind pursues her own desires: "She no longer felt need of the Goddess' blessing to do what she wanted, but neither would she be rushed" (178). Rifkind has no need of the Goddess' blessing because Rifkind has learned to trust herself in the way she already feels trusted by the Goddess. While Rifkind is planning her defense of the Well and awaiting the Bright One's return to her place of power, the moon, Rifkind reflects that "there was no one by whom Rifkind could swear an oath for her intuition, but she no longer needed reassurance from the Goddess for her judgments" (229). Rather than placing her in a position of dependency like that of a child toward a parental figure, her relationship with deity allows Rifkind to manifest her own power and decide her own actions. The view of deity as immanent places control in the hands of individual women, thereby enabling women to go into the world as effective agents.

Another facet of Rifkind's growth in her spiritual quest is her exploration of a different aspect of deity in the form of the Landmother. What is the Landmother? She is an earth mother goddess, but she is "not the gentle, fertile mother but the archetype of witches, the mother of magic and death" (360). Enormous and terrifying, she is described as having Medusa-like aspects: "Worm-like roots protruded everywhere, becoming a nightmare nest above her eyes, a parody of hair." In this novel, the Landmother's appearance is definitely a reminder that "she changes everything she touches, and everything she touches, changes."[3] Desperate to end the struggle between Domhnall and the demon, a battle which is perverting the life and land of the Hold, Rifkind as healer makes the painful decision to risk his life in order to raise the Landmother:

> No Goddess compelled her to raise the staff, then strike the ground with all her strength. She did it with love, despite

> love, and without knowing the result of her actions except that the Landmother alone had the reservoir of slow strength to vanquish the two opponents [359].

The Landmother is the Leveler, and by raising her, Rifkind indeed fulfills prophecy, succeeding in the epic promise of her quest. Rifkind's ability to raise the Landmother reveals an ability to connect with an older, primordial form of the Goddess, one who is both the nurturing mother and the terrible mother, like Avarra in *City of Sorcery*. Although the Landmother commits destruction in the remaking of the swampy Felmargue, she "wanted her children to have another chance. Her children could be difficult, but they were still her children" (365). This combination of reconstruction and forgiveness, embodied by the Landmother, is now passed on to Rifkind, raising her character to new levels of complexity.

Abbey stresses the importance of reconstruction and healing at the close of the novel. Returning to her former clansite, Rifkind discovers Muroa dead, and claims her cave as her own (369). Symbolically, she is claiming her place in a tradition of women healers. When two women seek her out in order to perform a healing, Rifkind acknowledges the need to take up the task: "She could not face more suffering" (272). As a condition, she requests that Kerdal, a leader of those who had slaughtered her clan, allow a new clan to live at the clansite, if she can purify the well he had poisoned. She does so, and her cleansing of the fountain symbolizes her ability to return to the source of her pain and heal it. Thus, Rifkind's journey completes a turn of the spiral; she has now learned to give life as well as take it, even to those who were her enemies. This hint of the healer's potential to affect society is explored more fully in the discussion of Vinge's character Moon.

Critics often misunderstand the Goddess and claim that women are merely exchanging one figure of domination for another. While I have noted that feminist spiritualists do demonstrate a variety of conceptions of the Goddess, a common thread which connects them is the need to find the qualities of deity within one's self. Rifkind's transformation from skilled but savage barbarian to a healer/fighter who serves while remaining independent centers around a belief in a Goddess who seems to be outside her, but whose energies she learns to realize as her own. While her outer quests consist of the need to defeat An-Soren and to find and defend the Well of Knowledge, her inner quest involves Rifkind's need to balance independence and service in regards to her Goddess. She never breaks or renounces her bond; rather, she grows into it, a powerful woman who uses her energies for the perpetuation of the life-giving properties of herself and her deity. The lesson demonstrated by Rifkind's quest is the need to balance destruction and creation, always focusing on what aids life.

Joan Vinge: The Goddess in the Machine*

Joan Vinge's *The Snow Queen* offers the image of a powerful young woman, Moon, who finds much of her strength in the values of her Goddess worshiping culture of origin, that of the Summers. She not only possesses psychic abilities, but also learns to find the ultimate source of the Goddess' power: herself. In doing so, she must fight against various forms of institutionalized patriarchal power: the Hegemony and the Hegemony-corrupted Winters, led by Arienrhod. Moon must also fight the temptation to use her own power to dominate others by becoming the replacement Arienrhod expects her to be. Vinge's creation of a strong female subject is integrally tied to the idea of a spirituality based not on domination but on personal integration and connection with others.

A reading of this novel reveals more than positive images of an individual woman who represents the reclamation and transformation of a biophilic, female-focused mythology. Like Bradley and Abbey, Vinge critiques patriarchal religion as an embodiment of a patriarchal worldview based on separation, thanatos, and eros as domination. Moon's quest to internalize her concept of Goddess and use it to save her world is made epic by Vinge's adaptation of mythology and by the repercussions Moon's vision has not only for her world, but for our own.

The Snow Queen incorporates three major uses of Goddess imagery, or figures, and of psychic powers: 1) the role of vegetation myth and the figure of the Triple Goddess; 2) the mythical figure of the sibyl and the sibyl machine; and 3) the idea of Goddess as machine. In addition to examining the role these elements play in structuring the novel, a discussion of these points helps the reader to understand why some women and men relate to personal and literary visions of the Goddess in a technological age, as well as broadens the concept of Goddess religion as nature religion.

Vinge's use of vegetation mythology, stories which explain the changing of the seasons and the cycles of the land, enlarges her heroine's quest to epic status, and makes the struggle in Tiamat universal in its implications of perpetual change as the structuring principle of nature. In doing so, she enlarges the ecofeminist theme that Bradley and Abbey only suggest. The most obvious evidence of vegetative myth is the exchange of

---

My thanks to the editors of FEMSPEC for their permission to reprint this material.

Winter and Summer rule on Tiamat, Moon's home planet. As Thelma Shinn points out, this exchange is a reference to the Demeter myth (*Worlds Within Women* 83), a connection also explored by Roberts (101–3). Further evidence is given by Carl Yoke, who details Moon's symbolic descent into the underworld, as symbolized by that Carbunclian den of iniquity, Persipone's (130). These references endow Moon with a mythic stature as she moves from innocent, unsophisticated girlhood to the woman who will reign as Summer queen. In addition to these references to vegetative myth, Shinn also notes that the name Tiamat refers to a great sea Mother Goddess (82); the connection of the sea to the moon can also be made, as Anne Rush demonstrates (*Moon, Moon* 6), possibly representing the cultural change of tides which Moon will cause, as Byrd asserts (239).

As in the previous novels, the Moon as Triple Goddess (Maiden, Mother, and Crone) is strongly present in the novel, though at times the myth is not expressed fully, or is used to contrast the potential of a character with her reality. More importantly, Vinge uses the Triple Goddess as an expression of a female empowerment which goes beyond the personal realm to effect change in the political one as well. Moon first appears as the Maiden. In her quest she must reclaim the role of the Mother, and also redeem the proper function of the Crone. Moon's quest has societal, as well as individual, impact. Arienrhod, the Winter queen from whom Moon was cloned, stands in contrast to this vision, allowing herself to be corrupted by Hegemonic (patriarchal) ideas of control, thus disrupting her natural role in the symbolic and social cycle.

Moon is clearly the new moon, the first crescent of the waxing moon, usually associated with Artemis and other maiden goddesses. Shinn's observation of Moon's rebirth via her return through the black hole reinforces the idea of the waxing moon emerging from the dark circle of the old moon (83). Like Artemis, Moon is a protector of wildlife, in the form of the mers, dolphin-like creatures; similarly, regardless of sexual relations, she remains virginal in her essential pureness of nature and focused purpose. She signals change and new beginnings for Tiamat, qualities associated with the new moon.

Arienrhod is the name given to a Welsh moon goddess. As a character, Arienrhod represents a warped form of the full moon aspect of the Triple Goddess, which is that of the Mother; rather than wishing to birth something new, she wishes to only give birth to a continuation of herself: her clone daughter. Also, she is power hungry and wishes to prolong her rule and her youth far longer than is naturally possible. Rather than yielding to change, the nature of nature, Arienrhod is static, and therefore unnatural. Her cultivation of the slaughter of the mers as a means to power is a measure of her corruption. She slaughters them for the life-properties of their blood, and exports the elixir to gain a position in the Hegemony and thereby enjoy its technology, an act which posits an opposition between nature and culture. The moon is tied to the sea, and Arienrhod's violation of the mers amounts to a breach of sacred trust in her role as planetary caretaker and figurative "mother" of the planet. Her misuse of power is similar to Acquilara's, but represents the warping of a different aspect of deity. In another instance of the moon symbolism at work, the diminishment of the full moon allows the new moon to rise, and Arienrhod is ultimately forced to yield her place to Moon.

Fate Ravenglass, maker of the Summer Queen's festival mask, is the embodiment of the Crone in this novel, an insight which Shinn overlooks in her discussion of Fate (86). This connection is made clear by her function in the story: to dismiss the full moon, Arienrhod, and usher in the new moon, Moon. In this sense she differs from other explorations of the Crone I have examined. Vinge is careful to use physical description to support her development of Crone imagery; Fate is nearly blind, as befits the dark moon. She symbolizes the world of inner, rather than outer, illumination. As maskmaker, she also replicates the dark moon's function of concealing or shadowing rather than revealing. Finally, Fate enacts the appropriate role of the Crone: change and death, the processes which Arienrhod fears the most. Thus, the lunar symbolism is fulfilled by the actions of the characters.

Vinge's portrayal of Moon as a sibyl, or transmitter of sacred knowledge, bears interesting analogies to its counterpart in myth, reinforcing her portrayal of Moon as a strong young woman whose journey into maturity is inspired by the truth revealed to her from an internal Goddess force. In Nor Hall's discussion of the sibyl, she points out the connection of the Pythoness, priestess of Apollo, with the presence of snakes (*The Moon and the Virgin* 174); the upswept "net of silver braids" which Moon possesses are rather snaky, and suggest a connection (*Snow Queen* 400). The sibyl uttered her prophecies while suspended over a deep cleft in the rocks, from which intoxicating vapors poured (Hall 177). Vinge parallels this practice by having Moon receive her peak transmission of knowledge in the Hall of Winds, where the winds arise out of the Pit, bringing the sibyl call with them (431–32). What Hall refers to as the sibyls' "umbilical root reaching down into the earthly wisdom of the underworld" (186) becomes the sibyl machine, which is "below this shaft that plunged into the sea, below this pinpoint city driven into a map of time, as secret as stone beneath the guardian seaskin of this water world" (*Snow Queen* 432). Moon's inspiration as a sibyl comes from the sibyl machine, the repository of all the knowledge of the Old Empire, passed down as blood knowledge through the line of sibyls. For ancient sibyls, inspiration was said to come from the Muses, the daughters of Memory (Hall 178).

The similarities to ancient sibyls are pervasive. As much as Vinge portrays Moon's prophetic abilities as rising from the computer bank of the sibyl machine, truly making her a daughter of technological memory, Vinge also sticks very closely to the ancient image of the sibyl, thus investing her technologically aided heroine with both the powers of a prophetess and the strength of an earth Goddess. The idea of mechanical inspiration remains intimately linked with that of the earth as a source of inspiration and power. This correlation reappears in the symbol of the trefoil, used on Tiamat to signify the contaminated and dangerous blood of the sibyl. Hall notes that the caves of sibyls were frequently painted with red ocher (183). In addition, the trefoil serves as a reminder of the triadic nature of the Goddess.

The end of Moon's quest in *The Snow Queen*, her discovery that her Goddess is the sibyl machine, does not negate the deific aspects of her Goddess. The revelation of the computer as Moon's sourcepoint does not fully relegate the Summer idea of the Goddess to the status of a backward superstition, or mere "motherloving."

First, the sibyl machine is such a powerful form of artificial intelligence that its sentience appears deific. It actually reaches further in space than the known universe of the Hegemony, a fact which is revealed in Vinge's sequel, *The Summer Queen* (1991). Like a type of higher power, the sibyl machine guides much of Moon's life in a sentient manner.

Although the creation of the sibyl machine is explained in *The Summer Queen*, Vinge manages to preserve the sense of mystery which surrounds this Goddess which has manifested herself in both metal and flesh. The machine is grounded in the bedrock of Tiamat, and cannot be separated from its ties to the land and the sea, the whole processes of the planet. The ecosystem in its diversity, especially the mers, must be preserved in order for the integrity of the sibyl machine to be maintained. The significance of Vinge's portrayal of this fleshly computer is found in contemporary visions of the Goddess which do not separate her from her appearance in the natural world; this is the concept of immanent divinity. However, humans have the capacity to upset the natural ordering of this intelligence, and thus threaten themselves as well. The link between Vinge's representation and the tenets of feminist spirituality become clear in a passage from Moon's visionary experience in *The Summer Queen*: "The Lady existed, the Lady watched over Her chosen world; those who peopled its lands and seas and kept Her peace were truly her beloved children" (888).

To see oneself as a "child of the Goddess" entails the ecofeminist view of recognizing one's responsibility to the earth and all its life forms. Like Moon, contemporary explorers of the Goddess need not ignore science and technology, nor should they ignore the wisdom of the past; instead, they must find the truth which lies behind both viewpoints. The unifying intelligence of the universe draws no arbitrary distinction between the natural world and the cultural production which arises from existence.

Importantly, like Magda and Avarra, and Rifkind and the Bright One, Moon's link with both machine and Goddess is an inner one, which allows for all of the spiritual dimensions associated with deity and devotee: specifically, free will and fate. Moon is driven by many forces beyond her control; her life seems to be fated by the will of the sibyl machine to save Tiamat from the destructive reign of Arienrhod, the collapse of technology caused by the pullout of the Hegemony, and the possible destruction of the sibyl machine due to the exploitation of the mers. These issues reflect the interwoven nature of social, natural, and technological concerns. Still, Moon's conscious decision to accept these challenges makes her more than a chosen puppet. Because Moon grows and can accept the forces of the sibyl machine inside her, we as readers can appreciate her as a character with depth and development. We can share her triumph as she answers the question no sibyl should be able to answer: "Where is your sourcepoint?" (*The Snow Queen* 432). Below her, yes, but also inside her.

Moon creates her power from the models she is given—the Goddess and the sibyl machine—by integrating nature and culture in a spiritual way. In *The Summer Queen,* Moon's growth is so pronounced that she further breaks down these artificial barriers, and teaches the sibyl mind compassion through sharing her human viewpoint with the sibyl mind, which Vinge clearly is describing as a Goddess: "But She was no longer pitiless, or soulless, or blind. A vast compassion filled Her, and She knew that because She had been healed, She must heal their wounds, if She could" (908). Goddess, human, animal, plant, inanimate matter; all are integrally tied together in a web of interconnection where all the of the parts are vital to the creation and maintenance of the whole.

Vinge increases the scope of speculative fiction by critiquing the dismissal of the world as immanently spiritual simply because we exist in a technological age which favors scientific, mechanical models for viewing the universe. Like many before her, she implies that any conception of the infinite is perforce limited. Therefore, one must choose the model which offers the most positive results for one's (or a society's) interconnection with other forms of life. The false, patriarchal dichotomy between nature and culture is challenged in the novel by Moon's biological link to the "cultural" Winters, and cultural link to the "biological" Summers. Likewise, Moon's Goddess-like stature denies the oversimplification and dismissal of the Goddess as "merely" the natural world or the focus of a "primitive" nature religion. Instead, Moon's quest demonstrates the understanding of the Goddess' attributes as the force behind the natural world and all resulting cultural production. How, in fact, could the creation of culture not be a natural process?

Vinge depicts patriarchal systems as oppressive due to their artificial separation of nature and culture, belief and science, an idea which Roberts explores in *A New Species* (96–99). Vinge critiques such systems, whether symbolized by groups or individuals, by presenting a heroine courageous enough to take risks in presenting an alternative view of living, and who actively protests the plans and activities of patriarchal structures. As Moon puts it, "Real power ... is control. Knowing that you can do anything ... and not doing it only because you can" (*The Snow Queen* 425). Like Rifkind and Magda, Moon's quest to understand the Goddess results in a new awareness of the (mis)uses of power.

Some feminists have criticized Goddess spirituality as a "woman's only" province which bases its power on the idea that alternative visions for living in connection with nature are biologically deterministic, reducing women to matter without mind. In contrast to this concern, Vinge's protagonist is not depicted as a mindless, nurturing womb, elevated to the status of godhead in a vulvacentric universe. Rather, she expresses a feminist mythology which simultaneously supports her as it forces her to rely on her own potential, an idea which is frequently expressed in the literature of feminist spirituality. Moon's unique position resembles that occupied by the resurgence of feminist nature religion perspectives in our own time and culture. When one realizes that the values of integration and interconnection held by a nature religion are extended to the world of culture as well, giving it a basis for choosing life-affirming uses of technology, one can view contemporary Goddess religion as a paradigm uniquely qualified for healing the splits which have resulted from the ethics of patriarchal separation and domination.

In their quests to understand the Goddess, these heroines undergo lessons in identity, balance, and power, lessons which women involved in contemporary feminist spirituality see as integral to an incorporation of the Goddess in their everyday lives. As Magda discovers, the search for knowledge is an ongoing process, one which carries with it the responsibility to use one's knowledge wisely. Important keys to wise usage lie in the development of sisterhood, and an understanding of the importance of how language shapes our concepts of reality. For many, to invoke the concept/belief/existence of "Goddess" is to commit a revolutionary act which challenges the foundation of western patriarchal culture. Having challenged those foundations, like Rifkind, women must develop all of their strengths, including the inner voice which tells when to fight, and when to heal. They must incorporate within themselves the strengths they find in the Goddess. And, like Moon, women must carry that strength into the societal struggle to eradicate the forms of power-over which threaten all life on our planet.

Feminists are aware of the use of language as a tool of power, and our search to understand its force and ability to shape our world is in itself a quest. The struggle to tell the stories of our own quests, or a fictional character's, reflects a transitional moment in western culture where the desire for creation transforms traditional modes into new tales, where we find the echoes of earlier legends whispering new truths.

The mythic nature of such stories need not be dehistoricized; quite the contrary, if myths reflect the effects of patriarchal encroachment and rule, then recognizing those elements makes the myth even more relevant for women wishing to re-create them as tools of positive psychological change. Not only are Goddess stories reflections of women's psychic experiences (e.g., the myth of Demeter and Persephone is an explanation for vegetative changes, yet also serves as an account of the mother-daughter bond), our current drawings on or experiences of these mythic patterns in our own lives is colored by both the patriarchal denial of, and the feminist search to restore, the Goddess principle in our worldview. Both levels are aspects of contemporary women's search for meaning through the symbol of the Goddess.

These speculative texts serve to give readers, especially female readers, examples of a type of heroic femininity which they may have never experienced in everyday life. Fantastic fiction, then, offers the potential to liberate the mind from the shackles of the dominant worldview. By inventing women who are successful in their fictional journeys to manifest the principles of the Goddess, authors such as Bradley, Abbey, and Vinge speak to the many women who are striving toward the same goal in contemporary society.

5
Wise Women and Healers

While Abbey's Rifkind, and to a greater degree Vinge's Moon, are shown as embarking on a path of service to heal their community/world, the novels end without delineating the scope of that service. However, in recent fiction by African American authors Toni Morrison, Ntozake Shange, Gloria Naylor, and by Pagan/Jewish author Starhawk, one discovers women who are, in varying degrees, knowledgeable about the supernatural, the spiritual, and the arcane lore of their foremothers, and who are depicted as using that knowledge to benefit their communities. Due to this knowledge, Denver (*Beloved*), Indigo (*Sassafras, Cypress, and Indigo*), Mama Day (*Mama Day*), and Maya (*The Fifth Sacred Thing*) achieve a certain status other women in their communities do not share.

In discussing the portrayal of each of these characters, I use the term "wise woman" to designate a woman familiar with the arts of herbalism, prophesy, healing, and other spiritual survival skills encompassed under the label "womanspirit" (see Introduction) and discussed here as remnants of ancient European and African diasporic religious practice. In this regard I go beyond the idea of this blending as "mythological" in the sense used by deWeever (9).

Wise women can be seen as the coordinators of various forces within the community, and in these novels there is a focus on the preservation of black and multicultural communities. These women help to keep the disturbances of the community within bounds, thus serving as a type of internal regulator. Their healing serves social functions as well as personal ones; under the guise of the wise woman, potentially disruptive forces are channeled into positive directions, allowing the community to stay united and to survive, thus preserving the delicate existence of threatened minority identity. Racism in America has ensured that this task is an ongoing one. As Barr has noted, black women are treated as alien in white patriarchal society (*Lost in Space* 99). As such, black women's writing operates from the triple voice of African, American, and female (de Weever 12).

African American women's novels frequently emphasize racism as a primary form of power-over, and their reliance on an African spiritual tradition which articulates immanent value. My inclusion of Walker's *The Temple of My Familiar* in Chapter 2 and Butler's *Wild Seed* in Chapter 4 stressed some of the parallels with the portrayal of immanent value in European American women's texts. By discussing Morrison, Shange, Naylor, and Starhawk together, a much greater focus on the issue of racism and healing is possible, which moves us from the area of personal empowerment to community/world change. Viewing themes covered in previous chapters, one finds a progression from the recovering of the lost past, the usefulness of allowing a new definition of power in order to foster personal growth, the female heroic quest in order to come to a personal understanding of Goddess spirituality, and now, a focusing outward to heal interpersonal relationships, the community, and even the world.

First, I will examine more closely some of the differences offered by the African and African diasporic religious traditions, especially in regards to the role of women. The traditions and adaptations of African religious traditions during the diaspora often allow[ed] women of African heritage to play a larger spiritual role in their communities than was allowed for women in white mainstream religion. While many of these beliefs, rituals, and roles became modified in the Americas by Christian doctrine, others survived more visibly in Voodoo and related folk practices. In one sense, the marginalization of Africans in American society allowed for more preservation of native customs than outright assimilation would have. Although slave owners often strove to eradicate the continuance of native cultural practices in America, this eradication was inconsistent, and aspects of African culture did survive (Mulira 35), often disguised to appear "harmless" to white masters. As noted earlier, I believe that this historical situation actually allowed African American women to maintain closer, though still diminished, connections to their roles as powerful, spiritual women, whereas the alienation of European women from their heritage as priestesses and healers was widespread by C.E. 1000, and received its culmination during the witch-burning craze. Thus, African American women authors have been able to draw on an ongoing process, whereas European American women authors have had to engage in more "recovery" (Sojourner, "The Goddess Heritage of Black Women" 58–61). Therefore, the presence of wise women and healers in African American women's fiction has the potential to allow many women to counter their "amnesia" and to remember a spiritual heritage whose effects carry self-transformation into community transformation. As bell hooks contends in regards to contemporary black fiction, "[t]his fiction is popular because it speaks to the hurt black folks are grappling with. Indeed, many non-black people also find healing maps in this work they can use in daily life" (*Sisters of the Yam* 11). Also emphasizing healing while noting a difference between Alice Walker's womanist perspective and that of Africana womanism, Dorothy Thompson suggests that "...the Africana womanist widens the circle to be more inclusive of cultural elements that [re]member the past— Africa, creating a connectedness for diasporic women in their various secondary cultures" whose purpose is ultimately to "liberate" (91). While logically Thompson intends this statement for women of African descent, I would argue that any practice which displaces Eurocentrism is liberatory for all peoples.

While an extensive discussion of African religious practice (before and after diaspora) is beyond the scope of my study, several elements are pertinent to the works under examination: the role of women; the emphasis on interconnection; the importance of community; and the presence of psychic phenomena and healing. These beliefs have been discussed as they appear in works by a variety of spiritual feminists, and touched on in my discussions of Walker and Butler, but they are foregrounded in this chapter because of their direct relationship to the figure and actions of the wise woman.

Women's highly visible participation in African religion, especially West African, can be partially explained by the historical presence of Goddess worship.[1] Personification of African deity is both male and female. While some female deities such as Mawu are clearly linked to childbirth, the feminine aspect of deity is never reduced to reproduction. Instead, goddesses such as Yemaya are creators in their own right, while other goddesses, such as Oya, embody the principle of destruction (Gleason). This representation is unlike [male] monotheisms, which result in a deity seen as separate from and superior to the natural world.[2] Benetta Jules-Rosette notes that "Indigenous African cults and churches have provided a special vehicle for women's self-expression ... [women] have held some of the most effective leadership roles" (185). While some women gain power from official roles, others may "directly assume two other forms of power: (1) mystical power, which operates in a fashion rather comparable to *mana*; and (2) direct control of situated interactions" (186). These spiritual skills can be combined usefully with interpersonal skills. Thus, in cults, "women ... [who] employ ritual leadership in combination with lineage and familial alliances ... [can] establish a power base that extends beyond the secret associations" (187). Further, even when roles are divided along gender lines, "the importance of ritual separateness often makes forms of women's leadership parallel to, and insulated from, the political leadership of men" (187). Such separation need not be seen as subservient or ineffectual, according to Jules-Rosette. In addition to leading rituals and instruction, women are frequently prophetesses and healers (196).

In America, women of African descent have played prominent roles in the history of their people. Sojourner Truth, Harriet Tubman, Francis Harper, and Mary McLeod Bethune are striking examples of religious and social achievement coming out of black Christianity, and suggest that an acceptance of powerful women has managed to survive exposure to Christian monotheism. However, sometimes a break with Christianity has to occur (hooks, *Sisters of the Yam* 185). The fascinating history of Marie LaVeau reveals the power wielded by African American women in such religions as Voodoo, which is a survival of West African religious practice. Jesse Mulira finds that in New Orleans "women generally made up 75 to 80 percent of the cultists," and "in all matters affecting actual worship in the voodoo cults, the queens and priestesses possessed supreme authority" (49). Marie's reign of forty years, which then passed to her daughter, the "second" Marie, saw her powers sought after by men and women, black and white, rich and poor. To this day, persons visit her tomb to request her aid (52–56).

The second relevant aspect of African religious practice is interconnection. John Mbiti observes:

> Chapters of African religions are written everywhere in the life of the community, and in traditional society there are no irreligious people.... To be human is to belong to the whole community.... A person cannot detach himself from the religion of his group, for to do so is to be severed from his roots, his foundation, his context of security, his kinships, and the entire group of those who make him aware of his own existence.... Therefore, to be without religion amounts to a self-excommunication from the entire life of society, and African peoples do not know how to exist without religion [2].

Margaret Creel notes that for Africans, "[a]ncestral patriarchs, matriarchs, diviners, the living dead, and other spirits were daily guardians of human behavior" (72). Given the importance of religious practice and ancestry, ancestor reverence is a logical outcome, as well as a corresponding emphasis on children, who not only provide physical vehicles for the return of the spirits of the ancestors, but who will also revere one as an ancestor at some future time. The widespread reverence noted by Mbiti includes the natural world: "Nature in the broadest sense of the word is not an empty impersonal object or phenomenon; it is filled with religious significance" (56). Coming from a belief in immanent deity, "this religious universe is not an academic proposition; it is an empirical experience, which reaches its height in acts of worship" (57). According to Luisah Teish, this belief in interconnection has survived the diaspora: "The African continues to regard children as wealth, to revel in the spirit of music and dance, to recognize the holiness of food, and to believe in the importance of proper burial, respecting the elders, ancestors, and the forces of nature" (*Jambalaya* 111). For some contemporary African Americans this sense has been lost, and bell hooks warns that "black people must reclaim a spiritual legacy where we connect our well-being to the well-being of the earth" (*Sisters of the Yam* 181).

This sense of interconnection underlies the widespread sense of community which African Americans have fought to protect from the destructive forces of white supremacist America. When the slave trade separated biological families, new kinship systems were created to care for the young, and are still reflected in the continuing terms "brother" and "sister." Voodoo-inspired revolutionaries and Christian-inspired abolitionists fought against slavery, and the civil rights movement spread through religious leaders such as Martin Luther King, Jr., and Malcolm X. Religion has provided a continuing basis for preservation and protection of the community. As Teish says of the LaVeau women, "[they] were golden rings. They linked Blacks to their African past and their Christian present. They linked women of different races and social classes to each other and tugged firmly against the chains of oppression" (*Jambalaya* 186–87).

Another African practice demonstrated by the wise woman is that of psychic phenomena and healing. Beverly Robinson asserts that "[f]olklorists and other cultural scientists recently uncovered evidence that enslaved Africans had a world view encompassing the balance of nature and did not separate mind and body" (218), and that "African American healing is rooted in belief and thus is a religious act, which places folk practitioners and their art in the world of the spiritual" (219). Folk practices range from midwifery, to herbalism, to receiving healing techniques through dreams, mediumship, and so forth. The healer might or might not have psychic abilities, such as astral projection, clairvoyance, telepathy, and precognition — all skills Teish experienced growing up "tipsy," or psychically aware (4). Such abilities have been well documented in many places, among them Zora Hurston's pioneering folkloric research.[3] Alice Walker even goes so far as to assert that "it is only among blacks (to my knowledge) that a trace of their [psychic persons] existence is left in the language. Rootworkers, healers, wise people with 'second sight' are called 'two headed' people" (*Living by the Word* 1–2).

Women as powerful agents, an interconnected world, the importance of community, and the validation of psychic powers and healing abilities are not uniquely African beliefs. My previous discussions make it clear that some claim these traits for ancient European cultures as well, while many spiritual feminists are more concerned with claiming them for all peoples in the present. What must be recognized is the existence of these beliefs in living tradition and practice among peoples of African descent, and the way in which a truly multicultural exchange of feminist spiritual practice can have healing benefits for many. The novels I have selected demonstrate how these principles can shape and validate female identity as a powerful force in community healing, with widespread implications for our world. In Morrison's *Beloved* and Shange's *Sassafras, Cypress, and Indigo*, we see initial and formative stages of the wise woman figure as she begins to understand and connect the community. *Mama Day* presents the mature wise woman, linking her with the idea of the Crone, as does *The Fifth Sacred Thing*, albeit from a multicultural perspective rather than an exclusively African American one. I consider Starhawk's novel last because I feel its multicultural emphasis ties together the alternating European, African, and Jewish American narratives which have been examined previously.

Toni Morrison: Denver, a Glimpse of the Wise Woman

The issues of maintaining an African heritage in spite of slavery, of preserving black community life, and of recognizing self-worth are all present in Toni Morrison's *Beloved*. The destruction of the "Sweet Home" boys by slavery, Sethe's willingness to kill her children, if necessary, to protect them from the degradation she experienced, and the struggle of her children, dead and living, to exist in spite of Sethe's decision, form the weblike plot through which Morrison considers the challenge of African Americans to come to terms with the past.

Although much of the plot (and criticism) centers on Sethe and her uncanny interaction with Beloved, the novel is, in several ways, an African American bildungsroman which delineates Denver's coming of age via a supernatural trial which results in her quest to the "outside" world in order to save herself and her mother. Critics tend to focus on Baby Suggs as the novel's primary spiritual figure, thus missing the importance of Denver's role. Through her quest, Denver not only saves her mother, but also heals a rift in the community and begins a life of her own. Morrison's use of magical realism[4] is a crucial aid in bringing Denver's quest to life and in depicting her as a wise woman by affirming her connection with her family, her strength, and her community ties. Morrison describes the presence of the supernatural in her work in very matter of fact terms:

> My own use of enchantment simply comes because that's the way the world was for me and for the black people that I knew. In addition to the very shrewd, down-to-earth, efficient way in which they did things and survived things, there was this other knowledge or perception, always discredited but nevertheless there.... It formed a kind of cosmology that was perceptive as well as enchanting, and so it seemed impossible for *me* to write about black people and eliminate that simply because it was "unbelievable" [Davis, Christina 414].

Here Morrison articulates the sense that these beliefs, while having undergone some decay or suppression, remain an integral part of the background of the African American psyche, and thus are present for the writer to draw from. Because her fiction critiques white patriarchy, it fits Barr's definition of a feminist fabulation, which includes magical realism (*Lost in Space* 12).

To prepare the reader to accept her role as a healer, a number of clues are given which indicate that Denver is a charmed child, and that her presence plays a spiritual as well as familial role. Denver's birth is replete with unusual circumstances and coincidences, typical of a hero's birth. Amy, a previously indentured white girl on the run, appears as the unlikely candidate to help Sethe, who is near death, give birth (32). As Sethe says to Paul D, "She's a charmed child from the beginning ... she pulled a whitegirl out of the hill. The last thing you'd expect to help" (41–42). Significantly, Denver decides to make her appearance in the boat as they cross the Ohio River in order to gain freedom. Telling her story to Beloved, Denver silently observes:

> This was the part of the story she loved. She was coming to it now and she loved it because it was all about herself; but she hated it too because it made her feel like a bill was owing somewhere and she, Denver, had to pay it. But who she owed or what to pay it with eluded her [77].

Denver's very life is a gift, but gifts must be used, or "paid for." Her payment is intimately related to the plan of action the reincarnated Beloved pursues with Sethe, though Denver does not realize it. Before that choice, however, Denver makes one other special payment which changes her life and singles her out. At age seven, while she is attending Mrs. Jones' school, Nelson Lord asks Denver "the question about her mother [Sethe's murder of Beloved] that put chalk ... out of reach forever" (102). Unable to respond due to her own fear and uncertainty about Sethe, Denver becomes deaf and mute, not even hearing the answer Sethe gives when Denver repeats the question to her (103). This silence, which gives "her eyes a power even she found hard to believe," lasts for two years, until Beloved's ghost tries to ascend the stairs. So that her mother can't kill her again, Denver, a girl who "took her mother's milk right along with the blood of her sister," stays isolated in the house, bound by Beloved's literal and figurative specter (152). Denver's unusual birth, traumatic deafness and muteness, and isolation mark her as special and "set apart" from the rest of the community.

Although familial interconnection is very important in African belief, slavery has severed the normal bond between mother and child in Sethe's family. She would rather kill her children than see them enslaved. Denver's love for Sethe is ambivalent: "I spent all of my outside self loving Ma'am so she wouldn't kill me, loving her even when she braided my head at night" (207). Such a reaction is not improbable for a child whose mother tries to murder her, no matter how understandable the reason. Although Denver survives, Sethe's actions separate the child from her mother. Denver must choose to reconnect with her mother and to "step off the edge of the world and die because if she didn't, they all would" (239). She is the only one rational enough to make that survival decision: "Now it was obvious that her mother could die and leave them both and what would Beloved do then?" (243). In a reversal of nurturing roles, Denver must heal by giving life to the mother who would have taken it away.

Because of Denver's isolation, her difference, and the alienation of her family from the community due to Sethe's actions, Beloved fulfills Denver's need for interconnection and represents the psychic lack which Denver must learn to fulfill through meaningful connection with other people in her quest. Inside her place of refuge, her boxwood bower, "Denver's imagination produced its own hunger and its own food, which she badly needed because loneliness wore her out. Wore her out" (28–29). So, when Beloved first appears in the flesh as the family makes their way home from the fair, Denver nurses her, "So intent ... she forgot to eat or visit the emerald closet." Later, she is hurt by the fact that she is not the main reason for Beloved's return (75). Denver is the only one of the household who really knows who and what Beloved is (76). She recognizes that Beloved is responsible for Sethe's choking in the clearing (101). Despite her knowledge of the danger Beloved represents, Denver clings to Beloved:

> Whatever her power and however she used it, Beloved was hers. Denver was alarmed by the harm she thought Beloved planned for Sethe, but felt helpless to thwart it, so unrestricted was her need to love another. The display she witnessed at the Clearing shamed her because the choice between Sethe and Beloved was without conflict [104].

Part of Denver's attraction to Beloved lies in the fact that Beloved's gaze helps to create a sense of self which Denver has lacked, the feeling of "being pulled into view by the interested, uncritical eyes of the other" (118). Thus, when Beloved "disappears," Denver panics, crying "because she has no self," having relied on another to create her locus of subjectivity (123). At first, Denver's accurate perceptions of Beloved's intentions cannot compete with her intense inner needs. This aspect of the story also implies the danger for African Americans of being destroyed by the haunting presence of slavery if no sense of personal identity is present.

Beloved gives Denver a sense of self, and paradoxically, that new found sense of self must take the steps which will destroy Beloved. This is the price for Denver's passage to freedom. Her decision is partially motivated by her love for Sethe and partially by her desire to save herself. As Beloved's "love" begins to drain the family both financially and emotionally, Denver must take action. Denver sacrifices Beloved because she realizes that freedom entails responsibility not only for the self but for others as well.

To do so she seeks external aid, and for Morrison this is a sign that Denver has come of age. Denver leaves her home, #124, the world of the past and the supernatural, and enters the outside world of the living present. Randi Kristensen, drawing upon the idea of "communitas," as articulated by Victor Turner, asserts that "Denver initiates the reconstruction of this communitas when she steps out into the world beyond 124" (40). For Kristensen, Baby Suggs had been the first to create a holy space of free individuals in expression of shared history and identity. Jealousy and resentment of Sethe had led to its sundering and Sethe's isolation. While it is not suggested that Denver will ever become the sort of "preacher" Baby Suggs was, she does step into her shoes by reuniting the community. This act also fits what Kristensen has described as fitting within the "Yemaya discourse," which emphasizes African based matrifocal connection as an alternative mode of resistance to western patriarchal separation imposed by slavery:

> Morrison's assertions of resistance to zombiefication [the dissoulution of African peoples under European exploitation] are all located in communal action, either grounded in interconnection or in the desire for it. This sense of interconnection in the New World context of historical slavery relies on the restoration of maternal relations, within the self and mirrored in community relations [18].

Denver's first visit to a community member is to Mrs. Jones, the teacher, and the visit "inaugurate[s] her life in the world as a woman" (248). Denver begins to read, to eat, and to work as a housekeeper, while Beloved devours Sethe (250). Janey, Denver's fellow housekeeper, learns of Beloved, and accepts her otherworldly status without hesitation. Teamed with Ella, a woman who refuses to let "past errors tak[e] possession of the present" (256), the townswomen are rallied to rescue the Sethe they had turned their backs on years before:

> Some brought what they could and what they believed would work. Stuffed in apron pockets, strung around their necks, lying in the space between their breasts. Others brought Christian faith — as shield and sword. Most brought a little of both [257].

Morrison's use of magical realism enables her to present the combination of folk magic and Christianity typical of African diasporic religious practice. Because magic is part of the everyday realm, the cultural climate readily allows the women of the community to believe Denver's story and aid in her task.

By trusting herself, Denver saves herself and her mother, and gains the help necessary to deal with Beloved's supernatural intrusion. She also takes the disruptive force of Beloved's return and uses it to heal the rift between her family and the community at large. After Beloved is driven away, Paul D returns to bring Sethe back to something approaching a normal life. Denver moves further into the world. Our last glimpse is of a woman on her way to a college education and romance (266–67). Typical of the wounded healer, her self-healing makes her a viable agent in the community. The importance of community healing cannot be overestimated, for here Morrison symbolically suggests the need to purge the internalized self-hate and denial which slavery has fostered in the African American psyche.

As Jacqueline de Weever comments, "the path to wholeness lies in claiming the slave past through identification with it, living with it, and then leaving it consciously and decidedly for the sake of life itself" (160).

By accepting the world of the spirit and of the past, but no longer collapsing herself into it, Denver comes of age in a broader world, and moves toward true psychic freedom. In doing so, she creates an opportunity for others in the community to put aside their differences and act as one.

Denver is not a wise woman in the fullest sense of the term, for she does not continue in a traditional healer's role, as will be seen with Indigo. However, Denver's grasp of her family's situation and her actions bring the problems she faces to a successful resolution, making her own journey toward wisdom and selfhood a successful one. She restores her mother, and thus helps to restore herself, by putting an end to a lethal disruption of the mother-child bond, both for herself and Beloved. By taking the responsibility of transforming herself and her environment, Denver demonstrates that healing can only come from those who are born into freedom, a birth which must come from the self.

Ntozake Shange: Indigo, the Traditional Healer

In contrast to Denver, Shange stresses that Indigo's devotion to the path of a traditional healer is motivated by the desire to serve African Americans as a race, especially African American women. Indigo accomplishes her task by developing her command of African diasporic religious practices such as the use of natural psychic talents, natural healing techniques, and innovative spellcraft. In her portrayal of Indigo, Shange maintains a strongly Africentic focus, but also suggests that these abilities are part of the heritage of all women.

Although a larger portion of *Sassafras, Cypress, and Indigo* is devoted to the characters of Sassafras and Cypress, a description of Indigo opens the novel and sets its tone:

> Where there is a woman there is magic. If there is a moon falling from her mouth, she is a woman who knows her magic, who can share or not share her powers. A woman with a moon falling from her mouth, roses between her legs, and tiaras of Spanish moss, this woman is a consort of the spirits.
> Indigo seldom spoke. There was a moon in her mouth [3].

It then comes as no surprise that things magical and spiritual appear as commonplace in the novel, particularly where Indigo is concerned. She not only talks with her dolls; she hears them talking to her, forcing her mother, Hilda Effania, to remark, "Something's got hold to my child, I swear. She's got too much South in her" (4). Unlike Denver's perceptions, which are depicted as arising from an unusual situation, Indigo's conversations with the spirit world are portrayed as being the result of a natural attunement to both place and race, the by-product of awareness of life's interrelatedness as found in cultures practicing earth-based spirituality. Her mother's remark suggests that the presence of Africans in the South has made it a place which fosters these practices.

Indigo's powers are taught by others, personally intuited, and received as gifts from the spirits. While Sassafras and Cypress contribute the novel's poems and recipes, Indigo produces the spells, such as "Moon Journeys" or "To Rid Oneself of the Scent of Evil" (5, 31) and herbal remedies (20). Some of this lore she learns from Aunt Haydee, who "had gone to the moon a lot" (6). She learns even more from trusting her intuition. As Teish points out in *Jambalaya,* a wise woman follows both the knowledge of tradition and her own inner knowledge (47). That is apparent in Indigo's fiddle playing, when she learns that "she had many tongues, many spirits who loved her, real and unreal" (28). Her playing instinct gives her the power to make members of the gang Junior Geechee Capitans back down, then initiate and accept her, thus earning her privilege in a male world (38–39). Intuition also enables her to hear the spirits and voices of ancestral memory, who grant her the ability to play the song of a person's soul: "The slaves who were ourselves aided Indigo's mission, connecting soul & song, experience & unremembered rhythms" (45). Indigo's trust in herself, her intuition, and the spirit realm makes others such as Pretty Man mark her as "a woman in charge of her powers" (45).

Like Denver, Indigo begins to identify herself as a woman during the course of the novel. First, she begins menstruating while at the home of Sister Mary Louise, an eccentrically Christian woman who does her best to serve Jesus, the flowers, and the children at the same time (17). In a boldly original reinterpretation of the story of Eve, Shange has Sister Mary bathe Indigo "in a hot tub filled with rose petals: white, red, and yellow floating around a new woman" (19). These colors, combined with Indigo's dark skin, suggest the four races, and imply that she may be seen as undergoing a redemptive spiritual transformation opening up new possibilities for all women. Sister Mary reinforces this idea by returning Indigo to the garden Eve had been cast from, "bleeding among the roses, fragrant and filled with grace." This scene presents a striking continuum of spiritually powerful womanhood, ranging from Eve to Mary "full of grace." Indigo is the new woman who has redeemed her female body and sexuality as sacred. Since Mary is often associated with the Virgin Mary, the only "pure" woman in Christian theology, the fact that Mary affirms menstruation, which is necessary for childbirth, indicates a reclaiming of the holiness of female reproduction. As a daughter of (this new) Eve, Shange encourages the female reader to include herself in this vision and to see magic in herself as a woman.

Indigo's second step toward womanhood also consists of a symbolic and empathetic identification with other women and with her African heritage. After her fight with Mabel, Pretty Man's girlfriend, over the fiddle, Indigo flees to the Caverns, but she still hears Mabel's screams as she is beaten by Pretty Man. At first, Indigo is shamed by her treatment of a sister, and the disruption she has caused in her small community: "Mabel was just some woman. One day Indigo would be a woman too" (49). Then, as she gropes along the walls, Indigo realizes that the rings she grasps were tethers for the chains and leg irons which bound slaves. The moment is revelatory for Indigo as she literally and figuratively embraces the slave past:

> The tighter Indigo held the chains in her hands, the less shame was her familiar. Mabel's tiny woeful voice hovered over the thick blood chorus of The Caverns. Indigo knew her calling. The Colored had hurt enough already [49].

She had always cared for the needs of "the Colored," trying to give them what she thought they needed:

> Access to the moon.
> The Power to heal.
> Daily visits with the spirits [5].

With her revelation, however, Indigo is moved to carry her bond with the spirit worlds into action in the African American community. She puts her dolls away and apprentices herself to Aunt Haydee, a healer and midwife, in order to serve the needs of black women. Again we observe the connection between community and maternal relations mentioned concerning *Beloved*. Her desire to focus on the needs of black women adds another dimension to her female heritage, a heritage already experienced by growing up in an all-female family of artists. Here we see that while Denver's connection with her community is more literal, a physical going into, Indigo's connection is one of lifelong service, a symbolic mothering which will help other women heal themselves and become mothers.

A phrase recurrent through Indigo's section of *Sassafras, Cypress, & Indigo* is "the slaves who were ourselves," which suggests at least two things: that "free" black people are still oppressed by the same system which fostered slavery, and the belief in reincarnation and ancestral relationship discussed earlier as part of African tribal religions. The first interpretation emphasizes mental slavery, past and present, a theme also found in *Beloved*. The second interpretation is supported by the story of "Blue Sunday," which occurs near the close of the novel. Property of Master Fitzhugh during slavery, Blue Sunday fought him at every turn for her sexual freedom, even to the point of transforming herself into a crocodile and mutilating him, then disappearing. We are told that after this episode, "The Fitzhughs no longer cultivated indigo as a cash crop." Indigo's name implies a connection between the two women (223). Women would call on Blue Sunday's songs when they were in labor, "when they risked mothering free children," asking her to "'give this child the freedom you know'" (223). In this same vein, women now call on Indigo's fiddle-playing for "relief from elusive disquiet, hungers of the soul" as well as when giving birth (222).

After Aunt Haydee's death, Indigo fights to keep the knowledge and role of the old woman alive in the community by taking her place as midwife and healer: "Hilda Effania knew Indigo had an interest in folklore. Hilda Effania had no idea that Indigo was the folks" (224). Through her connection with Blue Sunday and Aunt Haydee, Indigo places herself in a tradition of powerful female magic and healing. The implication is that Indigo will also be a wise Crone one day, who will pass down her stories of health, resistance, and survival. Her story affirms women as carriers of the voices of free ancestors who can speak to those in the present.

Indigo becomes a midwife, claiming her part in the larger African heritage of a preslavery freedom with its tradition of spiritual kinship and natural healing. This kinship is important in racial terms, but also is an affirmation of the creative powers of all women. Indigo uses the healing and magical arts to bring "free children" into the world, just as her sisters produce poetry and dance to inspire others and place themselves as creators of culture. She ponders, "Her sisters were artists. Would they understand she just wanted where they came from to stay alive?" (224). While all artists are wise women to the degree that their arts help to heal the mind, soul, or imagination, Indigo's gift is the wisdom to keep her wise woman heritage alive in order to literally heal other women and her community, and keep the legacy going.

Gloria Naylor: A Crone's Wisdom

Gloria Naylor's exquisite novel *Mama Day* centers around the tough yet gentle wise woman known as Mama Day. Critic James Saunders confidently asserts that "we must consider that clarity in itself was not Naylor's goal in writing *Mama Day*. As it is, the woman after whom the book is named is in possession of certain powers that defy explanation" (259). However, while one may debate points about narrative clarity in Naylor's novels, information about Mama Day's practices abound — after all, we have been examining many instances of womanspirit, a knowledge area this male critic has not chosen to draw from. Once examined in this regard, Mama Day's actions seem downright familiar.

Herbalist, healer, and magician, Mama Day wields considerable power in the island community of Willow Springs, which "ain't in no state" (64). Separated from the mainland, with no allegiance to any power but the ceaseless cycles of the seasons, Willow Springs exists almost as another world outside time, where magic is an everyday occurrence. Mama Day's stature echoes this sense of the eternal: "to show up in one century, make it all the way through the next, and have a toe inching over into the one approaching is about as close to eternity anybody can come" (6–7). Appropriately, the climax of the novel is an epic magical struggle to save the life of her grandniece, Cocoa. In a clearer fashion than Denver or Indigo, Mama Day has given thought to how her magic and healing work, and has paid a heavy price for that knowledge. While Indigo is a young woman who is discovering the joys of service, Mama Day, with her crone's wisdom, knows the role of sacrifice in life. On the continuum of wise women, Mama Day is one willing to suffer personally in order to serve the community, an idea we also saw among those questing for the Goddess in the previous chapter.

Like Indigo and Blue Sunday, Mama Day also has a legendary predecessor, Sapphira Wade. The portrayal of Sapphira Wade is twofold: She is a symbol of free African ancestry, but she is also a woman depicted in cosmic, Goddess-like terms; "She is the conflation of the need for a new woman-centered spirituality and ancient African ancestor worship" (Thompson 93). For example, Sapphira is of "pure African stock" (2), yet is "[a] true conjure woman: satin black, biscuit cream, red as Georgia clay; depending upon which of us takes a mind to her" (3). This quotation indicates an archetypal stature which allows her to be perceived by all races if they understand that "Sapphira Wade don't live in the part of our memory we can use to form words" (4). Helen Levy also notes that "[l]ike the Virgin Mary in her many manifestations, Sapphira takes on the complexions of the worshipper.... Unlike Mary, the ever-virgin handmaiden, the fully sexual Sapphira ... is independently creative and restorative ." (282).

As in Shange's novel, there is a sexualized and racialized rewriting of Mariolatry. Naylor suggests that what we imagine creates our reality if we will believe it, an issue which is crucial to the saving of Cocoa. Sapphira Wade "was the great, great, grand, Mother — as if you were listing the attributes of a goddess" (218). In addition, the name "Sapphira" is closely relate to "Sapphire," a name Patricia Bell Scott notes refers to a "caricature of the dominating, emasculating Black woman" (85). Here Naylor transforms this image of black womanhood into the positive one of a Goddess mother who looks out for her children. Capable of killing her white husband in order to procure the island for her descendants, one of whom is Mama Day, Sapphira Wade is the force Mama Day calls on to discover how Cocoa can be saved from the deadly magic Ruby has worked on her. Against Ruby, "Sapphira, Cocoa, and Mama Day form a sort of woman's trinity with mother, daughter, and spirit" (283).

Mama Day recognizes the power of interconnection and family as an organic state. Sewing on Cocoa's wedding-ring quilt, she reflects upon the pattern and connection of her family and heritage: "Could she take 'em all out and start again? …When it's done right you can't tell where one ring ends and another begins. It's like they ain't been sewn at all, they grew up out of nowhere" (138). The image is one of circular unity rather than linear progression.

Mama Day's own immense capabilities have come with a steep price tag. At the age of five, Miranda (Mama Day) learns that "there is more to be known behind what the eyes can see" (36). After their baby sister Peace dies from a fall down a well, she is left to care for her sister Abigail while their mother slowly goes insane. Like Denver and Indigo, Miranda must take on mothering qualities for herself and others. As a result, Miranda earns her nickname, "Mama Day," but also pays the price of losing her childhood and a normal adolescence:

> Gifted hands, folks said. You have a gift, Little mama … It ain't fair that it came with a high price, but it did … Mama and child. Mama and sister. Too heavy a load to take away … Everybody's mama now [88–89].

Mama Day earns her sense of self-worth through sacrifice and caring for her sister. Able to send marigolds and zinnias into flight by a wave of her walking stick (152), nonetheless only Mama Day seems to realize how gifts such as precognition are burdens as well: "I'm an old woman. And I'm tired, tired of knowing things I can't do nothing about" (174). Her acknowledgment of burden and sacrifice makes the character of Mama Day realistic and wise as well as magical.

As they would have in Africa, Mama Day's abilities grant her power and status within the community of Willow Springs. She serves as healer, and sometimes as judge: "Mama Day say no, everybody say no" (6). This strength of character is reflected in her style of medical practice; Mama Day radiates assurance and experience. Throughout the novel she is depicted as knowing the medicinal and magical value of every plant, root, or bark on the island. Smithfield, the town doctor from across the bridge, is forced to admit that "being a good doctor, he knew another one when he saw her" (84). Because accuracy on her part is necessary to heal effectively in her community, Mama Day knows the differences between her healing, gimmicky charms, and that which is truly operating on a nonordinary level of reality. Approached by France for a "quick fix" to her problems, Miranda notes to herself "the mind is everything. She [Frances] can dig all the holes she wants around Ruby's door ... Walk naked in the moonlight stinking with Van-Van oil — and it won't do a bit of good. 'Cause the mind is everything" (90). Miranda does not mistake the medium for the message. She tells Abigail about the magic seeds she has given Bernice, who wants a child: "And the only magic is that what she believes they are, they're gonna become" (6). Mama Day's wisdom and acumen exemplify the best of a crone's knowledge as a force in the community.

However, Mama Day also works magic which involves more than psychological accuracy. She manipulates forces in order to bring about desired and beneficent change. One of the novel's most dramatic instances of such magic is the ritual impregnation of Bernice. Enacted within the timeless space of the old house dating back to Sapphira's time, Mama Day passes a chicken egg from the chicken to Bernice:

> Space to space. Ancient fingers keeping each in line. The uncountable, the unthinkable, is one opening. Pulsing and alive — wet — the egg moves from one space to the other. A rhythm older than woman draws it in and holds it tight [140].

Rather than being grateful for the ensuing pregnancy, Bernice avoids Mama Day, too unsettled by the procedure to acknowledge its effectiveness. When the unwitting community nicknames the boy Chick, Bernice is aghast, and chooses the nickname Little Caesar instead. Ironically, Pear, Bernice's mother-in-law, attributes the pregnancy to Bernice finally forsaking Mama Day's "bush medicine" (149).

Part of a crone's wisdom lies in knowing when to give and save life, and when to destroy it. Mama Day's magic is never used capriciously, and only used for destructive purposes to defend those she loves and to rid the community of evil. Such is the case in Mama Day's destruction of Ruby after Ruby puts a spell on Cocoa which causes her to be filled with worms which are gradually devouring her. Scattering a silvery powder around Ruby's home, Mama Day calls three times for her to come out: "Well, three times is all that she'd required. That'll be her defense at Judgment: Lord, I called out three times" (270); Thompson notes this ritual marking "recalls African tribal ritual of marking the house of a criminal" (95). In fact, even before Ruby casts the spell, Mama Day subtly warns Ruby not to harm her family, thinking to herself "before I'd let you mess with mine, I'd wrap you up in tissue paper and send you straight to hell" (173). Shortly after Mama Day distributes the powder, a storm comes, and lightning strikes Ruby's house twice, causing it to explode on the second strike. In contrast to the manipulation with which Ruby enacts her spell, Mama Day's approach is forthright and even gives Ruby an opportunity to reveal herself.

More important than the use of magic in the novel is the emphasis placed on the reality of magic and the role of belief. Although the retribution against Ruby is emotionally satisfying, in order for Cocoa to be saved, George must believe in Mama Day's magic as real. In this sense, George also represents the skeptical reader, who must voluntarily approach Mama Day with belief. He also represents the male who doubts female power and knowledge. As such, his eventual conviction supports tradition, belief, magic, and female power. Abigail, her sister, comments:

> "George ain't never gonna believe this, Miranda. Go to him with some mess like this, and he'd be sure we were senile."
> "That's right. So we gotta wait for him to feel the need to come to us. I'll have to stay out at the other place. And when he's ready head him in my direction" [267].

When George finally goes to Miranda to hear her out, he accuses her of speaking in metaphors, upon which she reflects: "Metaphors. Like what they used in poetry and stuff. The stuff folks dreamed up when they was making a fantasy, while what she was talking about was real. As real as them young hands in front of her" (294). Levy correctly concludes that "[t]hrough Miranda's anguish, Naylor portrays the modern emptying of effective ritual communication from literature, as she dismisses the elegant, aesthetic concept of metaphor as belonging to the present leisure entertainment of intellectual literature" (283). In other words, readers who see that fabulation does indeed express reality as a means of commenting upon and changing it, are best able to understand the deeper messages of such texts, which resist reading along lines of traditional white male scholarship and analysis.

George cannot accept this reality at first, and leaves Mama Day's "mumbo jumbo" (295). After returning to Cocoa and lying next to her, he finds a worm on the tip of his penis, and is forced to believe in the reality of what has happened to Cocoa. He goes to Mama Day and attempts the task she has given him — to search inside the hen house. The task itself is unimportant except that his willingness to undertake it demonstrates his belief and love, which is what he finds in the henhouse. As he dies from the bursting of a weak vessel in his heart, his sacrifice saves Cocoa (300–02). Symbolically, George is sacrificed to the "henhouse," with its connotations of femaleness and domesticity.

In commenting on the many Jungian readings of this scene (with the henhouse as anima), Thompson remarks that there is an overlooked yet striking remnant of African diasporic religious practice present: the role of chickens in sacrificial rites (97). This comment provides a needed balance to those who wish to read the texts of those who write outside or on the margins of the western tradition. Levy argues that "George's lonely life represents the emotional costs to men as well as women of the mother's loss" (281). As such, he sacrifices himself to the mother principle in order to continue Cocoa's life, the sacred lineage of the Great Mother, Sapphira. Through George's actions, Naylor points to the harnessing of the powers of belief as miraculous and capable of effecting change in the material world.

As an example of the wise woman and healer, Mama Day is important for several reasons. As a mature woman, she understands the role of sacrifice, both of her own life and the lives of others, in order to achieve ends motivated by love. Her sacrifice leads her to spiritual understanding, which further gains her respect within the African American community. As a healer, Mama Day's practice involves the material, psychological, intellectual, and spiritual realms, and her wisdom lies in knowing which to use when. As is typical of African healing traditions, this knowledge is used not for selfish purposes, but to serve, preserve, and protect the community. To approach the novel without an understanding of the healing tradition drawn upon in the portrayal of Mama Day would not only erroneously cause the reader to dismiss the character as entertaining fantasy, but also to miss the emphasis Naylor is placing on the role of belief, creation, and freedom in creating the reality in which we live, and the role of the healer as an artist who can create a better reality.

Starhawk: The Revolutionary Crone

How does our understanding of reality reflect our choice of genre labels? This question, which underlies many of the discussions within this study, becomes even more intriguing when applied to an examination of Starhawk's first published novel, *The Fifth Sacred Thing*. Having discussed Starhawk's pivotal importance in the contemporary Pagan renaissance as both priestess and theorist, one must ask if the certain knowledge that a writer actually believes in psychic practices and other elements outside the dominant paradigm affects what we call a fictional work which treats those practices as real and accessible. Can this work be called fantasy? Is it even magical realism, when magic is not juxtaposed with consensus reality, but rather is presented as an organic outcropping of human potential?

Regardless of which label is chosen for this speculative work (and all names have some merit in this instance), *The Fifth Sacred Thing* is unique in that it takes the socio-religious principles articulated elsewhere by its author and shows them put to work in a society only slightly futuristic and removed from our own. By doing so, Starhawk suggests that a society based on the feminist spiritual tenets of cooperation, respect, and reverence for the earth is within our grasp, if we will just work to get it.

Through the figure of Maya Greenwood (a Pagan author rather broadly based on Starhawk herself, including her Jewish identity), as well as Bird (Maya's grandson) and Madrone (the granddaughter of Maya's lovers, Johanna and Rio), Starhawk interrogates the realities dictated by being willing to follow Pagan principles in a pacifist way, even to the point of risking death through nonviolent protest of the "other" lifestyle choice presented in the novel, one which is the logical extrapolation of current power-over practices of hierarchical, military, and religious domination.

An understanding of Maya's identity and ethics is important to an accurate interpretation of her religious and political significance in *The Fifth Sacred Thing*. First, she is a Jewish woman who has chosen Paganism/Goddess worship as her life's path, personally and in her writing (such persons sometimes refer to themselves as "Jewitch" in the movement). As such, she partakes of two groups traditionally marginalized in western culture. Second, she comes from the radical protest tradition of the sixties, with a vested interest in social change which Starhawk implies is not dead within the baby boomer generation, but for some, is ready to blossom forth into the creation of a new social structure. Finally, her sexual relationships and extended chosen family present a uniquely multicultural display in fiction. Maya is bisexual, with both Latino (Rio) and black (Johanna) lovers who are lifelong mates in a basically polyamorous relationship.[5]

More so than any other novelist thus examined in this study, Starhawk forces the reader to examine basic notions concerning racial mixing, relationships, fidelity, love, and cultural bridging through the character of

Maya. The breadth and scope of the challenges Maya and her relationships present suggest a conscious effort on Starhawk's part to present her ideas in an all-inclusive fashion, one which moves beyond mere "tolerance" to actual cultural interconnection.

In Maya's world, San Francisco circa 2048, a revolution occurred (2028) which has allowed the implementation of the basic ideals Maya Greenwood espoused in her books that had inspired a new pagan generation (again, much like Starhawk herself). Water is recycled, and gardens and streams flourish throughout the city, providing food and recreation. Windmills help provide power, and air gondolas connect the reaches of the city. Everyone works, and no one does without food, although often there is no surplus. There are no prisons; criminals are banished from the city to live with the "Wild Boar People" (277). Religious and cultural celebrations flourish: European, Hispanic, African, Chinese, and so forth, while Pagans, Jews, and Christians work side by side. Everyone has two of the three main languages: Mandarin, Spanish, and English. Decisions are made by committees, and all have a voice (though the meetings may be long and tedious, Maya is quick to note). All sexual preferences are welcome, and no one is persecuted. Computers use a consciously programmed crystal technology. This San Francisco is an ecotopia which restores both body and soul, and works to heal all other forms of life as well.

Against this vision is ranged the combined unholy trinity of the Stewards, the Millennialists, and "the Corporation" (102), a representative of the relentless force of global capitalist politics so pervasive and controlling that the actual corporate name is insignificant. The Stewards, military in origin, control the government , and are backed with "funds and religious prophecies" (72) by the Millennialists. Outside San Francisco, "You've got to work for the Stewards and obey the Millennialist Purities, or you can't even buy water and you lose your right to eat" (72). Against the four sacred elements of earth, air, fire, and water are contrasted the Four Purities: Moral Purity, Family Purity, Racial Purity, and Spiritual Purity (272). The first

> outlawed all sorts of fornication, rape, incest, and child abuse ... they didn't seem so bad. Until we found out that if you violated them, you officially lost your immortal soul, which made you fair game for rape and enforced prostitution, if you were a woman, and your children prey for all sorts of abuse [298].

The others remove women from professional fields, virtually outlaw all other religions than the Millennialist creed, and force people to identify themselves by selecting one racial category (298–99). In such a society, a woman who dares to get an illegal abortion, if caught, is either forced to become a breeder or a prostitute for soldiers (320). Lacking anything resembling the compassion many find in Christ's teachings, the Steward/Millennialist/Corporation trinity distills the worst aspects of Judeo-Christian western modes of imperialism, exploitation, and domination of women, minorities, and the earth. In Madrone's journey to Los Angeles, she sees their policies in action, where all must subscribe to them in order to eat or drink, unless they wish to run away to join the rebellion in the hills. This triumvirate force tries to crush all that the Four Old Women had stood up to create and protect when they began the revolution which culminated in the new San Francisco.

Starhawk's choice of Four Old Women — Maria Garcia, Alice Black, Lily Fong, and Greta Margolis — to dig in their heels, or pickaxes rather, against the Steward's declaration of martial law, is representative on three counts: the racial variety suggested by the names, and the age and gender involved. Older women, so discounted in contemporary society, are presented as the voices of radical change and wisdom. Here we see a shift from the often youthful to middle-aged protagonists of many of the other novels.

Throughout Starhawk's novel is the tension between the young, who are more likely to be tempted to use violence in self-defense against the Stewards, and the old, including Maya, who warn with the wisdom of the past that "the means shape the ends. You become what you do" (164). The decision of how to defend what they have created is at the heart of the novel's plot; for Starhawk, a decision to resort to violence is to side with power-over, a concept we already know she stands firmly against. Yet her fiction allows her to play out the losses and obstacles involved in putting nonviolence to the test in defense of a neo–Pagan dream. Further, the cooperative nature of this interracial alliance points to another persistent theme in the novel: the need for true appreciation of diversity, and a recognition that all humans and all ancestors have wisdom to impart. With her multiracial urban setting, Starhawk challenges us to think beyond black or white traditions, and to understand through her microcosm of San Francisco that only the solutions which have input from all races will provide healing for the world community. The actions of the Four Old Women serve as a metonymy for the linking of ecological, age, race, gender, and power issues in *The Fifth Sacred Thing*.

Woven with Maya's reflections are the narratives of Bird and Madrone, creating a textual braid which links young and old, male and female, healers and healed. Both Maya and Madrone are healers. Maya has helped to heal culture through her activism and writing, while Madrone focuses on healing of the body (which, in a paradigm of interconnection, also includes the mind). Bird, however, first appears as a man broken by the Stewards, bereft of his memory and his heritage. His struggle to break free of their effects on his body and mind (not once, but twice, when he is again taken prisoner) allows Starhawk to illustrate that fighting the forces of domination takes a unique kind of strength, one which is not limited to a gender or race. But the stories of both Madrone and Bird exist because of Maya's. Her legacy has created the opportunity for both to grow into beings who can resist the lures of violence, even the violence of revenge. A brief look at some of their struggles reveals different forms of strength and healing.

The varied experiences of Bird and Madrone reveal how different conceptions of power result in divergent experiences of sexuality. Both were raised to explore their sexuality openly and honestly, in various forms and pairings. Even their names and associated animals reveal a roundabout pun. Madrone's healing becomes associated with special bee-given powers, so between the two, we have Bird and the bees. When Madrone has sex with Hijohn, one of the rebels, she is dismayed by his selfishness and inability to please a woman, so she instructs him in some basic pleasuring techniques. Much to her surprise, Hijohn's lover, Katy, does not appreciate this help, saying to Madrone, "Everything you need, you think you have a right to reach for and take. Every impulse you have, you follow" (356). Madrone is stunned by Katy's jealousy, as she is not used to such possessiveness. However, Katy is partially correct: Madrone does act with her impulses, as though it is her right — she has been raised to live an instinctual life which honors the body, rather than denying it. Starhawk's presentation of her behavior makes the reader aware that many of our traditional notions of sexuality would have to be sacrificed to do so.

In contrast, both of Bird's imprisonments contain elements of sexual violence or coercion. When he first wakes to himself, ten years after being captured, he is shocked to find he has a teenage boy as a lover, not because he views homosexuality as abhorrent, but because he sees anonymous sex as distasteful (21–22). When he is tortured by the Stewards, much of it focuses on his genitals, and he feels raped (342). Yet even after this torture breaks him, he refuses to rape, and helps to trick the soldiers into letting one of the city's girls go. Rape is the unthinkable for Bird, but for the Stewards, rape is the logical extension of their worldview, as well as of the repression involved in the "Purities," a point Starhawk makes clear with the story of the rape/torture death of the young girl Poppy at the hands of a high-ranking official. In contrast, sexuality as sacrament serves as a healing tool for Bird, first in his enactment of the "Great Rite" (the Wiccan ritual of union between the Goddess and the God, sometimes rendered symbolically, and sometimes through intercourse) after his first escape (98) and again through a group sexual experience when he returns home the first time (146). Clearly, our conceptions of power help to determine our conception of the erotic, which can either harm or heal. In Audre Lorde's words, "Our erotic knowledge empowers us, becomes a lens through which we scrutinize all aspects of our existence, forcing us to evaluate those aspects honestly in terms of their relative meaning within our lives" (57).

Bird and Madrone also represent the continuum of the healer and the healed, with Maya's influence involved in both. Madrone, as a healer, sometimes goes too far in risking her own life in order to save another's. Maya warns her that this is the worst type of selfishness and egoism, to deny the Crone what is hers. Bird, in his despair over the betrayal of the city, sees himself as beyond redemption, losing himself in a sea of self-pity. But when he is selected to be Maya's executioner, he is saved by the sting and caress of the bees sent by Madrone:

> They had reached for him; they had not abandoned him. Not because he deserved compassion, but because by their very nature they were emissaries of a power that was always and everywhere offering itself, asking nothing in return …. That was the real gift, the true grace: not death, but love, the fifth sacred thing [473].

He then puts down the rifle and begins to sing. Soon the Stewards' men begin abandoning their ranks and defecting to the side of the city.

The soldiers abandon the Stewards because of the message Maya was given to use as a means of defending the city by winning over its enemies: "There is a place set for you at our table, if you will choose to join us" (218). Ironically, this message is brought to her by Elijah on Passover night, during which celebration Maya argues against them inviting "that old religious fanatic…. He's the Junipero Serra of the Bible, your typical racist imperialist bigot. Why the hell should we feed him?" (215). When he appears at her bed that night, she rails against him in lengthy fashion for failing Jewish women miserably and being "'an old fraud'" (217). Finally he tells her,

> I have been fed each spring by women. I have tasted the spring and the tears and the blood until something in me wanted to rise up and dance, to roll in the mud. I'm a changed man, Maya.…The Messiah I herald has become the redemption of the earth [218].

Embarrassed at presenting this message at the city's defense meeting, she thinks to herself, "for over half a century I've been spokeswoman for the

Goddess, and here at the crucial moment I turn up with a visitation from an Old Testament prophet. Am I merely getting senile?" (234). They agree that nonviolent resistance is the way, and although many die at the hands of the Stewards, Maya is eventually proven right that the Steward army, which is largely made up of men of color who will never share fully in the society they are fighting for, will defect to the city when they see that people of all races live in harmony, sharing the fruits of their labor. Thus, when Maya is held prisoner and begins talking to the young black and brown men who are her guards, they ask her if she is going to put a spell on them. Her reply is, "You are already under a spell, a spell I'd like to free you from"(460).

When Madrone is able to use her bee-augmented healing powers to help formulate an antidote to the addictive boosters the soldiers are given, their eventual defection is secured. By offering them a place at the table, and not seeing themselves as different from their oppressors, the people of the city force the soldiers into a recognition of their shared humanity, a recognition which benefits both parties.

In this regard, Goddess spirituality does not "conquer" the forces of patriarchy in a militaristic fashion, through overpowering it. Rather, the recognition of immanent value of every living being, a crucial tenet of Goddess spirituality, works as a power-ful lure for the disenfranchised. There is no doubt in the novel that the San Franciscans (those who hold to the sacred principles of immanent divinity) are in a contest, the outcome of which will determine not only their very lives but the efficacy and workability of their belief system. In this way, Starhawk suggests that those who share her beliefs must be willing to stand firm, even to the point of sacrificing their lives for these principles, but that, as Audre Lorde would say, "the master's tools will never dismantle the master's house" (110).

Additionally, Starhawk offers another way to view the continual process of blaming which continues to divide many who would/should be allies. Recall that most of the city's inhabitants, at least of the younger generation, are very ethnically mixed. As such, most have ancestors who were victimized — and most have ancestors who victimized others. At one point Lily, one of the Four Old Women, tells Madrone, "If you can somehow heal yourself, you help to redeem your ancestors. Who were, of course, also the torturers, the murderers, the rapists. We are none of us completely pure" (445). Bird is also made aware of this; as he sits broken down, surrounded by the ghosts of the unquiet dead, he hears the voices of those who were enslaved and destroyed, and he thinks, "*Diosa*, I have too many ancestors, one history of oppression would be enough to inherit. Leave me alone!" But they respond:

> Then listen, listen to us, we are your ancestors too. I sold my daughter to the slavers, I loaded the cattle cars, I smashed the temples of the heathens, I applied the lash, I raped. We are your ancestors, we are the unquiet dead. Feed us, heal us, listen to our stories. Or we will feed on you [458].

This statement is quite similar to Alice Walker's comment that "we are the African and the trader. We are the Indian and the settler. We are the slaver and the enslaved. We are the oppressor and the oppressed" (*Living by the Word* 89). Although he is not ready at that moment to accept this truth, Bird's ability to resist the orders to kill Maya even after he has been tortured causes the Defense Council to lift the only barrier in the city: that of gender, for the Council had been comprised solely of women (482). Although recognizing difficulty, Starhawk indicates that guilt and blame will only carry us so far on the path of change. Ultimately, a vision of unity means that we must each accept individual responsibility for change, for remembering the stories of victimized and victimizers, and for healing their unquietness — the human failings which exist within each of us, and which are more likely to erupt in brutality if we ignore or repress them.

In several ways Starhawk is the most utopian of the writers discussed in this study. The reader of *The Fifth Sacred Thing*, especially one who comes to the novel grounded in her nonfiction works (of which many traces appear in the fiction), is very aware that she not only believes in the moral correctness of her vision of the extrapolation of the tenets of feminist spirituality, but in the ability of humans to actually achieve something very like it if they will believe in the vision. As such, we have come full circle with this leader of the neo–Pagan movement, and with the idea that true magic is changing our minds, and by doing so, our lives. Having this realization we are still hard pressed to say with certainty the genre — utopian fantasy, or just-this-side-of realism — but with this fabulation, to use Barr's comprehensive term, Starhawk provides characters which bridge the divides of color, ethnicity, gender, and sexuality. The novel's closing image, that of the ouroboros, the snake of eternity which swallows its own tail, reminds us that the Goddess' image of healing and unity is an inclusive one.

Wise women see themselves as the ancestresses of future generations, and consider what legacy they are leaving to these future children. Will it be a biophilic vision of interconnectedness? Will it be a world where women refuse to be controlled by men, and demand our rightful places as powerful forces for healing and community on a global scale? Will it be a world where color no longer is used to divide us from creating a life-affirming world?

These four novels illustrate the variety of appearances the wise woman can make, and the range of the effects of her knowledge, skill, and courage on those around her. Thus, readers must be aware of the varied cultural manifestations of healing traditions and women's roles in them if they are to derive the fullest richness from reading such texts. What I find to be a significant component of the richness of these works is the lessons they have to teach us. African American culture draws great strength from hope balanced with a recognition of the realities of historical struggle; this is a useful strategy for all groups in struggle against the various cultural manifestations of power-over. In addition, these novels point to a strong heritage of female healing which can be reclaimed by women and men today, a heritage based on a love of the universe and a valuation of the life force as holy.

Works by European American female authors often end in a narrower focus on the self, and this reflects a particular male western intellectual tradition. While it is true that healing of the self is a first and highly important step, African American female authors write from a historical experience which reminds their readers, whatever their race, of the responsibility of carrying one's knowledge and powers into the community and the world. As Katie Cannon claims, "the womanist writing consciousness does not obscure or deny the existence of tridimensional oppression but rather through full, sharp awareness of race, sex, and class oppression we present the liberating possibilities that also exist" (135). Starhawk, as a Jewish American author, shares this bridge vision. Through the fabulist genres of magical realism, fantasy, and science fiction, writers such as Morrison, Shange, Naylor, and Starhawk remind their readers of the role of the imagination in the creation of reality. If we truly wish to be Goddess-like wise women, then we will use our minds to create what we wish to be and the world in which we wish to live.

6
Conclusion

Cauldron of Changes enriches literary studies by bridging the gap that currently exists between feminist theories of spirituality and literatures which display spiritual feminist practices and beliefs. In addition, this work crosses the traditional boundaries separating popular culture and the academy. Feminist spirituality is a realm which encompasses both theoretical articulations of thealogy and anonymous groups of women who gather in their backyards to honor the Goddess at the full moon.

Fiction displaying feminist spirituality is written by a variety of authors of various races and ethnicities. My work can be seen as a signpost at the crossroads of these divergent paths of spiritual expression, a marker in little–traveled territory. What this marker heralds is nothing less than the articulation of a redemptive vision for the 21st century. Ultimately, these works re–sacralize our perspective of the world, and reconceptualize power as balance and interconnection, not domination.

Female readers derive two benefits from these speculative and magical texts. First, they have the delight of seeing their spiritual selves and struggles represented in written form. Second, they may perceive instruction in the form of the possibilities envisioned and enacted by the protagonists depicted in the fiction. The point is not that the reader picks up a sword or hurls mage fire after a reading, but rather that she might experience growth and change as these texts assist in opening up new worlds of female existence for her. A woman with a talent for ritual leadership may be inspired by the stories of Maya, Rae, Morgaine, and Kassandra; an activist who desires to create healing may draw strength from the balance exhibited by Mama Day, Indigo, Miriam, Rifkind, Moon, and Tarma and Kethry. Others may be drawn to look at aspects of self they never knew they had, as do Anyanwu, Magda, and Aeron. Speculative texts aid in what Eller describes as the project of feminist spirituality:

> creating a new kind of womanhood, one that is not oppressive to [a woman] and does not require that she be disempowered. Her unique gifts as a person are socially validated through feminist spirituality, validated not simply as her quirky traits or even as admirable human powers, but as an expression of her divine femaleness. In the embrace of feminist spirituality, she and many others like her find a way to be "authentically female" and feminist at the same time [Eller 217].

The popularity of speculative fiction may be partly accounted for by this by-product of "textual healing." As Annis Pratt observes, "[i]f our minds and our literature as well as our recent past keep alive such impressive feminine possibilities, maybe we should conclude that the 'culture' that used to seem so overwhelming is but a threadbare coat of tattered clothing covering the sticks of a scarecrow that no longer frightens us" ("Book Reviews" 209).

The spiritual feminist quest is also historical, and paradoxically, mystical as well. As my arguments have indicated, all of the women involved in the feminist spirituality movement can be seen as questing, seeking for knowledge and insights that have been hidden or denied to them throughout patriarchal history, but which resurface and resurge when women seek to end their oppression. Yet this process, including even the varying conceptions of Goddess, evokes in many women tremendous fear and a sense of risk. What does verifying the historical existence of Goddess worship really do for women's liberation? Does celebrating female deity mean that we exalt those qualities which have been systematically devalued, and thus used to denigrate women? Can our cause afford to embrace the mystical and intuitive? Can it afford not to? Through the process of healthy questioning, women who are involved with Goddess–focused spirituality are without a doubt changing their concepts of female and feminine, and therefore of themselves as well.

As Monique Wittig exhorts in *Les Guérillères,* "remember a time when you were not a slave ... or, failing that, invent"(89). Thus, those who are concerned with the female psyche cannot afford to dismiss the importance of the idea of the Goddess in grassroots feminist consciousness as women seek to process new possibilities for themselves as spiritual beings. Seeing beyond the customary bifurcations imposed by the lenses of patriarchal cultures, women increasingly recognize that the struggle for change is a spiritual journey as well ... some would say that the foundation of change is spirituality in practice. And, as Carol Christ has demonstrated in *Diving Deep and Surfacing: Women Writers on Spiritual Quest,* articulating this quest is a challenge taken up by many contemporary women writers, and determining what they have to tell us of our heras or heroines on their paths holds significance for the lives of real women.

Where better than in speculative fiction to propose answers to these questions? Women writers are ensuring that the presence of the Goddess is felt not only at the grassroots but on the bookshelves as well. Women writers of fantastic fiction are exploring the spiritual dimensions of women's lives through their magical storytelling, and in turn are contributing to a further reawakening of female power.

The title of my work, *Cauldron of Changes: Feminist Spirituality in Fantastic Fiction* evokes this dynamic of textual, cultural, spiritual, and personal change. The image of the cauldron also conveys the idea of death and rebirth; both artists and practitioners of feminist spirituality are engaged in the process of creating a mythology which offers new life to women. My study of contemporary novels by American women writers reveals that they have undertaken this task of creating and re-creating feminist mythology which speaks to the spiritual needs of today's women. As Gloria Orenstein points out, this rebirth is only beginning, so we can only speculate about its effect on society. Clearly, the progression of this phenomenon bears close observation.

This book, then, serves to identify this spiritual interaction and its roots in fiction, theory, and practice. However, there are some inherent limitations in its conception and execution. My focus on the novel requires that works of short fiction, poetry, and drama be excluded. In addition, my decision to narrow my choice of authors to Jewish American, European American, and African American women, a decision based largely on my own areas of expertise, excludes the works of other ethnic groups in American and world literature. Also, in my treatment of each theme, I have chosen to deal with a few works in depth, rather than many superficially. I hope these limitations point to areas of further exploration for other spiritual feminist critics and theorists working with literature. Other directions this research may take include looking at these ideas in works by female authors who use male protagonists, and at their appearance or transformation in works by male authors.

The importance of the noncanonical works of genre fiction in my study should serve to emphasize the need to include these works in scholarly studies, as evidenced in the ongoing debate about the literary canon. Genre fiction's exclusion from the ranks of "literature" becomes increasingly questionable, a point argued by Marleen Barr in both *Feminist*

Fabulation: Space/Postmodern Fiction and *Lost in Space: Probing Feminist Science Fiction and Beyond*.

Linked to this aspect of the need for the academy to increase its awareness of contemporary world issues is a little asked question: In what ways does our work as academics better the existence of life on this planet? As a feminist scholar, I view the goal of feminism as a shift in the vision and exercise of power with the ideal that no group wields power over another, whether on the basis of gender, race, class, creed, lifestyle preference, species, or some other factor. The completion of this goal is perhaps not as important as the striving; otherwise, feminism will reproduce the same types of power-over practices which have traditionally been used by men against women, European against non–European, upper class against working class, and so forth.

Speculative fiction offers feminists the opportunity to examine the "fantasy" of the transformative effects of female power. The protagonists I have studied are in motion; they are agents of change who engage the conflicts around them in concrete form. They fight and heal, creating justice in their worlds. The literature offers a bold heroism for women, whether they fight their battles with the pen or with the sword.

The ongoing practice and theorization of feminist spirituality in our contemporary world reveals that many women, and even some men, are willing to embrace a new spiritual paradigm which offers the potential for reforming the perception of our interconnection on this world. To look at the fiction without the practice is to remain blind to the palette of possibilities which awaits the touch of the ordinary human to bring to creative life. These possibilities lie within ourselves, and this study points to the stages explored by women acting as artists and creators of their lives and the world. Our minds are the most important tools of change, and words cast the spells which change our minds.

Notes

Introduction

1. In using the terms fantastic and speculative interchangeably, I am drawing on Shinn's concept of "fantastic" literature (*Worlds Within Women* 2–3) and Barr's definition of "speculative" fiction as inclusive of science fiction, utopian fiction, and fantasy (*Alien to Femininity* xxi), while broadening both to include magical realism. In this sense Barr's later use of the term "fabulation" (*Feminist Fabulation*) is paralleled, while linguistically retaining the sense of insight, speculation, and elements of the fantastic evoked by these terms.

2. "Africentric" is used rather than the more familiar term "Afrocentric" in order to more concretely delineate a focus on the African continent.

3. A discussion of Goddess terminology follows in the next chapter.

4. Author unknown. Heard at a Reclaiming Collective Summer Intensive, 1989.

Chapter 1

1. I broadly define patriarchy as a social system which devalues women / denies them equal rights either through law, religion, economics, social custom, or any of a number of means. Though specific patriarchies differ from each other, they share the quality of domination of women by men, a domination which is often extended to differing groups of "others" (i.e., through racism, homophobia, speciesism, etc.).

2. A good synopsis of the women's spirituality movement from a participant's point of view is given by Diane Stein in *The Women's Spirituality Book* (St. Paul, MN: Llewellyn, 1986), 1–17.

3. In this work I am primarily working with the reaction against Judeo-Christian religious systems and their crucial role in grounding women's (and all others')

oppression. Thus, I omit the role of feminist critique and reform in Islam, Buddhism, and Hinduism. The investigation of goddesses in the cultures from which these religions arose is also a current project of feminist scholars. See Yvonne Haddad and Ellison Findly, eds., *Women, Religion, and Social Change* (Albany, NY: SUNY, 1985), and Carl Olsen, ed., *The Book of the Goddess Past and Present* (New York: Crossroad, 1988).

4. See page 30–31 for my discussion of the capitalization of "Goddess." For these reasons and consistency's sake, I have chosen to use the uppercase except in direct quotations or in references to goddesses, plural.

5. Naomi Goldenberg is generally credited with having coined this term to differentiate feminist spiritual exploration from androcentric theology (*Changing of the Gods* 96).

6. See the entry for "matriarchal" in Maggie Humm's *Dictionary of Feminist Theory* for further discussion of how feminists have used this term in varying ways (132).

7. Many scholars such as Monica Sjöö and Barbara Mor now argue that the first reverences of the human race were towards female divinity, deriving from the seemingly miraculous nature of women's birth-giving capabilities, as well as other cyclical processes.

8. Modern witchcraft generally credits Gerald Gardner (*Witchcraft Today*) with bringing the Craft out of "the broom closet" in 1954 with the repeal of the British Witchcraft laws in 1951, which had included the death penalty. He claimed to have found persons who had carried on the British pagan tradition underground in the manner of groups since the witchhunts. While Aidan Kelly's research indicates that Gardner may not have been completely factual, witchcraft is still growing as a creative religion based on the pagan traditions of Europe, though some would expand location further. Despite distortion by the media, witchcraft is in no way a Satanic practice; Satanism is a Christian heresy, and witchcraft is grounded in the pre–Christian era. Many witches prefer the term Wicca, which comes from the Old English *wicce*, to shape or to bend, because it evokes a slightly less volatile reaction from our predominately Christian culture. Others, like Mary Daly, who include semantic revaluation as part of their political practice, use the word "witch" with great glee.

9. The witches' version of the God is not that of the grey-bearded, almighty patriarchal father. Traditionally, the God is the son (in some mythological instances, brother) who becomes the Goddess' lover, then dies. In most early variations of this myth, the Goddess is viewed as eternal, and the God as dying and resurrecting with the seasons.

Chapter 2

1. Although in *The Book of J* (New York: Vintage, 1991), Harold Bloom argues for a woman as the author of Genesis, this is hardly how that text has been traditionally received.

2. My selection of novels for this chapter is representative, and certainly not inclusive. Spivack's *Merlin's Daughters* and Orenstein's *The Reflowering of the Goddess* refer to other novels with similar strategies.

3. See also Marija Gimbutas, Riane Eisler, Merlin Stone, and others.

4. The sources I have cited in my first chapters deal primarily with the change from Goddess to God worship as it occurred in Europe and the Near and Middle East. Work remains to be done on these changes as they may have occurred in the Far East, the Americas, and Africa. Naturally, these changes happened in various ways and times, with varying accompanying factors.

5. See *The Chalice and the Blade* by Riane Eisler, and *When God Was a Woman* by Merlin Stone.

6. Definitions of magic(k) vary among practitioners, but most include a change in consciousness, as in Dion Fortune's idea that magic "is the art of changing consciousness at will." Many writers on the subject spell magick with the *k* to indicate its difference from prestidigitation, or hocus-pocus.

7. Because of the influence of the Judeo-Christian tradition on western society, many who have rejected the gods of that tradition in favor of goddesses sometimes resort to "bashing" those traditions and deities. Carol Christ's words are a timely warning to those who might fall into anti–Jewish racism by conflating the actions of invading Hebrews with those of their descendants.

8. For example, Barbara Walker, whose contributions to feminist spirituality include such works as *The Woman's Encyclopedia of Myths and Secrets* and *The Woman's Dictionary of Symbols and Sacred Objects,* denigrates the idea of magical or other non-rational practices in her chapter on "Meaning" (*The Skeptical Feminist*). Thus, she restricts her definition of the real to those limits set by patriarchal thinkers.

9. When Luisah Teish came to LSU and presented a lecture which included ritual components, some academic feminists were shocked that she dared to actually talk about African diasporic religion, especially Voodoo, as something she believed in, rather than relegated solely to an intellectual level for dissection. One could also argue that racism played a role in such negative evaluations.

10. See Orenstein, Eisler, and Starhawk.

11. The idea of Maiden, Mother, and Crone as handy divisions of the Goddess, based on the cycles of the moon, occurs in many cultures, possibly as far back as the Stone Age (Sjöö and Mor, *The Great Cosmic Mother* 97–99).

12. See Janet and Stewart Farrar, *The Witches' Goddess* 141.

13. See Starhawk's discussion in *Dreaming the Dark*. Also, the Farrar's *A Witches Bible Compleat* (New York: Magickal Childe, 1984) does an excellent job of tracing survivals of the peasant ritual customs of the British Isles and their uses by contemporary Wiccans.

14. The apple, when sliced crosswise, reveals seeds in the form of a five-pointed star. In Europe the apple and the pentagram are traditional Goddess symbols.

15. Gardnerian witchcraft was the first tradition to enjoy popularity in the later twentieth century, and is named after its founder, Gerald Gardner (see above).

16. So when Charlotte Spivack, in her otherwise insightful chapter on *The Mists of Avalon,* asserts that "the goddess may not be actually worshipped in the modern world" (160), she blatantly ignores Bradley's numerous references to the contemporary feminist/neo–Pagan spiritual movements, and her indebtedness to them. For an interesting discussion of Bradley's personal spirituality, see Carrol L. Fry, "The Goddess Ascending: Feminist Neo-Pagan Witchcraft in Marian [sic] Zimmer Bradley's Novels," *Journal of Popular Culture* 27.1 (1993): 67–80.

17. In *Dreaming the Dark* (1–14), Starhawk employs the terms "power-over" and "power-within" (later, in *Truth or Dare,* she also adds "power with"). These terms have since entered the popular vernacular of spiritual feminists.

18. Bradley's novel has even inspired a group in Texas to formulate a coven, or Wiccan group, based on the presentation of magic and earth spirituality in *The Mists of Avalon*. In addition, Rev. Denise Tracy, a Unitarian Universalist minister, has developed a nine-session study guide to be used with the novel for groups exploring feminist spirituality.

19. For example, see Gerda Lerner's *The Creation of Patriarchy* (New York: Oxford, 1986).

20. For instance, after a group of Methodist and Presbyterian women held a conference on Sophia as a feminine image of divinity, United Methodist Bishop Earl Hunt commented that "This is material which must be eradicated from Christian thinking now."

21. Compare this instance to Camilla's questioning, which I discuss in Chapter 4. The wording of the question is markedly similar on Bradley's part, yet there is a significant difference. Camilla does receive an understanding of how she grew from her experience.

22. For example, the textual exchange represented in Martin Bernal's *Black Athena: the Afroasiatic Roots of Classical Civilization* (New Brunswick: Rutgers,1987) and Mary Lefkowitz and Guy Roger's *Black Athena Revisited* (Chapel Hill, NC: University of North Carolina P, 1996).

23. The collection of essays in which her work appears, *Black Women in Antiquity*, contains several works which argue this point.

Chapter 3

1. Spivack uses the term *feminine* in a fairly traditional Jungian sense, and while I do not share this usage, I replicate it here in quoting from her text.

2. For the story of the meeting of Tarma and Kethry, see "Sword Sworn," in Marion Zimmer Bradley's *Sword and Sorceress III* (New York: Daw, 1986).

3. In Lackey's *Magic's Price* (New York: DAW, 1990), the gay protagonist, Vanyel, is brutally gang raped.

4. Information furnished by the Baton Rouge Stop Rape Crisis Center, 1989. For more detail on acquaintance rape, see Robin Warshaw's *I Never Called It Rape* (New York: Harper & Row, 1988).

5. Need's origins are revealed by Lackey in *Winds of Fate* (New York: Daw, 1991).

6. For example, Joan Slonczewski's *Door into Ocean* (New York: Avon, 1986).

7. Unless one considers magic a technology in itself, another possibility, as Roberts argues in *A New Species* (92–101).

8. Rosemary Edghill's recent *Twelve Treasures* series is an example of the coded examination of racism in fantasy: not through the typical American view of white vs. black, but through interspecies oppression (in this case, elves over humans) whose analysis clearly parallels and invokes the dynamics and language of racism.

9. In fact, most theorists of feminist spirituality view war as a typical male enterprise of power–over, one where (usually) men give birth to death rather than life; Starhawk's *Dreaming the Dark* and *Truth or Dare* cogently discuss war in this fashion. However, in many of the novels I discuss, battle, while viewed with distaste because of its waste, appears as something of a necessity in imperfect worlds, and its appearance may reflect the nonutopian nature of the fiction. Perhaps the reader must simply recognize that there are differences between spiritual feminist theory and fiction, and understand the revolutionary nature of these protagonists, rather than dismiss them as following a masculinist model.

10. Starhawk discusses magic throughout her works; see also Diane Mariechild's *Mother Wit*.

11. Kennealy notes some of her sources, such as *Legendary Fictions of the Irish Celts, The Mabinogion, Magic Arts in Celtic Britain,* and *Preiddu Annwn* in the *Throne of Scone* (379). Each volume of the Keltiad also comes with a glossary and pronunciation guide. Of additional interest to the feminist reader is Jean Markale's *Women of the Celts* (Rochester, Vermont: Inner Traditions, 1986), as well as any works by John and Caitlin Matthews. I have noticed that many contemporary neo–Pagans feel an affinity with Celtic tradition, or are of Celtic ancestry as well.

12. In neo–Pagan jargon one finds the term "techno–Pagan," which refers to contemporary Pagans who advocate technology, especially computer technology, in their lives. Margot Adler discusses this attitude in *Drawing Down the Moon*, 392–98.

13. Compare to Simon James' discussion of Celtic society in *The World of the Celts* (London: Thames and Hudson, 1993) 52–73.

14. Again, we find the Arthurian legend being revised and adapted; as with Bradley's Morgaine, Kennealy's transformation of Morgan le Fay into "St. Morgan" marks a radical change.

15. In creating Arthur's lost treasures, Kennealy conflates traditional Arthurian grail legends with more disparate elements of Celtic folklore.

16. Elves or "fairies" come from the Sidhe found in Celtic mythology. However, some branches of contemporary Wicca claim a close traditional tie to the Celtic background, espousing a "faery" tradition. Starhawk, among other prominent neo–Pagans, was initiated in this path. For recent debates about its teachings, secrecy, and apostasy, see *Green Egg* 27.105 (1994): 68–70.

17. Abortion appears to be one of the few areas concerning which spiritual feminists consistently argue for a woman's ability to use the death–wielding powers of the Crone. As Eller observes, "'Pro–choice' falls right after ecology in spiritual feminists' descriptions of their political agenda" (*Living in the Lap of the Goddess* 194).

18. Baudino the author is also Gael Kathryns, a harpist interested in the healing uses of magical music. See "Whatever It Takes" *Folk Harp Journal* 74 (1991): 41–43.

19. The *Patternist* novels are those concerned with Doro and his various groups of psychic offspring.

Chapter 4

1. *Daughter of the Bright Moon* is stylistically inferior to *The Black Flame*; however, for the reasons noted in the text, I find the character of Rifkind worth discussing in spite of this flaw.

2. Rereading this sentence after hearing on the news (4/27/99) of genetically altered, cloned goats, I can only wish that science understood this principle.

3. This is a popular, anonymous chant widely shared in the movement.

Chapter 5

1. The role of women in regions of Africa under Islamic influence presents a rather different picture. As most slaves came from the relatively non-Islamic western regions of Africa, those traditions are evident in diasporic religious practice.

2. As Judith Ochshorn discusses in *The Female Experience and the Nature of the Divine* (Bloomington: Indiana UP, 1981) when the female is identified with the natural world by a sole focus on her childbearing capabilities, male monotheism deems her inferior and subjugate as well. When this is not the case, then one would expect to find a more elevated position for women in religious practice.

3. In fact, Barr refers to Hurston as a mother of feminist fabulation (*Feminist Fabulation* 22).

4. My operating definition of the term "magical realism" is fiction which displays the workings of that which is usually understood as magical or supernatural, incorporated into an otherwise realistic setting. Morrison herself was initially skeptical of the term: "I was once under the impression that "magical realism" was another one of those words that covered up what was going on. ...It was a way of *not* talking about the politics. ...It was a way of *not* talking about what was in the books. ...I have become indifferent, I suppose ... but I was very alert at the beginning when I heard it" (Davis, Christina 414). Clearly, I do not wish at all to remove political dimensions from the term or discussion, since I, like most spiritual feminists, believe the spiritual is political.

5. I use the term polyamorous here as many within the Pagan community define it: a core group of committed, bonded lovers who may have "satellite" relationships outside the core group.

Annotated Bibliography

Abbey, Lynn. *The Black Flame.* New York: Ace, 1980.
    The second novel with Rifkind as a focal character. Abbey, with a surer hand, gives us a more developed and pivotal Rifkind, one who grows and evolves in her relationship with the Bright One, and upon whom a quest for the Black Flame of the Well of Knowledge is thrust. The novel also explores Rifkind in various maternal roles.

―――. *Daughter of the Bright Moon.* New York: Ace, 1979.
    One of Abbey's earliest novels, Daughter of the Bright Moon details the journey of Rifkind from a healer's apprentice and chieftain's daughter who doesn't fit in with her own tribe, to a stronger and compassionate woman who serves as both healer and warrior for her Goddess, the Bright One. In this work she battles the mage An-Soren to save Dro-Daria.

Adler, Margot. *Drawing Down the Moon: Witches, Druids, Goddess— Worshippers, and Other Pagans in America Today.* Revised ed. Boston: Beacon, 1986.
    A landmark ethnographic study of neo–Pagans in America, reissued with results of her 1985 questionnaire. Covers a variety of groups and traditions, with distinctions clarified between witches and other neo–Pagan groups. Includes a resource guide.

Allen, Paula Gunn. *Grandmothers of the Light: A Medicine Woman's Sourcebook.* Boston: Beacon, 1991.
    A collection of Native American stories drawn from North American oral culture and focusing on women's shamanic tradition. Sections include woman-centered "Cosmogony," "Ritual Magic and Aspects of the Goddess," and "Myth, Magic, and Medicine in the Modern World." Allen's idea of storytelling as "medicine" for the modern world shows a matrifocal way of viewing women, nature, and power.

Allison, Dorothy. "The Future of Female: Octavia Butler's Mother Lode." *Reading Black, Reading Feminist: A Critical Anthology.* Ed. Henry Louis Gates, Jr., New York: Meridian, 1990. 471–78.

Allison offers an overview of Butler's novels, looking particularly at her female protagonists' independence and maternalism.

Andes, Karen. *A Woman's Book of Power: Using Dance to Cultivate Energy and Health in Mind, Body, and Spirit.* New York: Perigee, 1998.
Andes' book is written from the perspective of a personal trainer who decided to slow down the hectic pace of her life and study gentler forms of exercise, such as Middle Eastern dance. The first part covers a basic introduction to Goddess spirituality and dance. The second guides the reader through exercises with left- and right-brain instructions. Part three comments on the future, and includes resources for the reader.

Arewa, Caroline Shola. *Opening to Spirit: Contacting the Healing Power of the Chakras & Honouring African Spirituality.* London: Thorsons, 1998.
What distinguishes this book on the energy centers of the body, the Chakras, is an insistence that spiritual traditions be traced back to African roots.

Barr, Marleen, ed. *Alien to Femininity: Speculative Fiction and Feminist Theory.* New York: Greenwood Press, 1987.
Barr addresses what she sees as a difficulty: the male SF critic's dismissal of feminist SF, and feminist critics' distance from speculative fiction. Here she uses feminist theory to open readings of female SF texts. Divisions are: community, heroism, sexuality, and reproduction.

_____. *Feminist Fabulation: Space/Postmodern Fiction.* Iowa City: University of Iowa Press, 1992.
Barr examines the relationship between postmodernism and contemporary feminist writing, including in her idea of "fabulation" not only science fiction and fantasy, but other fictions as well. Further, she proposes that linking such genres within a study of postmodernism is a way to reclaim canonical space for feminist writers, rather than relegate them to a genre-prescribed ghetto.

_____. *Future Females: A Critical Anthology.* Bowling Green: Bowling Green State University Popular Press, 1981.
One of the earliest anthologies of criticism of women's science fiction, specifically locating itself in the field of feminist literary criticism. The essays cover discussions of women's roles, utopian and distopian influences, women writers, other genres, and a bibliography. Of special interest are contributions by noted SF/F writers Joanna Russ and Suzy McKee Charnas.

_____. *Lost in Space: Probing Feminist Science Fiction and Beyond.* Chapel Hill: University of North Carolina Press, 1993.
Barr expands her terminology to include "feminist fabulation," a concept breaking down the dividing lines between genres of science fiction and postmodernism. In doing so, she hopes to eradicate the barrier of critical isolation which segregates science fiction works from the literary/critical mainstream.

Barstow, Anne Llewellyn. *Witchcraze: A New History of the European Witch Hunts.* San Francisco: Pandora, 1994.
An analysis of the witch hunts which highlights the role of gender in the persecutions. Barstow also connects the role of gender in the witch hunts to the rise of violence against women in contemporary world culture.

Baudino, Gael. *Strands of Starlight*. New York: Signet, 1989.
   The first novel in her Elvin tetralogy, *Strands of Starlight* details the transformation of the wounded healer Miriam into the warrior (soon to be elf) Mirya. She vows revenge on the man who raped her, but in her quest learns complex lessons about healing, forgiveness, and fate. Introduces Baudino's concept of the Goddess as immanent deity capable of being perceived by the individual.

———. *Strands of Sunlight*. New York: Roc, 1994.
   The concluding novel of Baudino's tetralogy. This novel follows the character Natil, an elf, from the past into contemporary American society, where she introduces elfin change in the heart of Denver. Along the way, Baudino offers both sad and wry commentary on society and neo–Paganism, while holding out the hope that the Goddess offers renewal, but no easy answers.

Bernal, Martin. *Black Athena: the Afroasiatic Roots of Classical Civilization*. New Brunswick, NJ: Rutgers University Press, 1987.
   Bernal proposes that the roots of Greek civilization were derived from the Egyptian sources, and that this fact has been systematically ignored or derided due to racism among classical scholars.

Binford, Sally. "Myths and Matriarchies." *The Politics of Women's Spirituality*. Ed. Charlene Spretnak. Garden City, New York: Anchor, 1982. 541–49.
   Evaluates the tenets of those who assert that pre-patriarchal matriarchies have existed, and takes a very pessimistic view. Now, the sources referred to are rather dated in this debate.

Bloom, Harold, and David Rosenberg. *The Book of J*. New York: Vintage, 1991.
   Bloom and Rosenberg argue for a radical reading of the Yahwist (J) as a woman writer. Acknowledging that this could be a fiction, they note the differences between the Yahwistic strain and that of the other editors/redactors. A provocative position.

Bolen, Jean Shinoda. *Goddesses in Everywoman*. New York: Harper & Row, 1984.
   Bolen uses the Greek goddesses as archetypes of various aspects of women's experience, showing how her identification with each aspect affects a woman's relationships, work, parenting, and sexuality.

Bovenschen, Silvia. "The Contemporary Witch, the Historical Witch and the Witch Myth: The Witch, Subject of the Appropriation of Nature and Object of the Domination of Nature." *Articles on Witchcraft, Magic, and Demonology: Witchcraft, Women, and Society*. Vol. 10. Ed. Brian P. Levack. New York: Garland, 1992. 131–67.
   Bovenschen addresses contemporary women's appropriation of the label "witch." She finds such usage disturbing when it obscures the lines between history and mythology. She sees the term as indicative of, and in some ways reinscribing, women's oppression.

Bradley, Marion Zimmer. *City of Sorcery*. New York: DAW, 1984.
   Part of Bradley's Darkover oeuvre, *City of Sorcery* is a "Free Amazon" novel, which details the adventures of particular members of a group of women known to themselves as Renunciates, and more popularly as Free Amazons. Here, Magdalen Lorne, a woman pulled between Terran and Darkovan identities, is drawn to a search for a literal and figurative true sisterhood.

_____. *Firebrand*. New York: Simon and Schuster, 1987.
   Here Bradley does a project similar to her retelling of Arthurian legend — telling the unheard stories of the women involved in classic tales. In this case, Kassandra, the disregarded prophetess, recounts the unvoiced saga of the women and the male egotism of the Trojan war, as well as her own struggle between the voice of the Goddess and that of the God Apollo.

_____. *The Mists of Avalon*. New York: Ballantine, 1982.
   This powerful retelling of Arthurian legend through the eyes of Morgaine is regarded by many as Bradley's masterwork. The novel has even spawned its own study groups and covens. Morgaine's story becomes one of the struggle of a female-focused Pagan life versus the patriarchal Christianity which opposes it.

_____. *The Shattered Chain*. New York: DAW, 1976.
   The story of Magdalen Lorne's infiltration, and eventual joining of, the Free Amazons of Darkover.

_____. *Thendara House*. New York: DAW, 1983.
   Another Free Amazon novel featuring Magdalen Lorne.

Brownmiller, Susan. *Against Our Will: Men, Women, and Rape*. New York: Simon and Schuster, 1975.
   One of the most important early feminist studies of rape as a crime of power rather than sex. Brownmiller does a thorough job of historically contextualizing rape and its power dynamics, showing how we live in a rape culture.

Budapest, Zsuzsanna. *The Goddess in the Office*. San Francisco: Harper & Row, 1993.
   Going through the days of the week, Budapest assigns an energy, goddess, scent, color, and some spells and meditations to help women reclaim their "wild" selves in the sometimes sterile environment of the office. Some spells are lighthearted ("Money Cookies") while others are more serious (a variety of spells against sexual harassment).

_____. *The Grandmother of Time: A Women's Book of Celebrations, Spells, and Sacred Objects for Every Month of the Year*. San Francisco: Harper & Row, 1989.
   As indicated in the title, Budapest offers a guide to year-round celebration and ritual. Although many cultures are represented, West Africa is missing from this potpourri.

The Holy Book of Women's Mysteries: Part I. Los Angeles: Susan B. Anthony Books, 1980.
   The lively and directly feminist Z covers feminist witchcraft, sabbats, esbats, Dianic wicca, Goddess ritual, and psychic abilities.

_____. *The Holy Book of Women's Mysteries: Part II*. Los Angeles: Susan B. Anthony Books, 1980.
   A compendium of blessings, rituals, spells, and commentaries. Includes several sections on her view of the role of men within Dianic philosophy.

Butler, Octavia. *Wild Seed*. New York: Warner, 1988.
   One of Butler's *Patternist* novels, *Wild Seed* tells the story of Anyanwu the shapeshifter and her relationship with Doro, a psychic vampire who steals

people's bodies. Their love/hate relationship is finally transformed when Doro realizes the value of Anyanwu's ethics.

Byrd, Deborah. "Gynocentric Mythmaking in Joan Vinge's *The Snow Queen.*" *Extrapolation* 27 (1986): 234–44.
   Discusses how Vinge departs from the Christian aspects of Hans Christian Anderson's "The Snow Queen," instead relying on ecofeminist ideas, Goddess references, and critiques of patriarchal systems. Byrd argues that the characterization in the novel suffers from the didactic nature of Vinge's theme.

Cannon, Katie Geneva. *Katie's Canon: Womanism and the Soul of the Black Community.* New York: Continuum, 1995.
   Cannon takes Alice Walker's concept of womanism and applies it to theological and literary issues. Primarily she articulates the relevance of womanist Christian practice.

Carson, Anne. *Feminist Spirituality and the Feminine Divine: An Annotated Bibliography.* Freedom, CA: Crossing, 1986.
   This book is now out of print, with very few copies available through interlibrary loan. As the precursor to her second volume, it provides a similarly detailed breakdown of sources prior to 1980.

_____. *Goddesses & Wise Women: The Literature of Feminist Spirituality 1980–1992. An Annotated Bibliography.* Freedom, CA: Crossing, 1992.
   Divides spirituality into feminism, witchcraft, Christianity, and Judaism, fiction, children's literature, audio-visual, and periodicals. Very detailed and comprehensive source for all researchers.

Chernin, Kim. *The Flame Bearers.* New York: Harper & Row, 1986.
   Chernin has also written popular nonfiction works on women's relationship to self and body. Her first novel, *The Flame Bearers*, details the story of Rae Shadmi, who had the unique opportunity to inherit the gift of her grandmother's spiritual legacy, which dates back to the women of Canaan. In her struggle to accept or refuse her legacy, Rae embodies the challenges of women on the path of contemporary feminist spirituality.

Christ, Carol. *Diving Deep and Surfacing: Women Writers on Spiritual Quest.* 2nd ed. Boston: Beacon, 1986.
   The 1986 "Preface to the Second Edition" informs the reader what has changed in Christ's thought since the writing of the first edition — mainly issues of voice and totalizing women's experiences. Also discusses how she and others have used this text in a workshop/class format. The texts covered include works by Kate Chopin, Margaret Atwood, Doris Lessing, Adrienne Rich, and Ntozake Shange as they exemplify key experiences in women's spiritual exploration.

_____. *Laughter of Aphrodite: Reflections on a Journey to the Goddess.* San Francisco: Harper & Row, 1987.
   A book-length work which has as its basis a number of articles previously published by Christ, here expanded and unified. As such, it clearly defines the moments where Christ turned away from male-centered traditions and began exploring the Goddess. While never forsaking her intellectual range and

acumen, in this work Christ seriously begins to develop her personal voice in her thealogy.

_____. *Rebirth of the Goddess: Finding Meaning in Feminist Spirituality*. Reading, MA: Addison Wesley, 1997.
Many of the ideas encountered in this book will be familiar to those who have encountered Christ's many influential works. Her coverage of searching for the Goddess, Goddess history, interconnection, and ethics contains enough background for the new reader, while offering updated contemplations for the returning one. The Christ who finished this work is one who turned her back on academia and toward Greece, and the depth of spiritual growth reflected in that change underlies a freer and more peaceful tone in this work.

Christ, Carol, and Judith Plaskow, eds. *Womanspirit Rising: A Feminist Reader in Religion*. San Francisco: Harper & Row, 1979.
An anthology of essays on women and religion, both traditional forms such as Judaism and Christianity, as well as newer forms such as neo-Pagan witchcraft. Many of the contributors have since become prominent writers on feminist spirituality: Elisabeth Firenza, Starhawk, Z. Budapest, Mary Daly, Naomi Goldenberg, Elaine Pagels, Rosemary Ruether, and Phyllis Trible, among others. As such, the anthology represents the product of a decade's feminist exploration of new and old traditions.

Christ, Carol, and Charlene Spretnak. "Images of Spiritual Power in Women's Fiction." *The Politics of Women's Spirituality*. Ed. Charlene Spretnak. Garden City, New York: Anchor, 1982. 327–43.
Overlaps with material found in *Diving Deep and Surfacing*, as Christ examines the importance of women's stories while noting the distinctiveness of the female spiritual journey in fiction. Christ reviews Chopin and Lessing, and in part two, Spretnak turns to Kingston and Broner.

Cioffi, Kathleen. "Types of Feminist Fantasy and Science Fiction." *Women Worldwalkers: New Dimensions of Science Fiction and Fantasy*. Lubbock: Texas Tech Press, 1985. 83–94.
Cioffi delineates three main types of feminist SF/F genres: the Amazon tale, the bildungsroman, and the "world without men." The Amazon has special physical or mental powers which she uses as a warrior. In the bildungsroman, the protagonist emerges through trials with a clearer identity. The world without men is just that, allowing feminist SF/F writers to explore female-focused ways of being.

Collins, Sheila. "The Personal is Political." *The Politics of Women's Spirituality*. Ed. Charlene Spretnak. Garden City, New York: Anchor, 1982. 362–67.
Collins articulates one of the commonplace statements within feminism, that the personal is political. She traces the development of this feminist idea as a counter to patriarchal dualisms which prevent women's experiences from being political forces.

Creel, Margaret Washington. "Gullah Attitudes Toward Life and Death." *Africanisms in American Culture*. Ed. Joseph Holloway. Bloomington: Indiana University Press, 1990. 69–97.

A study of the Gullah (Carolina sea coast island) peoples of African descent and how traces of African cosmology eventually impacted their attitudes toward Christianity as liberation theology. Creel notes that a sense of community, anthropocentricism, a belief in the spirit world, and mysticism are hallmarks of this African legacy.

Daly, Mary. *Beyond God the Father: Toward a Philosophy of Women's Liberation*. Boston: Beacon, (1973) 1985.
A work which in her "Original Reintroduction" Daly describes as "prophetic in many ways," in that it signaled a break from the reformist feminist foundation of *The Church and the Second Sex*, her first book. Here she re-identifies deity as being, a verb, and writes of what women must do after having declared the death of "God the Father."

———. *The Church and the Second Sex: With a New Postchristian Introduction by the Author*. 1968. Boston: Beacon, 1975.
The "Postchristian Introduction" notes how Daly's thoughts have grown much more radical since the original publication of the work. Here she invokes a reformist position which critiques the church's support of sexual oppression, while calling for feminist change within its structure.

———. *Gyn/ecology: The Metaethics of Radical Feminism*. Boston: Beacon, 1978.
Gyn/Ecology stands out in the Daly oeuvre as the book which signals her departure from the more modulated tones of traditional academic scholarship/writing to a new voice which is more boldly feminist, creative, original. Here she begins her "Spooking," "Sparking," and "Spinning" of an alternative spiritual feminist paradigm, after her discussions of footbinding, suttee, female genital mutilation, witchhunts, and gynecology indict the rapacious misogyny of patriarchal cultures worldwide.

Daly, Mary, and Jane Caputi. *Webster's First New Intergalactic Wickedary of the English Language*. Boston: Beacon, 1987.
A mere summary could never do the *Wickedary* justice, as it is as much a process involving the reader as it is a book. Daly is in peak form as a "Revolting Old Hag" whose purpose is to reclaim and reinvent language to describe reality from a radical feminist perspective. With a flair for alliteration and humor, Daly and Caputi make readers laugh while enlightening them.

Davis, Angela. *Women, Race & Class*. 1981. New York: Vintage, 1983.
A must read as one of the classic studies of the conjunction of racial, sexual, and class oppression. Davis meticulously moves through slavery, abolition, suffrage, and the club movement, tying together previously neglected historical threads, then moves to a discussion of communism, rape, reproductive rights, and housework. This book serves as a corrective to a narrow, elite white feminism.

Davis, Christina. "Interview with Toni Morrison." *Présence Africaine: Revue Culturelle du Monde Noir* (1988). Reprinted in *Toni Morrison: Critical Perspectives Past and Present*. Ed. Henry Louis Gates, Jr., and K. A. Appiah. New York: Amistad, 1993. 412–420.
A wide-ranging interview which touches on Morrison's writing through

Beloved. Other topics include Morrison's relationship to an African tradition, her voice, and her reasons for focusing on black female characters and experience.

Delaney, Janice, Mary Jane Lupton, and Emily Toth. *The Curse: A Cultural History of Menstruation*. 1976. Revised ed. Urbana, IL: University of Illinois Press, 1988.
    One of the first studies of menstruation and its connection with taboos against women, its representation in popular culture and literature, and the marketing of menstrual products. The book also investigates how menstruation and premenstrual syndrome have affected views of women's equality.

de Weever, Jacqueline. *Mythmaking and Metaphor in Black Women's Fiction*. New York: St. Martin's, 1992.
    de Weever argues that African American women writers draw on European, American, and African mythologies in order to form a unique narrative voice which rises to a mythical level. Arguing that scholars have neglected or misread these texts because of sexist and Eurocentric bias, de Weever examines works by Gayl Jones, Paule Marshall, Toni Morrison, Alice Walker, and Toni Bambara.

Downing, Christine. *Goddess: Mythological Images of the Feminine*. New York: Crossroad, 1981.
    Downing looks at the figures of the classical Greek goddesses as various types from an autobiographical Jungian feminist perspective. In doing so, she writes about how women experience these types as stages and struggles in their lives.

_____. "Response to Gloria Orenstein." *Women's Studies Quarterly* 21.1-2 (1993): 38–41.
    Downing responds to Orenstein's cautions about ritual (see below) with an acknowledgment of the power of both teaching and ritual, yet she requests that Orenstein offer more suggestions about the feminist training of women to properly handle ritual powers.

Eagle, Brooke Medicine. *Buffalo Woman Comes Singing*. New York: Ballantine, 1991.
    Medicine Eagle, a Crow woman of mixed heritage, offers her book as a way of gifting people of all races with the heart of Native American earth-centered spirituality, in a way which can foster a spiritual practice of deep ecology. She believes this can be done through reclaiming feminine powers of nurturing and relationship. Included among the various rituals is a section devoted to helping women reclaim menstruation or "moon time" as a sacred time.

Ehrenreich, Barbara, and Deirdre English. *Witches, Midwives, and Nurses: A History of Women Healers*. Old Westbury, New York: The Feminist Press, 1979.
    One of the first sources to make the connection between the European witch-hunts and the targeting of women lay healers by the rising male-dominated profession of medicine. Traces gender-division in the history of medical training.

Eisler, Riane. *The Chalice and the Blade: Our History, Our Future*. San Francisco: Harper & Row, 1987.
    In this controversial work, Eisler asserts that archeological evidence from

Anatolia and other areas indicates that ancient culture has not always been male dominant (the "dominator" model), but rather has exhibited instances of equality, termed the "partnership" model. Eisler presents striking arguments that the alternative to patriarchy was not matriarchy, but a "gylanic" culture.

Eller, Cynthia. *Living in the Lap of the Goddess: The Feminist Spirituality Movement in America.* New York: Crossroad, 1993.
In this study, which combines ethnographic research, interviews, and popular culture, Eller tries to determine why women are attracted to the feminist spirituality movement and what benefits they derive from their involvement. Eller profiles the women involved, the connection with neo–Paganism, ritual, and magic, the stories of Goddess and women's power, and the role of politics. The most thorough study of its kind, truly breaking new ground in the sociology of religion.

Estés, Clarissa Pinkola. *Women Who Run With the Wolves: Myths and Stories of the Wild Woman Archetype.* New York: Ballantine, 1992.
A Jungian analyst and storyteller, Estés takes various tales and interprets them as guides for women's reclaiming of inner spiritual, creative, and psychological freedom.

Farrar, Janet, and Stewart Farrar. *A Witches Bible Compleat.* New York: Magickal Childe, 1984.
A combination of two formerly separate volumes of British witchcraft, as practiced by Gerald Gardner and Alex Sanders, influences on the Farrars. Covers Sabbats, esbats, and other various other rituals such as initiations. Includes origins and customs found in the British Isles.

_____. *The Witches' Goddess.* Custer, WA: Phoenix, 1987.
A nicely tripartite compendium of Goddess information. The first part covers various Goddess "types" such as the Earth Mother and the Moon Goddess. Part Two includes specific rituals for various Greek, Celtic, Egyptian, and Mesopotamian goddesses. The remainder is an A-Z reference on goddesses throughout the world, with short but informative entries and cross-references.

Fox, Selena. *Goddess Communion.* Mt. Horeb, WI: Circle, 1989.
Rituals for goddesses such as Isis, the Sea Goddess, Lady Liberty, Bast, and Mother Earth. Fox is priestess and founder of Circle Sanctuary, a nonprofit spiritual center and nature preserve in Wisconsin.

Frith, Gill. "Women, Writing, and Language." *Introducing Women's Studies: Feminist Theory and Practice.* Eds. Diane Richardson and Victoria Robinson. London: Macmillan, 1993. 151–76.
An overview of the different ways in which feminist criticism explores texts, and the varying "texts" which result from these divergent questions. Frith focuses on different readings of *Jane Eyre* in order to make this point clear to readers initially delving into feminist literary criticism.

Fry, Carrol L. "The Goddess Ascending: Feminist Neo-Pagan Witchcraft in Marian [sic] Zimmer Bradley's Novels." *Journal of Popular Culture* 27.1 (1993): 67–80.

Fry examines Bradley's works as exemplars of an expanding interest in neo-Paganism amongst fantasy writers. Fry is particularly interested in witchcraft, and so includes a brief overview of the craft. He covers Bradley's *Darkover* novels as well as *Mists of Avalon* and *Firebrand*.

_____. "'What God Doth the Wizard Pray to': Neopagan Witchcraft and Fantasy Fiction." *Extrapolation* 31 (1990): 333–46.
Another article which covers a basic introduction to neo-Paganism, and Marion Zimmer Bradley's novels. Katherine Kurtz's novels are also discussed.

Gadon, Elinor. *The Once and Future Goddess: A Symbol for Our Time*. San Francisco: Harper & Row, 1989.
Richly illustrated throughout, Gadon describes various manifestations of the Goddess in ancient culture, then moves to coverage of patriarchal influence on Goddess legend. Finally, she discusses how the Goddess has re-emerged in contemporary culture, with her connections to feminism and ecology.

Gage, Matilda. *Woman, Church, and State: The Original Exposé of Male Collaboration against the Female Sex*. 1893. Watertown, MA: Persephone Press, 1980.
This reprint offers to the contemporary audience one of the classics of feminist spiritual analysis by the sharp and insightful Gage, exploring issues related to the role of Christianity in the suppression of women, issues not explored again until the women's movement of the 60–70s. Gage explores the church's stand on marriage, celibacy, polygamy, witchcraft, and work as inherently sexist and self-defeating for women to follow.

Gardner, Gerald. *Witchcraft Today*. 1954. New York: Magickal Childe, 1982.
First published in 1954, three years after the English laws against witchcraft were repealed, this book broke the silence of the "broom closet" and thrust Gardner into the spotlight as a spokesperson for witches. Although some of the history Gardner presents in the book has come under fire for fabrication and inaccuracy, *Witchcraft Today* still sets forth some basic beliefs of British witches, as well as folklore.

Gearhart, Sally. "Womanpower: Energy Re-Sourcement." *The Politics of Women's Spirituality*. Ed. Charlene Spretnak. Garden City, New York: Anchor, 1982. 194–206.
Writing in 1976, Gearhart already saw the women's movement as being co-opted and defeated. To counter this, she postulated the idea of "re-sourcement" as a turning to new sources for energy in feminist change. This will happen by exploring new ways of knowing (womanspirit) and developing new values based on "woman power." Still relevant today is her summation of, and responses to, the criticism of spirituality as a foundation for change.

Gimbutas, Marija. *The Goddesses and Gods of Old Europe: Myths and Cult Images*. Berkeley: University of California Press, 1982.
In this work Gimbutas argues for the existence of a well-developed Old European civilization during the late Neolithic and Chalcolithic periods. She analyzes the artwork of ritual animal forms, and Goddess and God images.

_____. *The Language of the Goddess: Unearthing the Hidden Symbols of Western Civilization*. New York: Alfred van der Marck Editions, 1988.
Gimbutas patiently walks the reader through a vast array of artwork and

images from the Paleolithic and Neolithic times as she argues for these representations as signs of an egalitarian, peaceful culture of Old Europe. As such, she shows how these symbols constitute a language of a Goddess who lies at the center of life, death, and rebirth.

Gleason, Judith. *Oya: In Praise of the Goddess.* Boston: Shambhala, 1987.
A work on the tempestuous and often ignored West African goddess Oya. A detailed accounting of her worship, rituals, and stories.

Glendinning, Chellis. "The Healing Powers of Women." *The Politics of Women's Spirituality.* Ed. Charlene Spretnak. Garden City, New York: Anchor, 1982. 280–93.
Glendinning begins with a scathing critique of patriarchal medicine, many points of which hold true almost twenty years later. The bulk of the essay concentrates on healing practices which women can reclaim: midwifery, natural childbirth, death guides, laying on of hands, dream healing, and retreats.

Goldenberg, Naomi. *Changing of the Gods: Feminism and the End of Traditional Religions.* Boston: Beacon, 1979.
After concluding that "No Feminist Can Save God" (Chapter 2), Goldenberg turns to Jungian theory, rebel female religious figures, and finally feminist witchcraft as alternatives to replace patriarchal father-gods. She accurately covers both the appeal of and the challenges facing feminist witchcraft as a serious religious alternative.

Govan, Sandra. "Connections, Links, and Extended Networks: Patterns in Octavia Butler's Science Fiction." *Black American Literature Forum* 18.2 (1984): 82–87.
Govan, one of the earliest critics to recognize Butler's talent and introduce her to a wider reading audience, especially in terms of African American readership, here focuses on the issues of power as central to Butler's work. Govan also compares Butler's female protagonists.

_____. "Homage to Tradition: Octavia Butler Renovates the Historical Novel." *MELUS* 13.1-2 (1986): 79–96.
Govan shows how in *Wild Seed* and *Kindred*, Butler renovates the historical novel and the slave narrative through her melding of these genres under the rubric of science fiction and fantasy. As such, Govan recognizes that this allows Butler to introduce black history into a genre/readership not ordinarily exposed to it.

Grant, Jacqueline. *White Women's Christ and Black Women's Jesus: Feminist Christology and Womanist Response.* Atlanta: Scholar's Press, 1989.
Grant argues that while white feminists (to varying degrees) have seen only the sexism involved in Christology, black women have experienced Christ in a liberatory way because of their unique social experience of Christianity as self-affirming. Though sexism is a problem, Grant believes that womanist experience leads to different conclusions about the relevance of Christ than those reached by white feminists.

Greene, Gayle. "Feminist Fiction and the Uses of Memory." *Signs* 16 (1991): 290–321.
Greene considers memory in the fiction of Doris Lessing, Margaret Atwood, Margaret Drabble, Margaret Laurence, and Toni Morrison as it is used in feminist ways to indicate possibilities for change.

Haddad, Yvonne Yazbeck, and Ellison Banks Findly, eds. *Women, Religion and Social Change*. Albany, NY: SUNY, 1985.

    A collection of essays examining women's relationship to religions such as Islam, Hinduism, Buddhism, Spiritualism, and Christianity. Some entries also cover women and religion in relationship to various places, like Nigeria, and historical moments, such as the Chinese revolution.

Hall, Nor. *The Moon and the Virgin: Reflections on the Archetypal Feminine*. New York: Harper & Row, 1980.

    Hall's work comes from the Jungian and Freudian traditions and incorporates their uses of the "feminine" and "masculine." She devotes three chapters to the mother archetype, one to the Amazon, one to the Hetaira (companion) and three on "the feminine as sibyl, wise woman, and poet." Analyzes myths and fairy tales as they present "essential psychic facts."

Heller, Dana A. *The Feminization of Quest Romance: Radical Departures*. Austin: U of Texas Press, 1990.

    Asserting that previous analyses of questing have been skewed by bias toward male/patriarchal experience, Heller undertakes an examination of female-defined questing in a sampling of women's novels. She finds that these heroes are heroic to the degree they break from social roles and explore alternatives which have repercussions for all humans.

The Heresies Collective, eds. "The Great Goddess." 2nd ed. of *Heresies* 2.1 Issue 5 (1982): 1–136.

    The editors note in the preface to the 2nd edition that the first printing sold out in a few months, becoming a classic. This re-issue is a cornucopia of art, poetry, tales, and scholarship on a wide variety of Goddess-related issues. Writers such as Merlin Stone, Carol Christ, Kay Turner, Gloria Orenstein, and many others comment on art, history, ritual, women's bodies, and other spiritual issues.

hooks, bell. *Feminist Theory from Margin to Center*. Boston: South End, 1984.

    Hooks (a.k.a. Gloria Watkins) postulates a type of feminism (she prefers the term *feminist movement*) which comes from the margin: "part of the whole but outside the main body." Linking race, sex, and class, she addresses issues of sisterhood, feminist men, work, education, violence, and parenting. She is concerned with broadening the base movement of feminism.

——. *Sisters of the Yam: Black Women and Self-Recovery*. Boston: South End, 1993.

    One of the first self-help books aimed at an African American readership, and promoting a black feminist viewpoint. Hooks covers affirmations, work, stress, addictions, beauty, loss, and passion in African American women's lives.

——. *Talking Back: Thinking Feminist, Thinking Black*. Boston: South End, 1989.

    A collection of twenty-four short essays addressing a wide variety of issues, from the experience of being black and female in graduate school, to her choice of a pseudonym. A good choice for the reader wanting a quick overview of hooks' political stance.

Humm, Maggie. *The Dictionary of Feminist Theory.* 2nd ed. Columbus, OH: Ohio State UP, 1995.
> A guide to the terminology of feminist theory with an interdisciplinary basis, drawing on the fields of the arts, history, psychology, psychoanalysis, and sociology. Humm also includes references to important figures in feminist theory and theorists whose work has influenced key feminist thought. Interestingly, some of the additions in the new edition come from students who brought the most difficult jargon terms from their professors' lectures.

Iglehart, Hallie. "The Unnatural Divorce of Spirituality and Politics." *The Politics of Women's Spirituality.* Ed. Charlene Spretnak. Garden City, New York: Anchor, 1982. 404–14.
> Iglehart contends that the opposition of spirituality and politics that some feminists perceive is, in fact, a patriarchal construct predicated on hierarchical dualism. Sections on meditation and healing show how women can address other components of their oppression.

James, Simon. *The World of the Celts.* London: Thames and Hudson, 1993.
> A basic introduction to the Celts of both the British Isles and the continent. Includes over 300 illustrations offering insight into many aspects of culture, especially Celtic aesthetics.

Jules-Rosette, Bennetta. "Women in Indigenous African Cults and Churches." *The Black Woman Cross-Culturally.* Ed. Filomina Chioma Steady. Cambridge, MA: Schenkman Publishing, 1981. 185–207.
> Covers women in both leadership roles and unofficial but important positions. She also notes relationships to independence movements, as well as women's experience in ritual, conversion, leadership, and family.

Kaler, Anne K. "Bradley and the Beguines; Marion Zimmer Bradley's Debt to the Beguinal Societies in her Use of Sisterhood in her Darkover Novels." *Heroines of Popular Culture.* Ed. Pat Browne. Bowling Green, OH: Bowling Green State UP, 1987. 70–90.
> As the title implies, Kaler asserts that Bradley relied a great deal on the idea of the Beguines, a medieval women's collective society, as a model for the Renunciates or Free Amazons of her Darkover world.

Kathryns, Gael. "Whatever It Takes." *Folk Harp Journal* 74 (1991): 41–43.
> Kathryns is also Gael Baudino, fantasy writer (see above). Here she writes in a nonfiction mode as a harper who uses her music to produce healing. This article covers her recording of music for an MS patient.

Kelly, Aidan, ed. *Cults and New Religions: Neo-Pagan Witchcraft I.* New York: Garland, 1990.
> Kelly's introduction, in which he argues that virtually all the branches of witchcraft celebrated in neo–Paganism can be seen as Gardnerian, has earned him some criticism within the community. However, his point that the invention of religion does not make it less viable, is often overlooked. The volume consists of reprinted pamphlets (in my opinion, hardly the most representative) concerning witchcraft.

Kennealy, Patricia. *The Copper Crown.* 1964. New York: Signet, 1986.

This *Keltiad* novel details the meeting of Kennealy's spacefaring Kelts with their long-lost Terran relatives. The war with the Fomori resumes, this time with Coranian aid. Aeron decides to leave and search for the lost treasures of Arthur.

———. *The Silver Branch.* New York: Signet, 1989.

Although published after the other two *Keltiad* novels, *The Silver Branch* occurs first in the chronology of the "Tales of Aeron." Here we follow Aeron through her magical and military training, to the situation of war with the Fomori, and her eventual crowning following the assassination of her parents and husband.

———. *The Throne of Scone.* 1986. New York: Signet, 1987.

The concluding volume in the "Tales of Aeron" trilogy follows Aeron on her search for the treasures of Arthur. Her successful quest, and struggle to master the power they hold, is at the heart of this story.

Kennealy-Morrison, Patricia. *The Deer's Cry.* New York: Harper Prism, 1998.

This most recent of her *Keltiad* novels finally gives readers the history of her Kelts before they left earth. The conflict lies between Pagan Brendan and Christian Patraic (Patrick). Her "Notes on the Text" is a no-holds barred commentary on the writing of the novel which elucidates her opinions on Celtic and Christian history.

Koppelman, Susan. *Old Maids: Short Stories by Nineteenth Century U. S. Women Writers.* Boston: Pandora, 1984.

A collection which reveals that the stereotype of the "old maid" is instead rendered in women's writing as one of the few independent roles open to women in the nineteenth century. Includes headnotes detailing the publishing history of each author, and relevant biographical information.

Kovel, Joel. *History and Spirit: An Inquiry into the Philosophy of Liberation.* Boston: Beacon, 1991.

Seeing spirituality and "emancipatory," Kovel asserts that spirituality can be a way of uniting society and healing it of the various splits caused by the divisions of race, class, and gender. As such he sees spirit as distinct from specific religious traditions. Largely written from a psychoanalytic and Marxist orientation.

Kristensen, Randi Gray. "Rights of Passage." Dissertation, LSU 2000.

Kristensen's dissertation is a study of selected novels of African American and African Caribbean women writers as "maroon" novels. Maroon novels detail ways in which women of African descent have found ways of creating mental resistance to slavery and established means of conserving black interiority by "reconstructing self and community in an alternative structure."

Lackey, Mercedes. *Magic's Price.* New York: DAW, 1990.

A novel of Valdemar, where the Herald-mage Vanyel sacrifices himself to save the land. Lackey presents homosexuality positively in this and related works.

_____. *The Oathbound.* New York: DAW, 1988.
   Book 1 of the *Vows and Honor* duology is the first novel featuring Tarma, the warrior, and Kethry, the sorceress. Here they are drawn into battle with the demon Thalkarsh, and learn to trust each other, sharing strengths and weaknesses.

_____. *Oathbreakers.* New York: DAW, 1989.
   Here the duo go in search of the disappeared mercenary Idra. In doing so, they become involved in determining the future of the kingdom of Rethwellan. Here Kethry also finds the man who will be her husband, and thus help her to restart Tarma's clan.

_____. Personal Interview. March 1989.
   Conducted by Timothy Whittemore at a SF/F con in Baton Rouge, Louisiana. Lackey disclaims the term feminist, preferring to consider herself a humanist.

_____. *Winds of Fate.* New York: DAW, 1991.
   The first volume of the *Mage Winds* trilogy follows Elspeth, Princess, and Herald, as she seeks out forgotten mage-lore in hopes of defending Valdemar from Ancar of Hardorn.

Larrington, Carolyne, ed. *The Feminist Companion to Mythology.* London: Pandora, 1992.
   A collection of essays on goddesses of the Near East, Asia, Europe, Oceana, and America, as well as a section on the role of the Goddess in the twentieth century.

Lauter, Estella. *Women as Mythmakers: Poetry and Visual Art by Twentieth-Century Women.* Bloomington: Indiana UP, 1984.
   Lauter examines several poets and visual artists for suggestions that they are offering new archetypes reflecting contemporary women's lives. As such, she breaks from the view of archetypes as static, and instead points to the influence of collective culture.

Lefanu, Sarah. *Feminism and Science Fiction.* Bloomington: Indiana UP, 1989.
   Lefanu examines what the genre of science fiction has to offer feminist writers that other genres do not, and the degree to which it is a viable medium of political interrogation. The first section of the book is an overview of a variety of women writers and looks at such issues as heroinism, amazons, and utopias. The second half focuses on James Tiptree, Jr., Ursula Le Guin, Suzy Charnas, and Joanna Russ.

Lefkowitz, Mary R., and Guy MacLean Rogers, eds. *Black Athena Revisited.* Chapel Hill, NC: University of North Carolina Press, 1996
   A compendium of essays which respond to issues raised by Martin Bernal's *Black Athena* (see above). Overall, the tenor of the essays is one of refutation of Bernal's main points.

Lerner, Gerda. *The Creation of Patriarchy.* 1986. New York: Oxford UP, 1987.
   A detailed, well-researched account of Lerner's argument that the sexual subordination and enslavement of women gave rise to the idea of private

property and class society, slavery of other groups, and the institutionalized subordination of women even as they retained some roles of power. Lerner asserts that the presence of Goddess worship and priestesses did not circumvent this process.

Levy, Helen Fiddyment. "Lead on with Light." *Fiction of the Home Place* (1992). Reprinted in *Gloria Naylor: Critical Perspectives Past and Present*. Ed. Henry Louis Gates, Jr., and K. A. Appiah. New York: Amistad, 1993. 263–84.
    Levy discerns in Naylor's fiction a movement toward the depiction of community, especially community between women. Drawing on Elaine Showalter, Levy sees Naylor moving from imitation, to protest, to an "authentic voice."

Lorde, Audre. *Sister Outsider: Essays and Speeches*. Trumansburg, NY: Crossing Press, 1984.
    In this collection of fifteen essays Lorde proves her gift with prose to be equal to that of her poetry. Lucid and incisive throughout, several of the essays are already classics: "Uses of the Erotic: the Erotic as Power" and "The Master's Tools Will Never Dismantle the Master's House," for example.

McKinney-Johnson, Eloise. "Egypt's Isis: The Original Black Madonna." *Black Women in Antiquity*. Revised ed. Ed. Ivan van Sertima. New Brunswick: Transaction Publishing, 1992. 64–71.
    McKinney-Johnson elaborates on the many titles and ascriptions of Isis, and shows how ancient writers recorded the spread of her worship, especially through the Roman empire. She goes further by linking her with other deities, and tracing her iconography to that of images of the Madonna.

Mariechild, Diane. *Mother Wit: A Feminist Guide to Psychic Development*. Freedom, CA: Crossing, 1981.
    A work by a coven leader and practicing psychotherapist which includes a number of meditations and visualizations designed to help women expand their self-healing and psychic abilities. Concludes with an introduction to witchcraft.

Markale, Jean. *Women of the Celts*. 1972. Trans. A. Mygind, C. Hauch, and P. Henry. Rochester, Vermont: Inner Traditions International, Ltd.,1986.
    Markale first gives an overview of the roles of women in Celtic society, including a detailed discussion of marriage customs and laws. The greater portion of the book focuses on themes found in Celtic myth, such as "The Submerged Princess" and "The Great Queen." She then concludes by commenting on the possibilities such information holds forth for contemporary society.

Martin, Judith G. "Why Women Need a Feminist Spirituality." *Women's Studies Quarterly* 21.1-2 (1993): 106–20.
    Martin wishes to explain why many feminists find patriarchal religions and practices unsatisfying or even harmful, and turn instead to feminist spirituality for a new paradigm. That this essay, published in 1993, iterates basic issues articulated since the 1970s, reflects the continued resistance by some feminists to spiritual ideas.

Mbiti, John. *African Religions and Philosophy.* Revised ed. New York: Anchor, 1990.
   A classic text covering some basic aspects of the variety of African religions: time, god, nature, worship, the spirit world, marriage and kinship, the afterlife, magic, ethics, and religious figures. In the preface he notes that his revised edition does not attempt to survey all of the new materials written in the two decades since the original publication.

Mestel, Sherry, ed. *Earth Rites. Vol. 2: Rituals.* 1978. New York: Earth Rites Press, 1981.
   Although the volume is subtitled rituals, the book also contains poems, invocations, spells, and photos of artwork and ritual performances. The overall appearance of the text is very "low-tech," which suits the text's appearance as an early hands-on collection.

Morgan, Robin. *Going Too Far: The Personal Chronicle of a Feminist.* New York: Random House, 1977.
   Morgan's chronicle makes for good, on the scenes reading for a generation of feminists who missed the first wave of radical feminist protest. Morgan further concentrates on defining radical feminism, and concludes by offering comments on "metaphysical feminism."

Morrison, Toni. *Beloved.* New York: Knopf, 1987.
   What many consider Morrison's masterwork, the Pulitzer-winning novel stands as one of the most memorable renditions of the effects of slavery and its haunting presence in American society. Sethe's struggle to deal with the returned spirit of the daughter she killed rather than see enslaved forms the center of the novel.

Mulira, Jessie Gaston. "The Case of Voodoo in New Orleans." *Africanisms in American Culture.* Ed. Joseph Holloway. Bloomington: Indiana UP, 1990. 34–68.
   Mulira traces voodoo to its Dahomean roots. She observes that the magical side of voodoo has often overshadowed the religious side in the popular imagination. She focuses on New Orleans and the lives of several famous priestesses, including the legendary Marie LeVeau.

Murdock, Maureen. *The Heroine's Journey.* Boston: Shambhala, 1990.
   Murdock details what she finds to be woman's unique heroic journey. It particularly applies to those women who feel unfulfilled after having followed male models of success. She argues for the need for women to heal the split from their deep feminine selves. Her perspective is that of a Jungian feminist.

Murphy, Patrick D. "Feminism Faces the Fantastic." *Women's Studies* 14 (1987): 81–90.
   Another essay observing the unique opportunities fantastic fiction offers feminist writers. Murphy discusses Suzette Elgin's *Native Tongue,* Mary Mackey's *The Last Warrior Queen,* and Joanna Russ' *Extra (Ordinary) People.*

Naylor, Gloria. *Mama Day.* New York: Vintage, 1988.
   Naylor's third novel takes us to the magical place of Willow Springs, home of the mystical and powerful Mama Day, who serves the community through both traditional healing and spellcraft. Here she battles for the life of her

grandniece Cocoa, whose husband George must learn the roles of sacrifice and belief in order to save his wife.

Ochshorn, Judith. *The Female Experience and the Nature of the Divine.* Bloomington: Indiana UP, 1981.
Ochshorn suggests that the rise of monotheism is largely responsible for the suppression of women's power within organized religions. As such, the Judeo-Christian tradition breaks from its Near Eastern counterparts and solidifies women's exclusion from roles of power.

Olson, Carl, ed. *The Book of the Goddess Past and Present: An Introduction to the Religion.* New York: Crossroad, 1988.
A collection of essays on various goddess in the ancient world from Mesopotamia, India, Japan, North America, and Greece.

Orenstein, Gloria. "Letter to Christine Downing." *Women's Studies Quarterly* 21.1-2 (1993): 42–47.
Orenstein address some of the points in her original essay which Downing found "murky" or "reticent." She also offers the practical suggestion of teacher follow-up or availability for those students affected by feminist ritual used in the classroom.

_____. "The 'Problematics' of Writing about Sacred Ritual and the Spiritual Journey." *Women's Studies Quarterly* 21.1-2 (1993): 22–37.
Orenstein breaks academic taboo by daring to write about her experiences with a Samiland shaman and asserting their reality and the reality (and dangers) of working with the spirit world with only partial knowledge. She cautions feminists who want to experiment with ritual in the classroom without having this understanding. Her essay is striking in that she breaches the ordinary distance even feminist scholars often maintain from their subjects.

_____. *The Reflowering of the Goddess.* Elmsford, NY: Pergamon, 1990.
In this work Orenstein explores her concept of "feminist matristic" art, which stresses the conjunction of radical feminism and the Goddess. After discussing connections to ecofeminism, shamanism, and madness, she covers examples of feminist matristic artists in both visual and literary forms, as well as performance art.

Passmore, Nancy F. W. "A Consciousness Manifesto." *The Politics of Women's Spirituality.* Ed. Charlene Spretnak. Garden City, New York: Anchor, 1982. 163–71.
Passmore sees science as beginning to merge with metaphysics. She delineates a brief history of scientific thought, showing how it frequently undergoes changes and upsets. Passmore suggests that women can use this new merging of metaphysics and science as a way to valorize traditionally non-linear ways of knowing and interacting with the world.

Pratt, Annis. *Archetypal Patterns in Women's Fiction.* Bloomington: Indiana UP, 1981.
As the title suggests, Pratt draws on Jungian literary analysis to look for recurring patterns in women's fiction. Since she feels women's experience differs from men's, their literary patterns differ as well. Pratt looks at development, marriage, social protest, eros, solitude, and other patterns. A work often cited in the literature.

___. "Book Reviews." *Signs* 14.1 (1988): 204–9.
> Pratt reviews four works: Esther Labovitz's *The Myth of the Heroine*, Bonnie St. Andrew's *Forbidden Fruit*, Charlotte Spivack's *Merlin's Daughters*, and Thelma Shinn's *Worlds Within Women* (the latter two are included in this bibliography). One commonality she finds among these works is their ability to locate female power and resistance within women's fiction.

Richardson, Marilyn. *Black Women and Religion: A Bibliography*. Boston: G. K. Hall, 1980.
> Richardson covers works dealing with African American women's religious involvement, mostly within Christianity. The bibliography has some annotations, and covers books, articles, literature, music, art, and audio-visual materials.

Roberts, Robin. *A New Species: Gender and Science in Science Fiction*. Urbana, IL: University of Illinois Press, 1993.
> Tracing feminist science fiction from Mary Shelley onward, Roberts argues that science fiction has always provided a unique locus for the examination of female power, one that has been appropriated for feminist analysis of gender. Additionally, she offers chapters on the relevance of the artwork in the "pulps," female utopian literature, equality, Doris Lessing, and postmodernism.

Robinson, Beverly. "Africanisms and the Study of Folklore." *Africanisms in American Culture*. Ed. Joseph Holloway. Bloomington: Indiana UP, 1990. 211–24.
> After noting debate about the meaning of the term "folklore," as well as the unique problems inherent in a study of African influences in African American folklore, Robinson discusses tales, terms, and folk beliefs, including healing.

Rosinsky, Natalie. *Feminist Futures: Contemporary Women's Speculative Fiction*. Ann Arbor, MI: UMI Press, 1984.
> Rosinsky looks at speculative fiction by women writers in order to understand the influence of feminism on the development of the genre. She also examines how differing feminist belief systems (androgyny vs. essentialism) are represented in the fiction.

Ruether, Rosemary Radford. *Sexism and God-Talk: Toward a Feminist Theology*. Boston: Beacon, 1985.
> Ruether's pivotal work which lays out the issues of feminist theology from the viewpoint of one who believes that the church can be revised from a feminist perspective. She also indicates that Christianity has liberatory aspects which can be applied to issues such as exploitation of both land and people.

Rush, Anne Kent. *Moon, Moon*. Berkeley: Random House, 1976.
> A feminist text which purports to "remythologize" the moon. Rush first considers our current scientific perspective of the moon, then covers the moon as seen by ancient cultures. She next discusses the role of the moon in contemporary feminist spirituality. Interposed throughout are lunar art and lists of names associated with the moon.

Sams, Jamie. *The Thirteen Original Clan Mothers.* San Francisco: Harper, 1993.
   Drawing on knowledge passed down from her Kiowa grandmothers and further reclaimed through a study of women's medicine teachings, Sams offers the Thirteen Original Clan Mothers as each representing a truth, which she then associates with a lunar month. Each of these spiritual truths offers a way to connect with a female healing principle.

Saunders, James. "The Ornamentation of Old Ideas: Naylor's First Three Novels." The Hollins Critic 27 (1990). Reprinted in *Gloria Naylor: Critical Perspectives Past and Present.* Ed. Henry Louis Gates Jr., and K. A. Appiah. New York: Amistad, 1993. 249–62.
   Saunders traces literary borrowing in Naylor's early works. Specifically he locates her references to Ann Petry, Dante, and Shakespeare.

Scott, Patricia Bell. "Debunking Sapphire: Toward a Non-Racist and Non-Sexist Social Science." *All the Women Are White, All the Blacks Are Men, But Some of Us Are Brave.* Ed. Gloria Hull, Patricia Bell Scott, and Barbara Smith. New York: Feminist Press, 1982. 85–92.
   Scott critiques the stereotypes of black women that pervade the scholarship in social sciences. Myths of black matriarchy, class bias, racist and sexist assumptions flaw most studies about black women. *But Some of Us Are Brave,* co-edited by Scott, Hull, and Smith, was one of the first collections of its kind, covering a variety of fields and offering bibliographies and syllabi.

Sered, Susan. *Priestess, Mother, Sacred Sister: Religions Dominated by Women.* New York: Oxford UP, 1994.
   Rather than focusing on how religious structures often disempower women, Sered studies examples of religious practices in which women hold positions of power. A large portion of her analysis pertains to matrifocality and motherhood. Gender ideology and concepts of immanent deity also figure prominently.

Shaffer, Carolyn. "Spiritual Techniques for Re-Powering Survivors of Sexual Assault." *The Politics of Women's Spirituality.* Ed. Charlene Spretnak. Garden City, New York: Anchor, 1982. 462–69.
   Shaffer concludes that rape victims must find empowerment on spiritual as well as emotional and physical levels, in order to touch an inner core of strength which lies beyond victimization. She covers a variety of rituals used by rape survivors as means of healing.

Shange, Ntozake. *Sassafras, Cypress, and Indigo.* New York: St. Martin's, 1982.
   A beautiful and magical novel detailing the lives of three sisters: Sassafras, a poet and weaver; Cypress, the dancer; and Indigo, the healer. Shange's linguistic play is evident, and she combines letters, poems, recipes, and spells in this remarkable work.

Shinn, Thelma. "The Wise Witches: Black Women Mentors in the Fiction of Octavia E. Butler." *Conjuring: Black Women, Fiction, and Literary Tradition.* Ed. Marjorie Pryse and Hortense J. Spillers. Bloomington: Indiana UP, 1985. 203–15.
   Drawing on Annis Pratt's idea of rebirth, grail, and witchcraft archetypes as dominating women's fiction, Shinn examines each of Butler's novels for traces

of these mythical patterns. In doing so she draws on the idea of the witch as a wise woman, and notes that Butler's black witches use their gifts to help others.

_____. *Worlds Within Women: Myth and Mythmaking in Fantastic Literature by Women.* New York: Greenwood, 1986.
Shinn studies ancient cultural and science-fiction mythologies as they inform women's fantastic literature. As such, she looks at how these authors both use and revise myth in their writing. Like a number of other critics, Shinn sees speculative fiction as a genre uniquely suitable for feminist revision and creation. Includes discussion of works by over twenty authors.

Showalter, Elaine. *A Literature of Their Own: British Women Novelists from Brontë to Lessing.* London: Virago, 1977.
Rather than looking at female British novelists as they stand in relation to male literary tradition, Showalter's pivotal study argues for looking at these novelists as they form a uniquely female literary subculture. In addition to major writers, Showalter also discusses lesser-known novelists.

_____. *Sister's Choice: Tradition and Change in American Women's Writing.* New York: Oxford UP, 1991.
While rejecting the idea of a homogeneous American women's literary tradition, or even of an American feminist criticism, Showalter looks at various themes, revisions, and images which have occurred across a broad range of women's writing in the U.S. She includes in-depth analyses of *Little Women*, *The Awakening*, and *House of Mirth*.

Sjöö, Monica, and Barbara Mor. *The Great Cosmic Mother: Rediscovering the Religion of the Earth.* San Francisco: Harper & Row, 1987.
From an original pamphlet by Monica Sjöö entitled *The Ancient Religion of the Great Cosmic Mother of All*, through several rewrites into this American edition, co-authored with Mor, the authors stress the primacy of Goddess religion as the original religion of humanity, and indict patriarchal culture and religion as misogynistic, and life and woman-threatening. Illustrations alternate reproductions of ancient art with Sjöö's original works.

Slonczewski, Joan. *A Door into Ocean.* New York: Avon, 1986.
A tale of the female, peaceful, and ecologically sound culture of the Sharers of Shora, as they are attacked by the militaristic, hierarchical culture of Valedon.

Smith, Andy. "For All Those Who Were Indian in a Former Life." *Ecofeminism and the Sacred.* Ed. Carol J. Adams. New York: Continuum, 1993. 168–71.
Smith decries the tendency of New Age feminist appropriation of Native American cultures and religion while refusing to aid native cultures in their struggles, or to form ties with actual communities rather than romanticized ideas of Native peoples. This makes a mockery of what Native Americans have had to experience in terms of cultural exploitation and repression.

Smith, Jeanette C. "The Role of Women in Contemporary Arthurian Fantasy." *Extrapolation* 35 (1994): 130–44.
Covers the minimal, stereotypical roles of women in traditional Arthurian

literature, then turns to an examination of feminist retellings of Arthurian tales. She finds four themes typical: Goddess spirituality, independent women, female narrative focus, and self-directed sexual life.

Sojourner, Sabrina. "From the House of Yemanja: the Goddess Heritage of Black Women." *The Politics of Women's Spirituality*. Ed. Charlene Spretnak. Garden City, New York: Anchor, 1982. 57–63.
    After discussing the presence of several mother Goddess figures among African cultures, Sojourner writes about the history of the Libyan Amazons. She rounds out the essay by discussing the renewed interest in Yoruba religion among African American women, and with a call for further scholarship.

Spivack, Charlotte. *Merlin's Daughters: Contemporary Women Writers of Fantasy*. New York: Greenwood, 1987.
    Spivak postulates that one reason for the dismissal of fantasy literature by many critics is its relationship to the areas typically deemed feminine: the nonlinear, dreams, and the unconscious. Examining the works of ten female fantasy writers such as Andre Norton, Ursula Le Guin, and Marion Zimmer Bradley, Spivak argues for the genre's receptivity to feminist ideas. One of the few books solely covering feminist fantasy, rather than science fiction.

Spretnak, Charlene. *Lost Goddesses of Early Greece: a Collection of Pre-Hellenic Mythology*. Berkeley: Moon Books, 1978.
    Spretnak researched and composed "new" mythic stories designed to capture the prepatriarchal nature of early Goddess figures. Full-page illustrations accompany each myth.

_____, ed. *The Politics of Women's Spirituality: Essays on the Rise of Spiritual Power Within the Feminist Movement*. Garden City, New York: Anchor, 1982.
    An impressive, central collection which was one of the first of its kind to articulate the interest in spirituality as a means of challenging patriarchal oppression. The anthology includes essays from many of the women who have gone on to become major figures in feminist spirituality, while also including lesser-known writers.

Stange, Mary Z. "The Once and Future Heroine: Paleolithic Goddesses and Popular Imagination." *Women's Studies Quarterly* 21.1-2 (1993): 55–66.
    Incorporates a discussion of Jean Auel's Ayla into her critique of goddess scholarship which postulates an essentialist view of women as totally nonviolent and nurturing. Instead, she argues, the role of women as hunters is reflected in such goddess figures as Artemis.

Stanton, Elizabeth Cady. *The Woman's Bible*. 1895. New York: Arno Press, 1972.
    Much like her contemporary Matilda Gage, Stanton realizes that patriarchal religion is a cornerstone of women's oppression. Selecting books from the Old and New Testaments, Stanton annotates their contents with commentary on how each text contributes to the subordinate status of women.

Starhawk. *Dreaming the Dark: Magic, Sex, & Politics*. Boston: Beacon, 1982.
    Starhawk's master's thesis for the feminist therapy program at Antioch University West has become an oft-cited link between neo–Paganism and feminist activism. As the subtitle indicates, *Dreaming the Dark* refutes the claim

of some feminists that spirituality is apolitical. Defines her concepts of "Power-Over" and "Power From Within," and comments on groups and rituals.

_____. *The Fifth Sacred Thing*. New York: Bantam, 1993.
A visionary novel of how the principles of ecofeminist spirituality could change the future. Putting Starhawk's nonfiction theories about magic, spirit, and activism into the garb of well-constructed characters and compelling visions of the future, this work forces the reader to think about the world we craft with each day's choices.

_____. *The Spiral Dance*. Tenth Anniversary ed. San Francisco: Harper & Row, 1989.
One of the most widely read classics of neo–Paganism, here in a tenth anniversary version with a commentary on how Starhawk's ideas have changed and developed in the years since original publication. Includes meditations, rituals, and discussions of the Wiccan Goddess and God.

_____. *Truth or Dare: Encounters with Power, Authority, and Mystery*. San Francisco: Harper & Row, 1987.
Starhawk examines the three types of power: power-over, power from within, and power-with. She demonstrates how the psychology of warfare is entrenched within individuals and groups, and then devotes chapters to how we can, singularly and together, break free from this negative model and operate from consensus.

_____. *Walking to Mercury*. New York: Bantam, 1997.
Starhawk's prequel to *The Fifth Sacred Thing*, detailing the life of Maya from youth to middle age. Starhawk's novel investigates the often uneasy relationship between mothers and daughters; friendship, love, and forgiveness; as well as the ideals and excesses of the 60s and 70s.

Stein, Diane, ed. *The Goddess Celebrates: An Anthology of Women's Rituals*. Freedom, CA: Crossing Press, 1991.
A collection of various rituals by a wide variety of women, including such notables as Z Budapest, Starhawk, and Carol Christ. In addition to explanations of general ritual practice are specific rituals for mourning, menopause, sexual abuse, cesareans, regular births, and handfastings (weddings).

_____. *Stroking the Python: Women's Psychic Lives*. St. Paul, MN: Llewellyn, 1988.
An accessible book for the lay person who wishes to develop an understanding of various psychic phenomena such as the psychic body, reincarnation, astral projection, telepathy, etc. Continues Stein's reliance on both her own experience and the experience of other women alternative healers.

_____. *The Women's Book of Healing*. St. Paul, MN: Llewellyn, 1987.
Another lay-level text which introduces women to psychic healing skills and the use of crystals and gemstones. Again, uses Stein's anecdotes and those of other women practitioners.

_____. *The Women's Spirituality Book*. St. Paul, MN: Llewellyn, 1986.
This early work by Stein is a very basic introduction to the need for feminist spirituality, the Goddess, the seasonal sabbats, and short chapters on

visualization, healing, crystals, tarot, and I Ching, subjects which Stein explores more fully in later specialized books. Includes a number of illustrations.

Stone, Merlin. *When God Was a Woman.* New York: HBJ, 1976.
    Although later scholars have found flaws in some of Stone's anthropological extrapolations, this work remains a classic in the literature of feminist spirituality. Stone dethrones the traditional Adam and Eve story by arguing that it was part of an ongoing public relations campaign to put Goddess worship into ill repute, and thus to replace the first religion and deity with a male dominated one.

_____. *Ancient Mirrors of Womanhood: A Treasury of Goddess and Heroine Lore from Around the World.* 1979. Boston: Beacon, 1984.
    This is a valuable source for anyone interested in multicultural views of the Goddess. Rather than concentrating solely on European goddesses as so many texts do, Stone includes tales and descriptions from Chinese, Central and South American, African, Indian, Japanese, Native American, and Mediterranean cultures. Stone's own poetic contributions and rewrites ring true alongside her scholarly material.

Teish, Luisah. *Carnival of the Spirit: Seasonal Celebrations and Rites of Passage.* San Francisco: Harper San Francisco, 1994.
    A collection of rituals for the entire year. Drawn primarily from African and African diasporic traditions, but also includes Native American and pre–Christian European practices. Teish writes to foster a connection with the natural world and to encourage a sense of global family. Includes poems and stories.

_____. *Jambalaya: The Natural Woman's Book of Personal Charms and Practical Rituals.* San Francisco: Harper & Row, 1985.
    Combining equal parts autobiography, history, legend, poetry, and ritual, *Jambalaya* is Teish's contribution to an understanding of the African orishas (deities) as honored in African diasporic/Voudoo traditions. Includes a variety of rituals and correspondences for the orishas. Teish also explains the practice of ancestor reverence.

Thompson, Dorothy. "Africana Womanist Revision in Gloria Naylor's *Mama Day* and *Bailey's Cafe.*" *Gloria Naylor's Early Novels.* Ed. Margot Anne Kelley. Gainesville: UP of Florida, 1999. 89–111.
    Thompson takes Alice Walker's idea of womanism and revises it in terms of "Africana" womanism — one which refigures that definition by a marked reference to African influences and paradigms. Thompson is particularly interested in mythic revision in the two novels.

Tobin, Lee Ann. "Why Change the Arthur Story? Marion Zimmer Bradley's *The Mists of Avalon*." *Extrapolation* 34 (1993): 147–57.
    She argues that Bradley rewrites Arthurian legend, and in so doing decentralizes Christianity, posits Morgaine as a powerful feminist heroine (rather than the scapegoat), and uses Gwenhwyfar to illustrate how western culture disempowers women. Tobin offers an especially insightful reading of Gwenhwyfar's repression, rage, and strength in the novel.

Turner, Kay. "Contemporary Feminist Rituals." 2nd ed. of *Heresies* 2.1 Issue 5 (1982): 20–26.
    Turner finds ritual to be indicative of the actual changes experienced by women on a spiritual level. She examines several rituals and the empowerment processes which they embody. Following her article, there is a ritual written by Turner, "Song of Black Feather, Song of White Feather."

Valiente, Doreen. *Witchcraft for Tomorrow.* 1978. Custer, WA: Phoenix, 1987.
    Valiente, who worked closely with Gerald Gardner, the man largely credited for the resurgence of witchcraft as a 20th-century religion, here presents an introduction to the basic beliefs, tools, practices, and ethics of witchcraft. Includes a Book of Shadows covering basic rituals. Due to her background, this work is far more insightful than many of the beginner's books which have appeared in its wake.

Van Dyke, Annette. *The Search for a Woman-Centered Spirituality.* New York: New York UP, 1992.
    Defining lesbians as women free from male control, as "woman-centered," Van Dyke asserts that a variety of novels from various cultural traditions can be seen as promoting lesbian or woman-centered spirituality. She considers Leslie Silko, Paula Allen, Audre Lorde, Alice Walker, Starhawk, Marion Bradley, Sonia Johnson, and Mary Daly.

Vinge, Joan. *The Snow Queen.* 1980. New York: Dell, 1984.
    A Hugo award-winning science fiction novel which details the rise of a young cloned girl, Moon, to eventual rule over the planet Tiamat, where the technologically oriented Winters must give way to the anti-technology Summers, who worship a Mother Goddess. In the novel, Vinge deals with the question of spiritual and ecological values in a technological society.

_____. *The Summer Queen.* 1991. New York: Warner, 1992.
    Hugo nominated, the sequel explores the nature of the sybil net, which was revealed to be the "true" identity of the Tiamatan Goddess. However, as Vinge traces the nature of this artificial intelligence, its interdependence with the natural world, and its vulnerability to human greed and corruption, she breaks down easy divisions of nature/human/machine, leaving the reader an allegory which speaks to our own fragile ecosystem.

Walker, Alice. *The Color Purple.* New York: HBJ, 1982.
    Walker's famous epistolary novel chronicling Celie's journey from abuse to empowerment at the prompting of the powerful and loving Shug.

_____. *In Search of Our Mother's Gardens.* San Diego: H B J, 1984.
    An important collection of Walker's early essays, including her frequently cited definition of "womanist," as well as essays on her search for Zora Hurston's grave, beauty, and the title essay.

_____. *Living by the Word: Selected Writings 1973–1987.* San Diego, HBJ, 1988.
    A collection of meditative prose pieces on spiritual, political, and personal topics. A number are journal entries, including ones written during her travels.

_____. *The Temple of My Familiar*. San Diego: Harcourt Brace, 1989.
   Sometimes overlooked by readers who find *The Color Purple* or *Possessing the Secret of Joy* more accessible, this median novel is a treasure-trove of mysteries interwoven with past lives, Goddess worship, and the struggles of couples to form egalitarian relationships.

Walker, Barbara G. *The Skeptical Feminist: Discovering the Virgin, Mother & Crone*. 1987. San Francisco: Harper & Row, 1988.
   In this text Walker combines autobiographical reflections with feminist analysis of the ways in which patriarchal religions have served as the foundations of female oppression. Walker's discussions of feminist spirituality consider the images and rituals from a psychological perspective; her "skeptical" slant disavows concepts of magic, etc., which some spiritual feminists hold to be valid.

_____. *The Woman's Dictionary of Symbols and Sacred Objects*. San Francisco: Harper & Row, 1988.
   Walker's compendium assembles a plethora of symbols for the purpose of making known to women meanings which predate patriarchal ascriptions. She covers a variety of directional symbols; sacred, ritual, and deity symbols; and symbols from the animal, vegetation, and mineral kingdoms — or is that queendoms?

_____. *The Woman's Encyclopedia of Myths and Secrets*. San Francisco: Harper & Row, 1983.
   Here Walker again lends her hand to feminist dis-covering by removing layers of patriarchal/Christian mythological sediment from a host of characters, legends, events, symbols, and the like. In doing so she hopes to promote a new understanding and imagining of the female power which was erased by distorting history and mythology.

Warshaw, Robin. *I Never Called It Rape*. New York: Harper & Row, 1988.
   Warshaw combines the results of the *Ms.* report (from a nationwide survey) with other scholarship to define acquaintance rape, discuss its widespread nature, analyze its cultural origins, and offer advice for survivors of acquaintance rape. Includes an annotated bibliography of resources about rape and rape prevention.

Weinstein, Marion. *Earth Magic: A Dianic Book of Shadows*. Custer, WA: Phoenix, 1986.
   An introductory level book which covers the tools, deities, beliefs, and basic rituals of witchcraft. Weinstein uses "Dianic" in the sense of devoted to Diana, rather than in the sense of woman only or lesbian focused, as the term is sometimes used. Includes a discussion of Aspect Theory, and the relation of affirmation, manifestation, and magic.

Wittig, Monique. *Les Guérillères*. Trans. David Le Vay. 1971. Boston: Beacon, 1985.
   A classic novel which is sometimes pointed to as an example of *l'écriture feminine* (feminine narrative) for the ways in which it defies traditional linear narrative. Wittig presents a female army which physically, symbolically, and linguistically defeats the patriarchal social order.

Wolfe, Gary K. *Critical Terms for Science Fiction and Fantasy: A Glossary and Guide to Scholarship.* New York: Greenwood, 1986.
> Covers almost 500 terms drawn from science fiction and fantasy authors and critics. Noting that his work is not intended to prescribe or arbitrate terminology, Wolfe represents the array of usage currently present in the field. His introduction considers the critical backgrounds for the fields of science fiction and fantasy, providing a backdrop for their often conflicting definitions.

Wolmark, Jenny. *Aliens and Others: Science Fiction, Feminism, and Postmodernism.* Iowa City: University of Iowa Press, 1994.
> Wolmark believes that feminism, postmodernism, and ideas of the alien and the Other intersect in science fiction, providing commentary on gender relations in society. She examines these concepts in SF novels by Octavia Butler, Gwyneth Jones, C J Cherryh, Vonda McIntyre, Suzy Charnas, Sally Gearhart, Sherri Tepper, Pamela Sargent, Margaret Atwood, Pat Cadigan, Rebecca Ore, Marge Piercy, and Elisabeth Vonarburg.

Yoke, Carl. "From Alienation to Personal Triumph: The Science Fiction of Joan B. Vinge." *The Feminine Eye: Science Fiction and the Women Who Write It.* New York: Frederick Ungar Publishing, 1982. 103–30.
> Yoke argues that Vinge's protagonists are frequently alienated characters who are able to connect with others through an incorporation of new value systems.

Zaki, Hoda. "Utopia, Dystopia, and Ideology in the Science Fiction of Octavia Butler." *Science Fiction Studies* 17.2 (1990): 239–51.
> Zaki argues for including Butler under the labels of feminist and utopian science fiction. Zaki qualifies her assertion by noting that Butler, as an African American writer, offers a perspective which critiques some typical liberal feminist SF ideas and the omission of race as an issue.

Zimmerman, Bonnie. "What Has Never Been: An Overview of Lesbian Feminist Criticism." *Feminist Studies* 7.3 (1981). Reprinted in *The New Feminist Criticism: Essays on Women, Literature & Theory.* Ed. Elaine Showalter. New York: Pantheon, 1985. 200–24.
> An overview of how lesbians have developed a body of literary criticism, and some of the achievements and challenges ahead in the field. She notes that combating heterosexism among feminists is not as important as trying to define what a lesbian perspective is — itself an area of ongoing debate.

Index

Abbey, Lynn 5, 20, 26, 74, 108, 110, 120–130, 136–137, 175
African American 5, 9–10, 13–14, 31, 61–63, 68, 100–101, 104, 108–109, 138–142, 146–147, 149, 155, 163, 166, 182, 185–186, 188, 193, 196, 201
amazon 55, 58, 60, 108, 110–112, 114, 117, 120, 177–178, 180, 186
amazon tale 110–111
archetype 76, 79, 128, 183, 186

Barr, Marleen 2, 111, 122–124, 138, 141, 143, 162, 166, 176
Baudino, Gael 3–4, 10, 17, 20, 26–27, 67, 73–74, 76, 92–100, 107, 177, 187
Beloved 5, 137, 142–147, 182, 188, 191
bildungsroman 108, 110–111, 120, 142, 180
The Black Flame 5, 108, 120–121, 126–30, 175
Bradley, Marion Zimmer 3–5, 17, 19–20, 26, 30–33, 43–60, 65, 69, 74–75, 88, 108, 110, 112–20, 177–178, 183–184, 187, 196, 198–19; see also *City of Sorcery*; *The Firebrand*; *The Mists of Avalon*
Butler, Octavia 3–4, 73–74, 100–107, 138–139, 175–176, 178, 185, 194–195, 201

Chernin, Kim 4, 17, 20, 34–43, 48, 50, 53, 55, 65, 69, 17

Christ, Carol 1, 4–5, 8–9, 15–16, 20–21, 23, 32–35, 38, 43–44, 47–48, 51, 57, 66, 71, 78, 96, 158, 166, 179–180, 185–186, 197
Christianity 4, 8–9, 14, 16, 22, 23–24, 30, 43–48, 51, 53–54, 59, 65, 66, 67, 93, 99, 117, 138, 140–141, 146, 148, 178–181, 184–186, 188, 192, 193, 198, 200
City of Sorcery 5, 26, 108, 112–120, 124, 129, 177
The Copper Crown 86, 188
Crone 44, 51, 95, 112–113, 116–118, 132, 150, 160

Daughter of the Bright Moon 5, 26, 108, 120–126, 175
deity 5, 8, 14, 22, 24, 33–34, 43, 48, 50, 56–57, 59–60, 65, 81, 85, 94, 104, 108, 115, 117, 121–122, 126–130, 132, 134, 139, 141, 165, 177, 181, 194, 198, 200
Dreaming the Dark 11, 16, 26, 45, 49, 72, 82, 196

Eller, Cynthia 6–7, 10–11, 13, 15, 19, 25, 29, 49, 73, 95, 123, 127, 165, 183
erotic as power 160, 190
European American 4, 9–10, 12–14, 19, 25, 31, 62, 100, 108, 111–112, 138, 163, 166

204 Index

fabulation 111, 141, 143, 154, 162, 166, 169n, 176
fantastic 2, 4, 13, 34, 37, 63, 69, 72, 76–77, 100, 111, 126, 136, 166, 191, 195
fantasy 1–2, 29, 37, 62, 73–78, 81–82, 86–87, 93, 96, 110, 112, 154–156, 162–163, 167, 176, 180, 184–185, 187, 195–196, 201
feminism 2, 7, 9, 71, 120, 167, 179–181, 184–186, 189, 191–193, 201
feminist spirituality 1–3, 5–12, 14–15, 18–20, 22, 25, 27–29, 37, 49, 54, 61–63, 70, 73, 82–83, 85–86, 92–94, 108, 112, 120–121, 128, 133, 135, 162, 164–167, 179–180, 183, 190, 193, 196–198, 200
The Fifth Sacred Thing 5, 11, 137, 155–162, 197
The Firebrand 4, 17, 30–33, 43, 54–60, 178, 184
The Flame Bearers 4, 17, 30–32, 34–43, 46, 49, 54, 56, 60, 103, 179

Goddess: definitions of 22; history 14–17, 32–33; movement 7, 10–12; and quest 108–112; rituals 19–24

healing 5, 11–12, 19, 27–28, 35, 62–63, 67, 73, 77–78, 85, 90–92, 96–100, 103–106, 109–110, 123, 126, 129, 135, 137–139, 141–142, 146–147, 150–151, 153, 155, 158–159, 161–165, 176–177, 185, 187–188, 191, 193–194, 197–198

heroic quest, female 109–110
history, rewriting 3–4, 13–19, 30–70

immanence 56, 63
immanent deity 8, 108, 177, 194
interconnection 2, 4, 16, 21, 36, 42, 46, 49, 52–53, 61, 65, 67–69, 78, 83, 93–95, 98–99, 104–106, 108, 127, 134–135, 139–141, 144, 146, 152, 157, 159, 164, 167, 180

Jewish 6, 10, 13, 30, 35–37, 42, 54, 142, 156, 160, 163, 166

Kennealy (-Morrison), Patricia 3–4, 73–74, 86–92, 188

Lackey, Mercedes 3–4, 73–86, 188–189
lesbian 1, 10–11, 15, 76, 79, 199–201
lunar 25, 51, 121, 132, 193

magic 3, 25, 27, 33–35, 37, 42, 54, 69, 74, 76, 82–83, 86, 88–89, 91, 97, 128, 146–147, 149–154, 156, 162, 175, 177, 183, 188, 191, 196–197, 200
magick 34, 171n
Maiden 44, 51, 117, 123, 131
Mama Day 5, 26, 137, 142, 150–155, 164, 191, 198
matriarchy 15, 183, 194
matrifocal 4, 15–16, 32, 44, 48, 55, 93–94, 98, 145, 175
menstruation 7, 21, 148, 182
The Mists of Avalon 3–4, 30–32, 43–54, 56, 59–60, 126, 178, 184, 198
monotheism 139–140, 192
moon 5, 12, 23–26, 39, 44, 86, 108, 111, 116–117, 120–137, 147–149, 164, 175, 182–183, 186, 193, 196, 199
Morrison, Toni 3, 5, 86, 137–138, 142–147, 163, 174n, 181–182, 185, 191
Mother Goddess 22, 65, 104, 123, 128–129, 131
myth 17–19

Native American 10, 12–14, 19, 24, 175, 182, 195, 198
Naylor, Gloria 5, 26, 137–138, 150–155, 163, 190–191, 194, 198
neo-Pagan 19, 24–25, 46, 49, 86, 94, 158, 162, 173n, 175, 180, 183–184
New Age 10, 28

The Oathbound 4, 73, 75–81, 85, 189
Oathbreakers 4, 73, 75, 81–86, 99, 189
Orenstein, Gloria 1, 16, 18, 20, 23, 30–32, 36, 38, 40–43, 60, 69, 73, 166, 182, 186, 192

Pagan 5–6, 20, 24–25, 46, 49, 52, 54, 86, 92, 97, 137, 156–157, 173, 174, 178, 188
patriarchal 4, 7–8, 11, 13–17, 20–21, 23–26, 28–31, 33–34, 36–39, 44, 46, 48–50, 53, 55–57, 59–60, 64, 69, 71–79, 93–98, 100–101, 103–106, 111, 113–115, 117–118, 120–125, 127, 130–131, 134–136, 138, 145, 165, 178–181, 184–185, 187, 190, 195–196, 200

patriarchy 4–5, 8–9, 14, 21, 28, 30, 32, 34, 43, 48, 54, 56–58, 64, 68, 70–72, 88, 90, 96, 99, 104, 111, 117, 124–125, 143, 161, 169n, 183, 189
power, types of 71–74
psychic 2, 7, 11, 13, 20–21, 26–29, 37, 46–47, 63, 77, 86, 100, 102–103, 110–113, 116, 118–119, 124, 130, 136, 139, 141–142, 144, 147, 156, 178, 186, 190, 197

quest, female heroic 109–10

racism 5, 9, 12, 26, 35, 37, 61–63, 66, 82, 114, 138, 172n, 177
rape 2, 21, 55, 76–77, 79–80, 83, 94, 96–97, 99, 157, 159, 178, 181, 194, 200
ritual 7, 11, 13, 19–27

Sassafras, Cypress, and Indigo 5, 137, 142, 147–50, 194
science fiction 1–2, 43, 62, 73–74, 86, 101, 110–112, 163, 166, 176, 180, 185, 189, 193, 196, 199, 201
Shange, Ntozake 1, 5, 137–138, 142, 147–150, 151, 163, 179, 194
The Silver Branch 73, 86–87, 98, 188
slavery 100–102, 138, 141–142, 144–146, 149–150, 165, 181, 185, 188, 190–191
Snow Queen, The 5, 108, 112, 130–135, 179, 199
speculative fiction 2–4, 13, 15, 18, 34, 69, 72–74, 77, 92, 100, 106, 110–111, 124, 128, 134, 165–167, 176, 193, 195
The Spiral Dance 11, 22, 25–26, 49, 52, 83, 90, 94–95, 100, 116, 126, 19
Starhawk 3, 5, 11–12, 16, 20, 22, 24–28, 38, 45, 49, 52, 72–73, 82–83, 90, 93–95, 100, 116, 126, 137–138, 142, 155–159, 161–163, 180, 196–197, 199; see also *Dreaming the Dark*; *The Fifth Sacred Thing*; *The Spiral Dance*, *Truth or Dare*; *Walking to Mercury*
Strands of Starlight 4, 17, 26, 73, 92–100, 177
The Summer Queen 131–134, 199
symbol 3, 5–6, 9, 33, 43–44, 46–48, 66, 69, 73, 111, 116, 118, 124, 133, 136, 151, 184

Teish, Luisah 10–12, 21, 24, 26, 37, 141, 148, 198
The Temple of My Familiar 4, 17, 30–32, 61–69, 108, 138, 200
thealogy 11, 94, 118, 164, 180
The Throne of Scone 86–88, 91, 188
Triple Goddess 24, 123, 130–131; see also Maiden; Mother; Crone
Truth or Dare 11, 28, 49, 72, 82, 90, 112, 197

Vinge, Joan 3, 5, 74, 108, 111, 129–137, 179, 199, 201
Voodoo 138, 140, 191

Walker, Alice 4, 17–20, 30–33, 37, 61–69, 99, 138–139, 141, 162, 179, 182, 198–200
Walking to Mercury 11, 197
wicca 10, 24–25, 27, 49, 86, 92–93, 178
Wild Seed 4, 73, 100–106, 138, 178, 185
witchcraft 10, 17, 24–26, 49, 93, 170n, 177, 180, 183–185, 187, 190, 194, 199–200
witchhunts 8, 16–17, 24, 64, 67, 93, 112, 181–182
womanspirit 8, 13, 27–29, 63, 137, 151, 180, 184

www.ingramcontent.com/pod-product-compliance
Ingram Content Group UK Ltd.
Pitfield, Milton Keynes, MK11 3LW, UK
UKHW042002140426
5217IPUK00015B/931